ACTS OF UNION

ACTS OF UNION

Scotland and the Literary Negotiation

of the British Nation,

1707–1830

LEITH DAVIS

STANFORD UNIVERSITY PRESS

Stanford, California

1998

Stanford University Press
Stanford, California
© 1998 by the Board of Trustees
of the Leland Stanford Junior University

Printed in the United States of America

CIP data appear at the end of the book

For Rob,

September 6, 1997

ACKNOWLEDGMENTS

The researching and writing of this book were made possible with the generous support of a Simon Fraser University President's Research Grant and a Social Sciences and Humanities Research Council of Canada Research Grant. The Department of English and the Dean of Arts at Simon Fraser University also supported my request for research leave in fall and spring, 1993–94, and the Simon Fraser University Publications Committee Rapid Response Fund provided funding for the index and the cover illustration.

Acts of Union is intended as a contribution to an ongoing dialogue on Scottish and British identity. It has gone through a number of manifestations, and I would like to acknowledge numerous people who have been helpful at various stages. I thank David Lloyd, who showed me a different way of reading literature, facilitated my first encounter with Ossian, and supervised my thesis. Geoffrey Carnell called my attention to the persistence of Lord Belhaven. Carol McGuirk shared her thoughts on Burns through e-mail and in person; her work has also been an example to me. Ian Duncan provided valuable suggestions on the entire manuscript.

In addition, I am very grateful to all those who read and commented on the manuscript at various stages and encouraged me to continue: Mary Ann Gillies, Margaret Linley, Betty Schellenberg, Janet Smitten, and Jeff Sorensen. My graduate student assistant, Jason King, was meticulous in carrying out a range of tasks. I am fortunate to have had his help. My graduate class of spring 1993 and the undergraduate students in my Burns courses in 1995 and 1996 provided a stimulating forum in which I could explore some of the ideas in this book. Needless to say, any errors that occur are my responsibility entirely.

One of the best things about this book is the opportunity for new friendships which it afforded me. Julie Moss and Neil Greer, Sarah Rideout and Louise Roy, Corinne Morris and Richard Perkins (and now Owen) opened their hearts and their homes to me during my many visits to Edinburgh. The book is finished, but the visits will continue.

Finally, I thank Rob McGregor for all his encouragement, love, and irrepressible humor. Without him, this book would have been much less enjoyable to write.

Parts of *Acts of Union* were originally published in modified form in the following articles: "'Bounded to a District Space': Burns, Wordsworth, and the Margins of English Literature," *English Studies in Canada* 20:1 (March 1994): 23–40; "Origins of the Specious: James Macpherson's Ossian and the Forging of the British Empire," *The Eighteenth Century: Theory and Interpretation* 34:2 (1993): 132–50; and "Re-Presenting Scotia: Robert Burns and the Imagined Community of Scotland," in *Critical Essays on Robert Burns*, Carol McGuirk, ed. (New York: G. K. Hall, 1998), excerpted by permission of G. K. Hall & Co., an imprint of Simon & Schuster Maemillan.

L.D.

CONTENTS

ACTS OF UNION

Acts of Union

Communities are distinguished not by their falsity/genuineness,
but by the style in which they are imagined.

—BENEDICT ANDERSON
"Imagined Communities: Reflections on the Origin and Spread of Nationalism"

May wee be Britons, and down goe the old ignominious names of
Scotland and England.

—THE EARL OF CROMARTIE
*Quoted in William Ferguson, "Scotland's Relation
with England: A Survey to 1707"*

The recent resurgence of claims regarding national identity around the globe
has attracted the attention of scholars from a number of disciplines.[1] The origin and the nature of national belonging are now concerns not just of the
fields of political science and economics but of cultural studies and literary
criticism as well. *Acts of Union* has evolved out of and is indebted to this continuing cross-disciplinary debate. It examines the instabilities inherent in the
idea of the nation by focusing on the literary production of one of the first
examples of the modern nation: Great Britain.[2]

Ever since its formal establishment in 1707, Great Britain has been a site
of contest—not always on the material level, but certainly on the discursive
level—between the nations from which it was constructed. Although the Earl
of Cromartie could optimistically urge the dissolution of the names of Scotland and England into the title of Britain, in fact those old names continued
to exert their ideological presence after the political union. Concentrating on
the relationship between Scotland and England in the century after 1707, this
book examines the British nation not as a homogeneous stable unit, but as a
dynamic process, a dialogue between heterogeneous elements. Far from be-

ing constituted by a single Act of Union, Britain was forged, in all of the variant senses of that word, from multiple acts of union and dislocation.[3]

Accordingly, this book examines work by Scottish and English writers from 1707 to 1830, concentrating on the ambiguous expressions of national identity inscribed in their texts. The Russian literary critic Mikhail Bakhtin posited the dialogic nature of the discourse of an individual subject, a result of the opposition between unifying, centripetal and diversifying, centrifugal forces (pp. 270–71). I suggest that such a dialogism exists in the discourse of the nation, where the nation is imagined simultaneously as both unitary and contested. I have shaped this study around discursive encounters between Scottish and English writers, proposing that these encounters are formed by and also inform Britain's dialogic national identity. Specifically, I consider the literary efforts of Daniel Defoe and Lord Belhaven; Henry Fielding and Tobias Smollett; Samuel Johnson and James Macpherson; William Words-worth and Robert Burns; and Thomas Percy and Walter Scott. Not only does the work of each of these writers reflect the instabilities inherent in writing about the nation, but the engagement of each writer in discourse with his contemporary also illustrates the negotiation of British identity that occurred throughout the eighteenth and early nineteenth centuries.

This book has a wider aim than simply to plot out specific moments during which writing served not only to trouble but also to renegotiate the Union of Great Britain, for it sets the articulation of British national identity within more general questions concerning postcolonial theories of the nation. While I employ postcolonial theory to interrogate the imagining of the British nation, I also want to use the case of Britain, one of the earliest established nations, to interrogate postcolonial theories of nationalism.

As will become apparent, my study is most immediately indebted to recent work on the cultural conditions of nationalism initiated by Benedict Anderson's *Imagined Communities: Reflections on the Origin and Spread of Nationalism*.[4] In this work, Anderson sets out to examine nationalism in relation not to "self-consciously held political ideologies," but to "the large cultural systems that preceded it, out of which—as well as against which—it came into being" (p. 12). For Anderson, the nation is "an imagined political community," imagined as "both inherently limited and sovereign" (p. 6). Anderson proposes that with the disintegration of particular cultural systems (the coherence of the religious community; the idea of a sacred language; the belief in the dynastic realm; and the concept of time as cyclical), gaps were left that were filled by national identification: "the search was on . . . for a new way of linking fraternity, power and time meaningfully together" (p. 36). This profound change to nationhood was also hastened by the shift to a print culture:

"Nothing perhaps more precipitated this search, nor made it more fruitful, than print-capitalism, which made it possible for rapidly growing numbers of people to think about themselves, and to relate themselves to others, in profoundly new ways" (p. 36). Anderson's work is important in pointing out how the public sphere of the literary world served as an important site for imagining the nation.

Anderson also offers a new perspective on the history of nationalism. Whereas most studies of nationalism before Anderson suggest that the phenomenon derived from European models, Anderson argues that a modular kind of nationalism was established in the Americas in the late eighteenth century. (The French Revolution, itself influenced by the American Revolution, was also important in this process.) This modular nationalism was taken up by populist nationalist movements in Europe, then was subsequently superseded by an "official nationalism" conceived of by aristocracies and dynastic realms that were afraid of marginalization by the populist ideology. Britain, however, proves an important exception to Anderson's analysis. By the 1820s, which Anderson identifies as the beginning of the new age of nationalism in Europe, Britain had already had over a century of negotiating a national identity based on contradiction. In this process, print culture served both to allow Britons "to relate themselves to others, in profoundly new ways," and also to realize the profound differences that existed within their nation.

Anderson has been criticized by Partha Chatterjee for universalizing the development of nationalism through his "sociological determinism" (*Nationalist Thought*, p. 21). Like Gellner, suggests Chatterjee, Anderson "confines his discussion to the 'modular' character of 20th century nationalisms, without noticing the twists and turns, the suppressed possibilities, the contradictions still unresolved" (p. 22). No matter how he is attempting to read nationalism differently, he ultimately relies on and repeats the same epistemological framework as other critics of nationalism. According to Chatterjee,

> the problem of nationalist thought becomes the particular manifestation
> of a much more general problem, namely, the problem of the bourgeois-
> rationalist conception of knowledge, established in the post-Enlighten-
> ment period of European intellectual history, as the moral and epistemic
> foundation for a supposedly universal framework of thought which
> perpetuates, in a real and not merely a metaphorical sense, a colonial
> domination. (p. 11)

In an attempt to avoid universalizing nationhood through relying on a paradigm of Self versus Other, Chatterjee emphasizes the importance of looking at nationalism as a crooked line between two points, observing: "It is in the shifts, slides, discontinuities, the unintended moves, what is suppressed as much as what is asserted that one can get a sense of this complex movement, not as so many accidental or disturbing factors but as constitutive of the very historical rationality of its process" (p. vii). Chatterjee unmasks the paradox of nationalism by examining the case of India. Nationalism in India, he argues, is based on a fundamental ambiguity, being addressed both to the people, in order to foster their confidence in their own capabilities, and to England, in order to demonstrate that England had no right to rule India.[5] But Chatterjee himself falls into the trap of essentialism, not in his portrayal of the colonized, but in his portrayal of the colonizers; this essentialism is suggested by his unproblematized use of the word "England." Although Britain (not just England) served as the mirror into which India was supposed to gaze for self-recognition, that mirror was itself quite fragmented.[6]

Like Chatterjee, Homi Bhabha also reads the nation as an ambiguous construct. Employing elements from theories of deconstruction, he suggests that ambiguity exists in the very discourse which imagines the nation into being. Accordingly, in *Nation and Narration*, building on Tom Nairn's discussion of the pathology of nationhood, he sets out "to explore the Janus-faced ambivalence of language itself in the construction of the Janus-faced discourse of the nation" (p. 3). The essays by various authors in that volume examine the nation as a "process," a phenomenon in the "act of 'composing' its powerful image" (p. 3), rather than as a fixed entity. Bhabha's own collection of essays, *The Location of Culture*, also probes the "cultural construction of nationness as a form of social and textual affiliation" (p. 140). Bhabha's work is useful in pointing out the ambiguities that exist in any articulation of the nation. But, again, the case of Britain can provide a corrective perspective on postcolonial ideas of the nation. My reading of the literary negotiation of Britain in the eighteenth century suggests that those who participated in the imagining of Britain in the eighteenth century were only too conscious that they were in the process of composing their image. Most of the representations of the nation that I will examine struggle with finding a way in which to simultaneously acknowledge and also downplay internal difference. As I will suggest, this struggle eventually centered itself in the domain of culture, where it would later trouble attempts to establish an official and imperial nationalism.[7]

Chatterjee's and Bhabha's assessments of the nation provide a perspective on the nation as a conflicted space; this perspective can be usefully historicized and contextualized, however, with reference to the British example of nationhood before the nineteenth century. Britain was struggling with the "heterogeneous histories" (*Location*, p. 148) within its midst even as it was being created. Its national identity was forged as a negotiation between the incommensurabilities of its internal populations. Some of these, like the Highlanders, were forcibly silenced, while others were allowed to speak only in a particular fashion; but they nevertheless served as elements that could unsettle the illusion of consensus at any time.

The case of Britain serves as a historical example of how from its beginning the nation has been a constantly contested space.[8] In studying nationalism from a postcolonial perspective, then, we need to look at the example of Britain in the eighteenth century for a concept of national identity based not on homogeneity (although that notion arguably came to the forefront later in the nineteenth century with the influence of official nationalism), but on difference.

Before offering an overview of the specific literary dialogues I will pursue here, I want to begin by considering the effect of the Union on the self-representations of the two founding nations of Great Britain and by examining the way these self-representations have been interpreted. The English imagined community before the Act of Union was largely based on a tradition of court literature. Geoffrey of Monmouth articulated the prevailing English national myth centered on Brutus, who, after he left Troy, was supposed to have established himself in Britain. Roger Mason observes that the "Brut tradition . . . came to form the basis of an English national epos which, continued, expanded and elaborated by a host of medieval chroniclers, helped to underwrite—however paradoxically—the continuity of English experience and the antiquity of English kinship" ("Scotching the Brut," p. 61). Colin Kidd notes that by the late fifteenth century this myth had been supplemented by a claim made by Sir John Fortescue: "the exaltation of the English constitution as a happily mixed *dominium politicum et regale*" (p. 12). Liah Greenfeld suggests that England's sense of its own nationhood grew steadily with the association of the Protestant Church and the state, as the English came to see themselves as God's chosen people, while Richard Helgerson examines how this sense of national identity was represented in Elizabethan literature. Despite the confidence of the English national imagining, after the Glorious Revolution of 1688–89, the English found themselves contending with a serious problem of national identity. England had gained a unique political character as a limited monarchy, but it also found itself saddled with a ruler who was undeniably un-English—indeed, who could not speak the mother tongue. For the English, the unification of Scotland and England meant a readjustment of national identity, but one made less threatening by the fact that they had not seen themselves as a pure ethnic nation; the absorption of Scotland was accompanied by some ethnic tension (the Scots, especially the Highlanders, were categorically seen as less civilized), but England remained the seat of economic and legislative power. For the Scottish national identity, however, the consequences of union were more dramatic.

Like England, Scotland existed as an imagined community long before the Union.[9] Colin Kidd points out that "the 'Scottish' kingdom, which emerged between the ninth and twelfth centuries to unite an ethnic diversity of Picts, Scots, Galloway Britons, Saxons and Flemish and Norman knights, found its identity in Scoto-Celtic monarchy, whose foremost expression was the royal genealogy recited as part of the coronation ritual by a Highland sennachie or bard" (p. 15). The Declaration of Arbroath (1320), which established Scotland's independence from English rule, can also be seen as promoting an ideal of popular nationhood (Harvie, p. 9). Literary works like John Barbour's *The Bruce* (1374–75) and Blind Harry's *Wallace* (1477) articulate a specific Scottish national identity against that of England. But Scotland's political status changed, first with the Union of Crowns in 1603 and again after the parliamentary union in 1707. After the Act of Union, Westminster determined Scotland's economic and social policies with an eye for what would benefit Britain as a whole, not Scotland. Or, as Rosalind Mitchison put it, "From 1689 onwards Scotland was ruled by a set of monarchs chosen by English politicians for English political purposes, and by a series of ministries thrown up in the changes of political power in England who were usually ignorant of and indifferent to the problems of government in Scotland" (p. 24). The Scots were left without a distinct legislative body, although they maintained their separate religious, legal, and educational systems.[10]

Contemporary critical assessments of the effects of the Union concentrate either on explaining away the political contradictions caused by the Union or on highlighting Scotland's anomalous position in opposition to England's national "normalcy." In *Britons: Forging the Nation, 1707–1837*, a work that succeeded in putting British history on the bestseller list, Linda Colley sews Britain together into a seamless fabric of Protestant and then imperial interests after the Union. Where Colley employs a number of different historical texts in the course of her assessment, Howard Weinbrot's *Britannia's Issue: The Rise of British Literature from Dryden to Ossian* celebrates the specific achievement of British literature as a "*concordia discors,*" a melting pot that "stimulates literary greatness" as it successfully incorporates difference (p. 1).[11] But both Colley and Weinbrot employ a narrative that repeats, despite the authors' best intentions, the Whig interpretation of British history as a series of events that eventually led to a united identity for Scots and English as Britons.[12]

Critics concentrating specifically on Scotland alert us to Scotland's anomalous position after the Union as a nation without the political apparatus of nationhood. Most frequently these critics employ metaphors of internal division to describe Scotland's national situation. In an early assessment of Scottish identity, *Scottish Literature: Character and Influence*, for example, G. Gregory Smith noted a kind of schizophrenia in Scottish letters. He identified it as "Caledonian antisyzygy," a split between the worlds of realism and of fantasy and suggested that such a split was inherent in the Scottish character: "It goes better with our knowledge of Scottish character and history to accept the antagonism as real and necessary" (p. 19). More recently, in *The Paradox of Scottish Culture*, David Daiches resurrected the notion of the bifurcation of Scottish identity, pathologizing it as a "dissociation of sensibility" caused by thinking in one language and writing in another (p. 21).[13] Kenneth Simpson, too, follows this trajectory, arguing that Scottish identity is based fundamentally on a division caused by political circumstances: "Both the talent and the need for the assumption of voices are most apparent in Scottish writing from roughly 1740 onwards, precisely the years when the social and cultural effects of the Union were beginning to catalyse in a crisis of identity among Scots" (p. 3). Simpson explains the oppositions which occur within specific texts as projections of the authors' internalized multiple voices. Simpson's explanation, although more nuanced that those of earlier critics, ultimately reads texts as transmitters of psychic distress caused by political contingencies. Tom Nairn points out the fundamental fallacy in such logic, based as it is on an ideal of romantic nationalism: "since the ideal-world (roots, organs, and all) is all right, and has unchallengeable status, it has to be Scotland which is all wrong; therefore Scottish society and history are monstrously misshapen in some way" (p. 122). On a different tack, Robert Crawford's *Devolving English Literature* questions the logic of juxtaposing the "ideal-world" with Scotland's anomalous state, as he explores the multiple ways in which this apparent margin actually defined the center of the cultural realm of Britain. As Crawford argues, "while for centuries the margins have been challenging, interrogating, and even structuring the supposed 'centre', the development of the subject of 'English Literature' has constantly involved and reinforced an oppressive homage to centralism" (p. 7).[14]

Recognizing the merit in such earlier studies, I want to embark on a different reading of literature within Britain, regarding it not just as a representation of a successful (or failed) historical unification and concentrating not just on the literature of one side of the national divide as either complicit or oppositional. Rather, I read the texts in this study as embodiments in themselves of the negotiations that have historically constituted the nation of Great Britain. Like Katie Trumpener's recent *Bardic Nationalism: The Roman-*

tic Novel and the British Empire, I am concerned with national identity as a dialogic process.[15] Where Trumpener surveys a vast amount of material from all of the Celtic peripheries and concentrates on cultural nationalism's contribution to the construction of the novel, however, my study focuses on the Scottish case, examining the negotiations of specific pairs of writers with each other and the dialogism internalized in their work. The kind of dialogism to which I refer can be illustrated with two examples—one Scottish and one English.

At first glance, two of James Beattie's works, *The Minstrel* (1768), a lyric poem, and *Scoticisms, Arranged in Alphabetical Order, Designed to Correct Improprieties of Speech and Writing* (1787), a self-help book for Scots wishing to purge their vocabulary of vernacular expressions, seem to illustrate Daiches's "dissociation of sensibility."[16] In *The Minstrel*, Beattie praises Scotland and its primitiveness. In *Scoticisms*, he tells readers how to eliminate the evidence of their Scottish heritage in speech and writing. The former work gestures toward praising Scottish poetic identity; the latter professes to want to remove the linguistic characteristics of that identity. Yet the ambiguities existing in each work qualify its professed intent and complicate any critical identification of antagonistic elements.

Beattie said the purpose of *The Minstrel* was "to trace the progress of a Poetical Genius, born in a rude age, from the first dawning of fancy and reason, till that period at which he may be supposed capable of appearing in the world as a Minstrel, that is, as an itinerant Poet and Musician;—a character which, according to the notions of our forefathers, was not only respectable, but sacred" (*Poetical Works*, p. 3). Consequently, he follows the development of the "Poetical Genius" through his early delight in nature, "each gentle, and each dreadful scene" (l. 191) to his education in science, philosophy, and the sorrows of human nature. Beattie addresses his comments to those who would disdain his setting his tale in the wilds of Scotland. He compares Scotland's "bleak and barren hills" with the superficially more attractive gold- and gem-filled Chilean mountains; in the former, there are peaceful vales and pure skies, but in the latter, "plague and poison, lust and rapine grow" (ll. 50–52). Beattie makes clear his intent to diverge from classical scenarios. His shepherd minstrel lives in

> A nation famed for song and beauty's charms;
> Zealous, yet modest; innocent though free;
> Patient of toil; serene amidst alarms;
> Inflexible in faith; invincible in arms.
>
> (*ll. 96–99*)

In the subject matter of his poem Beattie applauds the simplicity of Scotland, but he also subverts his praise of Scotland with his insertions of Englishness. He employs an English form, choosing the Spenserian stanza. His main character has the Anglo-Saxon name Edwin. And, strangely, he avoids using the word "bard" with its Celtic resonances, preferring the more courtly "minstrel," which Thomas Percy identifies with Anglo-Saxon culture. Even Beattie's name for Scotland, "Scotia," suggests a mythical classical realm, not the actual nation north of the Tweed.

Similar ambiguities appear in *Scoticisms, Arranged in Alphabetical Order, Designed to Correct Improprieties of Speech and Writing*. Beattie declares his purpose in compiling the work: "To put young writers and speakers on their guard against some of those Scotch idioms, which, in this country, are liable to be mistaken for English" (p. 2). He excuses the rigidity of the code he exercises, saying he has lately observed "a strange propensity, in too many of our people, to debase the purity of the language, by a mixture of foreign and provincial idioms, and cant phrases; a circumstance, which has in other countries generally preceded, and partly occasioned, the decline of learning, and which of course must be matter of regret to those who wish well to British Literature" (pp. 3–4). According to Beattie:

> There is a time when languages, as well as men, arrive at maturity; and, when that time is past, alterations are commonly for the worse. Our tongue was brought to perfection in the days of Addison and Swift: but has now lost not a little of its elegance, particularly in the articles of simplicity, vivacity, and ease. (p. 5)

The referent for the possessive of "our tongue," however, is unclear. It is as if the Scottish and English languages have already fused in his mind into "British Literature."

This brings up the most puzzling aspect of all: for whom is Beattie writing this book? His last comments are made to the "English reader":

> These idioms are thus huddled together, by way of exercise to young Scotch people, who may have been reading this pamphlet. But the English reader will not suppose, that the people of education in North Britain speak so uncouth a dialect. Many of them use a correct phraseology. (p. 5)

Although Beattie has put together this book for study by those who use the dialect, he is also writing for an English audience. In fact, he seems to want to assure the English reader that there is no audience for the book among many Scots, because "people of education" in Scotland do not require correction. The idioms "huddled" together are the legacy of a once independent Scotland. But *Scoticisms* also promotes Scottish identity. Beattie promises that his intervention is only temporary and that future populations may not make the same judgment calls as he does. He leaves room for a future of impressive Scottish writing: "When greater writers and speakers arise in this country, I shall not object to their taking greater liberties" (p. 5). In addition, he makes a point of commenting on how Scottish words are infiltrating the English language; significantly, the verb form of "narration," "narrate," is among these: "To *narrate*.—To relate. *Narrate*, and *to notice*, have of late been used by some Eng. writers" (p. 59). The Scots seem adept at promoting the use of verbal forms of nouns, as is apparent in the statement: "To *militate* against a doctrine.—To make against. This Scoticism, like some others, (*narrate, adduce, restrict, &c.*) seems to be getting into the language of England" (pp. 54–55). Beattie's *Scoticisms* also contains the memory of Scottish subversion within it as he uses the sentence, "He was born in *the forty-five*.—In forty five, or in 1745, or in the year 1745" (p. 87), to illustrate the improper use of "the" with dates. The selection of 1745 may have been arbitrary, but its effect is to remind readers of the occasion when the differences between the countries threatened to disunite them and when not just scoticisms but also Scottish soldiers came all too close to "getting into" England.

The subversion is reduced to a linguistic misunderstanding, however, in the following passage:

> I do not *mind* that I ever saw you before.—Remember. *To mind*, is, in
> Eng. to attend to,—or to put in mind. "Troth, Sir," said a young Scotch
> ensign to his commanding officer, "I do not *mind* your order." "Not mind
> my order!" said his superiour, (who was an Englishman) "By—I'll make
> you mind my orders, and obey them too." The one was no doubt guilty
> of a great fault, owing, however, to a failure of memory. The other
> thought the fault much greater, and owing to want of attention or
> respect. (pp. 57–58)

This passage asserts Scottish difference, but it also explains it away as a misunderstanding, as, indeed, Beattie himself both asserts and denies Scottish identity at the same time.

It is part of my contention, however, that the contradictions visible in work like Beattie's are not unique to Scotland, although they are perhaps made more visible in Scotland's case by the existence of the separate Scots language. Such contradictions concerning identity exist, as Bhabha suggests, in every statement of nationhood. Although the Scots may register a distinct form of what is known variously as "dissociation of sensibility" or "antisyzygy," contradictory impulses can be found in the work of English writers who also attempt to articulate a national identity. In *Understanding Scotland: The Sociology of a Stateless Nation*, David McCrone defines Scotland as a "stateless nation," suggesting that because of its peculiar position, Scotland can serve to challenge the traditional model of nationalism and to offer a new model of national affiliation.[17] Rather than read Scotland as an anomaly of national development, however, I suggest that Scotland displays only more prominently the tensions and ambiguities that result from trying to articulate any national identity. Moreover, if Scotland is a "stateless nation," it is possible to think of the wider unit of Britain as a nationless state, as it has always been fraught with contradictions that refuse to settle into any coherent national identity.

Indeed, we see in the texts of English writers, too, evidence of a fundamental instability of identity. Daniel Defoe's "The True-Born Englishman," for example, written six years before the Union and published in "ten authorized editions and twelve pirated editions in the first year" (Backscheider, *Ambition and Innovation*, p. 49), expresses underneath the surface of satire an anxiety about the nature of English identity. Defoe suggests that the English race is "uncertain and unev'n / Deriv'd from all the Nations under Heaven" (*Selected Writings*, 13: 42). He continues:

> Thus from a Mixture of all Kinds began,
> That Heterogeneous Thing, *An Englishman*:
> In eager Rapes, and furious Lust begot,
> Betwixt a Painted *Briton* and a *Scot*;
> Whose gend'ring Offspring quickly learn'd to bow,
> And yoke their Heifers to the *Roman* Plough;
> From whence a Mongrel half-Bred Race there came,
> With neither Name nor Nation, Speech or Fame.
> In whose hot Veins new Mixtures quickly ran,
> Infus'd betwixt a *Saxon* and a *Dane*.
> While their Rank Daughters, to their Parents just
> Receiv'd all Nations with Promiscuous Lust.
> This Nauseous Brood directly did contain
> The well-extracted Blood of *Englishmen*.

> *(13: 42)*

Defoe's version of the English primal scene is violent and sordid, suggestive of prostitution and venereal disease. The Englishman is an impure monster sewed together from various parts, a rootless and speechless "Thing." Without an identifiable origin, the English lack a given "Name."

Consequently, in the "Explanatory Preface" to the ninth edition of the poem, instead of valuing purity, Defoe sets out a different kind of national identity: "Our *English* Nation may value themselves for their *Wit*, *Wealth*, and *Courage*, and I believe few Nations will dispute it with them; but for long Originals, and ancient True-Born Families of *English*, I would advise them to waive the Discourse. A *True English Man* is one that deserves a Character" (13: 24). He presents a picture of a nation in constant flux, urging his readers not to despise foreigners because "what they are to-day, we were yesterday, and to-morrow they will be like us" (13: 24).

In this preface, Defoe also argues for the advantages of heterogeneity. Responding to accusations that he was "abusing" the English nation, he notes that although the Welsh, Irish, and Scottish nations are "as clear from the Mixtures of Blood as any in the World," he expresses his preference for "mix'd Blood" and claims that "if I were to write a Reverse to the Satyr, I would examine all the Nations of *Europe*, and prove, That those Nations which are most mix'd, are the best, and have the least of Barbarism and Brutality among them" (13: 22). Defoe is developing a typology of nations here: England is heterogeneous and assimilative, hence stronger and more "civilized" than the more pure Celtic nations. He continues: "We ought rather to boast among our Neighbours that we are part of themselves, of the same Original as they, but bettered by our Climate, and, like our Language and Manufactures, derived from them, and improved by us to a perfection greater than they can pretend to" (13: 25). But, paradoxically, Defoe also suggests that the Celts and the English are derived from the same "Original." What becomes apparent in Defoe's work are the contradictions behind the articulation of national identity: the English are both the same as other nations and different.

The instability Defoe points to was exacerbated by the Union, which fixed attention on the differences within the nation of Great Britain. As this book will argue, the initial Act of Union was reconsidered and re-created at various important junctures as historical events demanded the reexamination of the basis of the shared nation. And at each point, the fissures upon which the national structure was built became evident once more.

From its beginning, and continuing into the present day, the nation of Great Britain has been a dialogic negotiation between its various elements. In the chapters that follow I consider how the work of Scottish and English writers over the eighteenth century attempted to articulate an identity by sometimes denying but more often acknowledging the contradictions within that identity. Such a claim is best made by studying actual dialogues between different writers, and I have structured this book accordingly around five such historical pairings from 1707 to 1830.

An integral part of my history of the articulation of Britain concerns the progressive establishment throughout this period of a cultural arena separate from that of politics. In *Culture and Society*, Raymond Williams argues that the concept of culture developed in the late eighteenth century in response to the "new kinds of personal and social relationship" resulting from industrialization and the democratic ideas ushered in by the American and French revolutions (p. 17). For Williams, culture is both "an abstraction and an absolute," merging "two general responses":

> First, the recognition of the practical separation of certain moral and intellectual activities from the driven impetus of a new kind of society; second, the emphasis of these activities, as a court of human appeal, to be set over the processes of practical social judgment and yet to offer itself as a mitigating and rallying alternative. (p. 17)

David Lloyd points out the ideological use of this "court of human appeal," arguing that culture becomes separated precisely in order to serve as a salve to mounting contradictions in the political realm: "The political function of aesthetics and culture is not only to suggest the possibility of transcending conflict, but to do so by excluding (or integrating) difference, whether historically produced or metaphysically conceived, insofar as it represents a threat to an image of unity whose role is finally hegemonic" (p. 19). Tracing what he calls the "ideology of the aesthetic," Terry Eagleton adopts a similar perspective on the cultural realm: "The construction of the modern notion of the aesthetic artefact is . . . inseparable from the construction of the dominant ideological forms of modern class-society, and indeed from a whole new form of human subjectivity appropriate to that social order" (*Ideology*, p. 3). In the case of Britain, the separation of the cultural from the political realm did indeed serve to foster the dominant hegemony, as culture became a site onto which the heterogeneities (whether of national affiliation, geography, class, or gender) of different political identities could be projected and integrated.

But Eagleton makes allowance for the oppositional nature of the aesthetic, too: "The aesthetic, understood in a certain sense, provides an unusually powerful challenge and alternative to these dominant ideological forms, and is in this sense an eminently contradictory phenomenon" (*Ideology*, p. 3).[18] Indeed, as we will see, this cultural terrain was also subject to battles for occupation. The literature produced by both Scots and English writers often represents through its dialogical form the national struggles it was intended to resolve ideologically. Writers from north of the Tweed attempted in diverse ways to stake their claim in culture as a means of both social and monetary advancement.[19] Their occupation and specific transformations of the literary arena were contested by other writers—both English and Scottish—who employed different models of national culture. For discussion of this dynamic relationship in the cultural realm, we can turn to Pierre Bourdieu's analysis of the aesthetic field as a *"field of forces,"* but also as a *"field of struggles* tending to transform or conserve this field of forces" (p. 30). Bourdieu examines these struggles as reflective of actual relations of power:

> The network of objective relations between positions subtends and orients the strategies which the occupants of the different positions implement in their struggles to defend or improve their positions— strategies which depend for their force and form on the position each agent occupies in the power relations. (p. 30)

The literary dialogue over the nature of Britain was never static. It changed in accordance with changes in the political events of the time. The chapters that follow trace the struggles and symbolic renegotiation of the relationship between Scotland and England during the century after the Union, examining how political struggles came to be located in the cultural realm. The first two chapters examine the ambiguous relationship between the political and cultural realms as they are in the process of separating from one another. These chapters necessarily cover quite a range of material in an attempt to determine how claims for literariness developed from a more general concept of print culture, although they focus on debates between two individual writers. Chapter 3 considers the political implications of one particular debate over the origin of culture in Britain. The final two chapters concentrate on the struggles occurring within the realm of literary culture itself, and the conclusion examines the role of Scotland in the establishment of a canon of English literature.

Chapter 1, "Writing the Nation in 1707: Daniel Defoe, Lord Belhaven, and the 'Vast Conjunction' of Britain," examines the political debate surrounding the Act of Union. I consider the articulation of Scottish identity by Scottish anti-Union pamphleteers, especially Lord Belhaven, and suggest that their ambiguous view of the Scottish nation contested but ultimately paved the way for cultural as well as political union. I compare their views with those of Daniel Defoe, who presented an idea of the nation as an all-encompassing heterogeneous system that could be made cohesive through the act of writing. Ultimately, Defoe's vision of Britain as a "vast Conjunction" of different elements won out, but inscribed within it is also the realization that the union must be continually repeated or it will vanish.

In Chapter 2, "Narrating the '45: Henry Fielding, Tobias Smollett, and the Pretense of Fiction," I argue that Fielding and Smollett used the novel form to highlight some of the same political concerns as nonfictional forms such as journalism. The novel form, however, allowed a more apparently objective space in which to encourage the integration of the national differences that had reemerged violently with the '45 Rebellion. Fielding's novel *Tom Jones* develops themes similar to those of his journalism during the Rebellion, as he attempts to reshape and contain the uprising in the fictional realm. However, the assertions of national unity in *Tom Jones* are troubled by the presence of the Gypsy King, a symbol of absolute difference who exists on the margins of the apparently settled nation. Smollett, too, seeks to smooth over the effects of the Rebellion. *Roderick Random* avoids discussion of the Rebellion per se, but, it does problematize the relationship of the various heterogeneous elements in Britain. According to their contemporary Samuel Johnson, Fielding and Smollett were responsible for inventing a new kind of fiction. Part of the appeal of this genre was its simultaneous representation and imaginative integration of political difference in the cultural realm.

Chapter 3, "Origin of the Specious: James Macpherson, Samuel Johnson, and the Forging of the Nation," continues to examine the efficacy of a cultural realm that was removed from yet also reflected political tensions. The debate between Macpherson and Johnson over the origins of British culture must be seen in relation to the growing Scottish influence in England, suggested by the cultural prominence of Scottish Enlightenment writers and by the political ascendancy of Lord Bute. I argue that Macpherson's reshaping of the past was designed to restore the Highlanders' self-esteem in post-Culloden Britain, but also to appeal to a sense of the British nation. *Fingal* and *Temora* suggest a mythic point of origin that Highlanders, Lowlanders, and English can share. Furthermore, in his later histories and political pamphlets, Macpherson postulates that ethnic differences between the Celts and the English evolved historically and will therefore disappear. His work, then, both promotes Scottish influence in Britain and assuages fears of Scottish dominance. Johnson's *Journey to the Western Isles of Scotland* is an attempt to correct Macpherson's view of Scotland's prominence in the past. However, at the same time, Johnson's narrative demands the reader's attention to both the situation of Scotland and the Highland predicament in the present. Macpherson's and Johnson's debate represents a new stage in the renegotiation of the Union, as it forced the British reading public to consider the consequences of the history of culture. This chapter also considers the intervention of James

Boswell into this dialogue. In his *Journal of a Tour to the Hebrides*, Boswell negotiates a place for Lowland Scots as cultural mediators in Britain.

Chapter 4, "The Poetry of Nature and the Nature of Poetry: Robert Burns and William Wordsworth," examines Wordsworth's renegotiation of Burn's work after the Scottish poet's death as illustrative of the contest for control of the British cultural realm at the end of the eighteenth century. From his position on the geographical, economic, and cultural periphery, Burns was acutely aware of the incommensurable differences not just within Britain but also within the Scottish nation. Burns himself negotiated a position between critiquing the hegemony and participating in it. Accordingly, his poetry draws attention to the differences within the nation but notes at the same time the acts of poetic and readerly imagination that are necessary to create a sense of national identity. Burns's position as a marginalized character defying and at the same time defining the literary and political center made him particularly appealing to Wordsworth. But Wordsworth was also troubled by the preeminence of Edinburgh writers in the literary arena. Part of Wordsworth's project in establishing his own poetic role in Britain consisted of negotiating Burns, as a representative of Scotland and Scottish writing, into his own work.

Chapter 5, "Citing the Nation: Thomas Percy's and Walter Scott's Minstrel Ballads," examines how, through his negotiations with Thomas Percy and with his Scottish predecessors, Macpherson and Burns, Walter Scott imagines alternative histories of Britain and of English literature. In the *Minstrelsy of the Scottish Border* (1801–3), Scott wanted to establish a different identity for Scotland than could be found in the fabrications of Macpherson or the rustic lyrics of Burns. He discovered an antidote to what he perceived as their limited imaginings of the nation in Percy's authoritative *Reliques of Ancient English Poetry*. Scott both identified with Percy's project and differentiated his work from that of Percy by concentrating on the matter of Scotland. In addition, Scott constructed a different history of Britain than that found in the *Reliques*, one that emphasized the heterogeneous nature of the nation. The 1801–3 *Minstrelsy* suggests that the ballads can be used as evidence of this heterogeneity. In the 1830 edition of the *Minstrelsy*, however, published after his financial downfall, Scott puts the construction of literary history into question by showing its relationship to material and market considerations. In the "Essay on the Imitation of Ancient Ballads" contained in that edition, Scott offers an alternate genealogy of British literary history that renegotiates the authenticity of the center.

My concluding chapter, "Runes of Empire: Scotland and the Margins of English Literature," considers the use made of the representation of national difference in Britain in the institutionalization of English literature. Drawing on the work of Thomas Carlyle and Matthew Arnold, I consider the place Scotland plays as a marker of difference that can be assimilated and that provides a model for the assimilation of other disparate groups in the British empire.

It is important to point out some things that this book does not do. First, it does not deal with the other Celtic countries, Wales and Ireland. They are mentioned only tangentially, although they certainly warrant closer attention than I am able to give them here. I have concentrated exclusively on the relationship of Scotland and England to provide geographical and historical continuity. Moreover, I suggest that the particularities of Scotland's relationship with England make it an interesting case, with the Union occurring as it did, during the embryonic stage of the birth of the modern nation. Unlike Wales, Scotland was an established nation with a parliament of its own. Unlike Ireland, Scotland was not predominantly Catholic and therefore irredeemably Other.

Second, there are, of course, hundreds of works of literature written in the eighteenth century that are not covered by this study. Compared to the range offered in Weinbrot's *Britannia's Issue: The Rise of British Literature from Dryden to Ossian* or Trumpener's *Bardic Nationalism: The Romantic Novel and the British Empire*, for example, the selection here may seem at first glance narrow. However, this study has a different purpose than to survey and chart the course of a British national literature; it aims to question the fixity on which an idea of a national literature, or indeed of a nation, is based by concentrating on what can be considered pertinent dialogues between Scottish and English writers. It is my contention that British national identity was created out of the displacement of cultural difference; I have therefore selected historical moments when cultural difference was foregrounded. By examining the kinds of dialogues concerning the idea of a British nation at these moments, I suggest, we can begin to understand the contradictions at the heart of Britain.

Another area that this book does not cover is what Raymond Williams, in *Marxism and Literature*, calls truly oppositional texts: oral texts, radical pamphlets, and such discourses. I am more concerned here with interrogating the successful hegemonic discourses than in detailing oppositional ones, although I look forward to future developments in that area.

I should emphasize that the arguments offered here are themselves a result of critical dialogism. My interpretations of the texts are informed by a practice of close reading that considers the "difference" located within the assertions of written language. My readings also borrow from New Historicism a concern to combine and entangle issues of writing, literature, and politics, to express what Stephen Greenblatt calls a "poetics of culture." Along with the New Historicists, I am interested in challenging the assumptions behind the traditional distinction between the artistic object and the context in which it appears.

Finally, my approach has been influenced by work that questions colonial narratives of domination juxtaposing a "fixed" idea of Self against a stereotyped Other.[20] In keeping with the aims of postcolonial criticism, I hope that this study participates in what Bhabha calls "a logic of supplementary subversion similar to the strategies of minority discourse" (*Location*, p. 162). The examination and unraveling of the ambiguities behind the hegemony of the nation is not a form of material intervention, and poststructuralist postcolonialism, as Aijaz Ahmad points out, can in fact "domesticate, in institutional ways, the very forms of political dissent" which it ought to be supporting (p. 1). However, instead of just displacing "an activist culture with a textual one" (p. 1), I hope that the examination offered here can contribute to the dialogue aimed at resisting the growing danger of myths of the nation. I also hope this book may provide some insight into the past that will be useful in rethinking the future political and cultural relationships between the entities of Scotland, England, and Britain. Such a rethinking is especially crucial at the present time in the wake of the current political changes in Britain.

CHAPTER I

Writing the Nation in 1707:
Daniel Defoe, Lord Belhaven, and
the "Vast Conjunction" of Britain

In *A Union for Empire: Political Thought and the British Union of 1707*, John Robertson makes a claim for a new perception of the Union of England and Scotland. Where previous interpretations by historians after William Ferguson have regarded the Union as a "simple political job, cobbled together by two sets of politicians whose ambition was set no higher than the confirmation of the Hanoverian succession in both countries," Robertson and the contributors to his collection argue that the Union must be understood "within an intellectual as well as a political and economic context" (p. 1).[1] Robertson suggests that although economics and politics are important factors in the creation of the British nation, they cannot be divorced and regarded separately from an enabling discourse.

In keeping with this new contextualization of the Union, I explore in this chapter the discourse that informed the negotiations and the changing relationship between Scotland and England. Specifically, I examine the tension between the Scottish anti-Union pamphleteers' image of the Scottish nation, one which draws on the mythic or historical past, and the representation of a new Britain as a heterogeneous nation joined through the medium of writing, a construction suggested in the work of Daniel Defoe. When Defoe refers to the Union as a "vast Conjunction," he connotes both the unification of the two nations and the medium—language—by which they were made to appear united.[2] By examining Defoe's dialogue with his opponents, especially Lord Belhaven, I consider how, in Homi Bhabha's terms, the "cultural construction of nationness" occurs by means of "social and textual affiliation" (*Location*, p. 140).

According to Raymond Williams, hegemonic forces act upon residual ideologies by "reinterpretation, dilution, projection, discriminating inclusion [or]
exclusion" (*Marxism and Literature*, p. 122). In Britain at the time of the
Union, the dominant economic forces, those that Defoe embraced, were tipping the balance toward the Union. Defoe reinterpreted and incorporated
residual ideas concerning national identity into what would become a dominant discourse of heterogeneity. Belhaven, a Scottish aristocrat and an im-
proving and protectionist landlord, drew on myth and history in his representation of the Scottish nation. Defoe, as an English tradesman, realized that
such national images stood in the way of the economic expansion of England
and Britain; for Defoe, prosperity necessarily entailed roping conflicting interests together.[3] Accordingly, he reimagined the Scottish lord's concept of
national identity into the all-inclusive idea of Britain by emphasizing the
unifying power of language. More than this, Defoe incorporated Belhaven's
utterance into his own writing; Belhaven's is one of the few speeches to appear in Defoe's extensive *History of the Union Between England and Scotland*
(1709).

However, Defoe's narration of the heterogeneous nation could not completely suppress its opposition. Belhaven's speech continued to circulate in
anti-Union circles throughout the century in various manifestations. The political conjunction of Britain, as Defoe was to realize, can never be static, but
has always to be anxiously repeated. Born of dissent and ambiguity, the "vast
Conjunction" of the British nation is also subject to dissolution; a "conjunction," after all, is a phenomenon that joins, but also divides, as it indicates a
fundamental difference between the two parts it brings together.

As Linda Colley notes, there has been little attention given to "the importance of print in unifying Great Britain and in shaping its inhabitants' view
of themselves," despite the rapid growth in print culture at the end of the
seventeenth century (p. 40). The period from the 1603 Union of Crowns to
the completion of the Act of Union saw a continuous academic debate on the
historical and cultural claims of Scotland and England as their economic and
political interests drew closer together.[4] Published literary work came to play
a larger part in the debate, as the printed word become increasingly important in reflecting and subsequently influencing economic and political concerns; the possibilities for the dissemination of public information and debate
were greater now than at any other time previously.[5] William Bragg Ewald
has identified the era of Queen Anne as formative in the development of
journalism and the manipulation of public opinion through print. We see evidence for a growing circulation of political issues through print culture reflected in the increase in numbers of newspapers. J. A. Downie has com-

mented on "the sheer volume of political propaganda that the party presses managed to turn out" in the beginning of the eighteenth century (p. 1). In addition, a concern for political affairs was also generated by the publication of political poetry.[6]

The Union, then, was situated in the context of this expansion of print and the growth of the reading public. Bruce Levack comments on the enormous amount of published material that was devoted to the Union, the biggest internal policy issue since the Licensing Act expired: "The volume of recorded opinion on the union, in the form of speeches, letters, proclamations, and pamphlets, is truly astonishing. Between 1603 and 1707 there was no other issue in the history [of] either nation, with the one exception of the English civil war, which attracted more attention and created more controversy than the union" (p. 14). William Ferguson confirms the interest in reading about the Union: "Demand for this literature of contention did not need to be created. The large number of pamphlets produced, some of them hefty tomes, is indicative of a keen public interest" (*Scotland's Relations*, p. 222). Moreover, for Ferguson, the Act of Union debate was a watershed in the history of public debates because it foregrounded political issues: "Previous exercises of this kind had concentrated on religious and theological themes to which politics was subordinated. . . . The Union debate for the first time gave political consideration priority" (*Scotland's Relations*, p. 239).

In addition to pamphlets circulated outside the legislative doors, printed documents circulated between Parliament and the outside world became a matter of attention. Ferguson says that the "fury" regarding the treaty for Union "erupted in Parliament, but it did not begin or end there. Parliament was certainly the focus of interest; its proceedings were eagerly followed by the public, and virtually for the first time speeches made there flooded from the presses" (*Scotland's Relations*, p. 185). Similarly, printed petitions were distributed to Parliament. Although he is cautious about the effect of such petitions, William Law Mathieson identifies a number of cases in which the Scottish population voiced their disagreement with their parliamentary representatives:

> Public opinion as opposed to incorporation was first formally expressed
> on October 29, when every member on entering the House received a
> copy of certain instructions which had been given by the magistrates and
> town-council of Lauder to their representative, Sir David Cunningham
> of Milncraig, requiring him to dissent from all the twenty-five articles,
> and protesting that, if he supported the treaty, his vote should be void;
> and the member of Dumfriesshire was instructed by 31 of his con-

stituents to the same effect. The first addresses to Parliament against the
Union, five in number, were presented on November 1; and from this
date to January 10 the House was occupied almost every day with the
reading of petitions from parishes, burghs and shires, beseeching the
Estates in nearly identical terms not to sanction any incorporating union.
(p. 133)

Attention to printed debates becomes particularly important in establishing a more accurate picture of the uncertainty surrounding the passage of the
Union. The idea that the Union was an inevitable process is a retrospective
judgment, according to Murray Pittock, a result of what he terms "incre-
mental history" (*Poetry and Jacobite Politics*, p. 1).[7] There were many sharp
turns in the road to union, and public opinion played a not inconsiderable
part along the way. Ferguson highlights the effect of the public participation
in the debates: "the intensity of public feeling in both countries cannot be ignored. It certainly was not overlooked by the politicians of the time. Nor was
it negligible in its effects" (*Scotland's Relations*, p. 222). We can see this con-
firmed in contemporary accounts of the effect of the press on public opinion.
The editor of the *Flying Post or Post Master* comments on October 29, 1706,
for example, that "many of our Traders, who at first seem'd fond of [the
Union] have now imbibed other Notions" because of the "Pamphlets . . .
spread about here." The citizens of Scotland actively participated in the debates about the future of their nation. Despite the results of political maneu-
vering, we must not lose sight of the public discourse regarding the Union,
for it was this discourse that shaped the self-image of the nation in the years
following the Union. The new British nation was constructed from the dialogue that took place regarding its potential existence.

Defoe, in particular, exploited the interest in the printed word to convey
his idea of the nation as a conjunction of heterogeneous interests. We can see
evidence of his developing an appreciation of the power of print before he
encountered Belhaven and the Scottish pamphleteers during the time when
he started working for Robert Harley after being rescued from imprisonment
for debt. Defoe served as a liaison between Harley and the citizens of the nation, setting up a number of bases throughout England from which to gather
information and to distribute pamphlets and newspapers.[8] He toured the
country, establishing "an intelligence network that allowed the extensive dis-
play of political views held by the minister in an attempt to influence public
opinion in the widest possible sense" (Downie, p. 2). One of the most important tools in Defoe's network was a Saturday news journal that began on
February 19, 1704, as *A Weekly Review of the Affairs of France: Purg'd from the*

Errors and Partiality of News-Writers and Petty-Statesmen, of all Sides. After volume one, number eight, the word "Weekly" was dropped. A subtitle, "With some Observations on Transactions at Home" was added with volume two (February 27, 1705), indicating an interest in affairs closer to home. The title changed again with volume three to *A Review of the State of the English Nation*, and with volume four, number twelve, after the Union, it became *A Review of the State of the British Nation*.[9] Although the *Review* began as a justification of English actions in France, its purpose quickly broadened to creating national consensus through regular dissemination of the printed word.

Defoe took pains to make the *Review* appear to be a dialogue involving people from across the nation. The *Review* formed a hub around which information and opinions circulated in frantic haste. Readers who wrote letters, says Defoe, demanded "to be answer'd to Day before to Morrow, and are so far from staying till the Story is finish'd, that they can hardly stay till their Letters come to Hand; but follow the First with a Second, that with Clamour, and this sometimes with threatening Scoffs, Banters, and Raillery."[10] Defoe presents himself as beleaguered with the responses he got: "Thus I am Letter baited by Querists, and think my Trouble to write civil, private Answers to teazing and querulous Epistles, has been equal, if not more troublesome, than all the rest of this Work." However, he notes that this was an integral part of his project, and he attempted to make "something solid, and something solemn" from even the lightest questions.[11] Defoe aimed for a kind of journalism that separated itself from old-style orations, establishing instead a national community.[12] At best it was a fictional claim, however, for Defoe himself wrote many of the letters included in editions of the *Review*.

Defoe's interest in using print culture to create a nation of heterogeneous citizens united by concern for trade and expansion was challenged by the Union. He had been concerned about the Scottish situation well before he was sent up to Edinburgh, following events in Scotland avidly and discussing them with his Scottish friends in London. He had suggested to Harley as far back as the summer of 1704 that more immediate attention to the Scottish situation was needed: "A Settl'd intelligence in Scotland, a Thing Strangely Neglected There, is without Doubt the Principall Occasion of The present Missunderstandings between the Two kingdomes" (*Letters*, p. 14). As anti-Union feeling grew during the summer of 1706, particularly after George Lockhart, one of the Scottish commissioners, made the terms of the treaty public, the need for a "Settl'd intelligence" became more serious (*Letters*, p. 126). Finally, in the fall of 1706, Harley sent Defoe to be on location during the sitting of the Scottish Parliament. In a letter to Harley dated September 13, 1706, Defoe set down his understanding of his task and the tools with which he had to manage it. Notably, he emphasized the work of written words in his promotion of the Union. He would take pains, he says, "By writeing or Discourse, to Answer any Objections, Libells or Reflections on the Union, the English or the Court, Relateing to the Union" (*Letters*, p. 126).

From 1706 to 1709, Defoe devoted his attention to writing poetry, pamphlets, and issues of the *Review* to promote the Union. He had completed two *Essays at Removing National Prejudices Against a Union With Scotland* when he lived in London, chiefly with an English audience in mind. The subsequent four essays on the same subject changed considerably in tone as they became directly involved in answering Scottish pamphleteers. In subjecting the arguments of the pamphleteers to processes of "reinterpretation, dilution, projection, discriminating inclusion [or] exclusion" (Williams, *Marxism and Literature*, p. 122), Defoe further developed his rhetoric regarding the nation, attempting to promote his conception of a heterogeneous Britain united by the pen.

A common rhetorical thrust for Defoe is to reduce political disagreement to linguistic misunderstanding. In the third *Essay at Removing National Prejudices*, Defoe goes to great lengths to explain exactly how he understands the "happy conjunction" that is to occur, giving a precise understanding of what he means by the word "union": "here I think it can not be improper to explain how extensive I think *the word Union* to be in this Case; and how *even by the Treaty*, it ought to be understood" (p. 6). He counsels those who interpret it differently to "turn to their Books, and putting together all the Etymologies, receiv'd Significations, customary Acceptations, and common readings of the words *Union* and *Incorporation*, tell us what they understand by them, and how the true meaning of the Words, and the new suggestions of separate Existence in the Government can Consist" (pp. 6–7). Relying on etymology and analogy to undo the arguments the pamphlets were raising about Scottish independence, he suggests that common understanding regarding language could lay the basis for national concord.

Again, in the *Sixth Essay at Removing National Prejudices*, Defoe's method of refuting the danger of dissent is to turn the problem into an issue of language. He addresses the problem of petitions being taken to the Scottish Parliament. The petitions, says Defoe, claim that Parliament is "*Acting contrary to the Fundamental Rights of the Nation; that their Votes are Inconsistent with the Constitution of* Scotland, *Enslaving them to* England, *and Surrendering the Liberties and Freedoms* of the Scots Nation; in plain Words, *Betraying their Native Country to the* English, *and destroying that foundation which is their Duty to preserve and defend*" (p. 8). The citizens have been "misled" by what they have heard or read regarding the Union. Furthermore, Defoe argues that the petitions of the citizens cannot be taken seriously because they do not conform to the meaning of the word "petition"; the presentations to Parliament are not "prayers" but rather demands: "*As to the Words* or Terms of the Petition. As every Sermon ought to Conform to the Text, every Book to its Title, every Application to the Doctrine, so every such Application to Authority, ought to Conform to the Title, which always bears the term Humble in Front of it" (p. 7). The petitions are not humbly presented, therefore they are not petitions.

Throughout all of these *Essays*, Defoe incorporates and changes the arguments of his opponents into his own perspective. *A Fourth Essay, at Removing National Prejudices . . . With some Reply to Mr. Hodges and Some Other Authors, Who Have Printed Their Objections Against An Union with England*, like the third *Essay*, deals directly with pamphlets being distributed in the public sphere. In particular, it attacks James Hodges's *Rights and Interests of the Two British Monarchies, Inquir'd Into, and Clear'd* (1703). Hodges, although an advocate of federal union, drew on the arguments for Scottish sovereignty, asserting that Scotland was the most ancient of existing monarchies: "none of the [previously] mentioned Kingdoms or Dominions had the Honour of a Free Government of so long continuance, as is that of *Scotland*" (p. 9). Furthermore, the Scots are an unconquered race, "whereas *England* hath been four times conquer'd, to wit by the *Romans*, the *Saxons*, the *Danes*, and the *Normans*; The *Scots* are the only People of *Europe*, whom, tho' none more violently assaulted, yet neither *Romans*, who conquer'd all the rest, nor any other Nation, have ever been able to conquer, since the first Setling of their Government." In fact, the Scots had managed to preserve their "National Freedom and Independency, for . . . above one third of the World's Age from the Creation" (p. 10). Hodges goes to great lengths to prove that although the Scots would suffer the loss of their independence and trade from incorporating with England, the English, too, would suffer from a multitude of difficulties, including a "Deluge of all manner of Trades-People from Scotland" who would undersell them (p. 59).

In his refutation of Hodges in his *Fourth Essay*, Defoe sidesteps the issue of Scotland's ancient history but attempts to assure the Scots that a British constitution would protect them from abuses of government as well as, if not better than, a Scottish constitution. Hodges had claimed that upon union, Scotland would be dissolved into England, its interests lost. Furthermore, he had suggested that the Scottish commissioners had no power to dissolve Scotland because "taking a National Oath, obliges the *Scots* to keep themselves a distinct Nation" (p. 13). Defoe argues that the Scottish members of Parliament were acting in the best interests of the Scottish nation by joining with England. Thus, he solves the problem of the Scottish nation by suggesting a paradox: Scottish people can be best served by no longer being Scottish.

Like the third and fourth, Defoe's fifth and sixth *Essays at Removing National Prejudices* are also concerned with the pamphlet literature of his opponents. In the *Fifth Essay*, subtitled *"With a Reply to Some Authors Who Have Printed Their Objections against An Union With England,"* Defoe says he took up his pen again because he was surprised at the lack of sound understanding of the Union: "The Management of this present Treaty, I mean, without Doors, has something in it peculiarly odd, and to me very surprizing; Reason and Argument, nay even Demonstration cannot reach it; Men will argue against, nay Banter, and be Witty upon the several Branches, & yet at the end of the Discourse profess, They do not Understand them" (Preface). Defoe laments the fact that "Words can have no Effect on such Persons, no Argument can touch them" (Preface). In fact, however, it becomes obvious that he believes that words and arguments have touched some people. Defoe's concern in this essay is the immense impact the work of other writers is having on the general population.

Many sections from the *Essays* were reprinted in the *Review*, as the *Review* also became an important part of Defoe's campaign to write the nation into union.[13] The *Review* always emphasized the insignificance of national differences in the face of the possibility of union. Most important, the *Review* created a frame in which Defoe could present the Union as an inevitable, linear process, a tale unfolding to its awaited climax. He himself suggests this analogy, as he presents himself as the author of the narrative events of the Union. Responding to his readers' dissatisfaction with his dwelling on the question of union, Defoe laments: "Indeed this is the Fate of all the poor Authors that ever did or shall write; the World will never relish a long Story, be there never so much Variety in it" (p. 677).

One of the biggest trials for Defoe's attempt to write the "long Story" of a union of heterogeneous interests was the image of an independent Scottish nation presented by Scottish pamphleteers. Laurence Dickey and David Armitage discuss the difference between the English perspective on economics demonstrated in the work of Defoe, for example, and that of certain Scots like Andrew Fletcher and the merchants who promoted the Darien scheme.[14] I suggest that another difference between the English and Scottish perspectives was that the image of the nation in the work of Scottish pamphleteers was at odds with the English design for the construction of the British nation. For the Scots, the major issues of contention during the Act of Union debate were religion, trade, and the political self-determination of the Scottish nation.[15] Many Scots rejected the idea of union, although not all Scottish writers who denounced the Union were against some kind of affiliation with England. A number of them advocated a federal union but vehemently op-

posed an incorporating union. Regardless of their ultimate intentions for
Scotland, however, these anti-Union writers routinely emphasized two aspects of Scotland's national identity: its genealogical purity and its independent history.[16]

The concept of Scotland's genealogical purity can be seen in William
Wright's *The Comical History of the Marriage-Union Betwixt Fergusia and Heptarchus*, for example, which contrasts Scotland (Fergusia) as a nation of "ven-
erable Antiquity" (p. 3) with the "young and lusty" (p. 7) England (Heptarchus). The negotiations between them are presented as a courtship ritual,
as Heptarchus, after making "a great many Civilities and handsome Comple-
ments," exclaims: "I'm passionate to possess that Shining Beauty and Virtue, I
have so long beheld and admired in you" (pp. 9–10). Fergusia is suspicious
about allying herself with such an upstart, and understandably so, for she is
warned by Heptarchus's sister, Juverna, that he is "so strong, that Parchment
will not bind him" (p. 8). Fergusia presents to Heptarchus her terms, which
he refuses, claiming that he can never be happy until the two are "intirely Incorporated" (p. 12). Fergusia's interpretation of incorporation is "*that You'd
devour Me, and burie Me in the midst of Your self, and I be turned into Your very
Flesh and Blood*" (p. 12). She outlines more obstacles and claims she needs
time to deliberate. The pamphlet ends with "Fergusia's Advice and Caution
to Her Sons," in which she admonishes them to weigh her reasons for not
marrying and to consider that "*Your Predecessors have perpetually been deluded
with fatal Mistakes, in all their Transactions with their Neighbours*" (p. 29). She
urges them not to make the same mistakes and end up being "wise behind
the hand" (p. 30). The pamphlet draws on the same images of purity and heterogeneity that Defoe used in "True-Born Englishman." Heptarchus is presented, as in Defoe's poem, as a mongrel nation:

> He was of Old, very much oppres'd, and intirely subdu'd first by the
> *Casarians*: then, upon their Declension, by the *Fergusians*, against whom
> he call'd in, to help him, a barbarous Pagan People out of *Alemania*, who,
> of Servants and Confederates, made themselves his Masters. He was
> afterwards oppres'd by the then fam'd Nation of the *Lochlans*: And at last,
> by a bravading French Bastard, he was hector'd to an entire Submission,
> in so far, that he kept nothing of himself, but the old Name: So that this
> Gentleman has all the Blood of these annex'd People in his Veins, and
> also all their conquering Vigour. (p. 4)

Wright equates mixed blood with vigor, but, unlike Defoe, presents such a
combination as dangerous. In contrast to Heptarchus, Fergusia appears as an

aristocratic woman of pure pedigree. She has been independent for a long time and "has cherish'd all her Sons, for a long Tract of Time, to their Satisfaction and Content" (p. 3). She has preserved her hereditary honor: "her Chastity, tho' several times attack'd, yet was never violated; save that once, a long time ago, her barbarous Neighbour, *Edwardo*, did commit a Rape upon her" (p. 3).

Similar images are presented in James Clark's *Scotland's Speech to Her Sons* (1706), which also draws out the filial sympathy of the inhabitants of Scotland: "I can keep no longer Silence . . . there is not one within the land, who is not sensible, who sees not with his eyes, that I am stript naked of my Ancient Honour and Glory, and covered with Disgrace and Contempt among Neighbor Nations" (p. 1). According to this pamphlet, the problem lies not just with English insolence, but with the "sordid Mercenary spirits" of Scottish people. Scotland appeals to her citizens as "sons": "Is there no Scots blood in your veins? are Scots Spirits sunk into silliness? . . . ye be so unnatural and devoid of Respect to your Old Mother, so sadly beaten at all hands, as to do nothing for my Relief and Reputation." Like Wright's *The Comical History*, Clark's *Scotland's Speech to Her Sons* draws on the metaphor of rape: allegiance with England compromises the pure "Reputation" of the Scottish nation. Both pamphlets involve their readers in an act of imagining in the present, as those readers are positioned as heirs to an anthropomorphized nation.

In addition to the concept of the nation as a filial association, Scottish pamphleteers were also concerned with Scotland's historical independence. One of the most important documents concerning Scotland's history during the Union controversy was George Ridpath's 1695 republication of Thomas Craig's *Scotland's Sovereignty Asserted* (originally published in Latin in 1605). The subtitle of the tract explains the subject of contention: "Being a Dispute Concerning Homage Against those who maintain that Scotland is a feu, or fee-leige of England and that therefore the King of Scots owes Homage to the King of England." In the preface, Ridpath expresses his desire to republish Craig's work "for the Honour of Scotland, and the Information of Foreigners who are frequently misled as to our Affairs, and particularly on this Head, by English Historians" (p. xi). Ridpath addresses the accusation that this publication will "revive old Quarrels" (p. xi), but says that there is no reason "why Scotsmen should not now defend with their Pens, what their Ancestors maintained so gallantly with their swords" (p. xii). He claims that Scots are both "Noble Warriours" (p. xii) and "very Ingenious" (p. xiii). Craig's original work refutes the claim that Malcolm of Scotland and the Isles paid homage to Edward the Confessor.[17]

The issue of Scottish sovereignty became even more important in 1704 with the introduction of the Act of Security by the Scottish Parliament and its acceptance by the English Parliament. William Atwood, a Whig attorney, published *The Superiority and Direct Dominion of the Imperial Crown of England, over the Crown and Kingdom of Scotland* in 1704. He concluded that Scotland was a fief of England and bound by the English Act of Settlement. It is his duty, he suggests, to lay before those negotiating the treaty

> part of that evidence, which may be thought, rather than force of Arms, to have induced the brave Nation, which now possesses Scotland, as well as their Predecessors Picts and Britons, both Princes and People, not only in words, but notoriety of Facts, to have acknowledged the superiority, and direct Dominion of the Crown of England over all the parts, which have fallen under the domination of the Kingdom of Scotland; in testimony of which their kings have paid homage both Feudal and Liege, and the people have sworn Allegiance to our kings. (p. 3)

By alluding to the "predecessors" of the Scottish people, the "Picts and Britons," he questions the idea of the ethnically pure nation at the same time as he attacks the Scottish constitution. Atwood's document was condemned in 1705 by the Scottish Parliament and ordered to be burned.[18] But the dialogue continued, as James Anderson's *An Historical Essay, Shewing That the Crown and Kingdom of Scotland is Imperial and Independent* set out to refute the "bold assertions and glittering proofs" of Atwood's treatise. Anderson takes a different tack, however. Instead of culling evidence from previous histories, like Thomas Craig's, to prove his argument, he reproduces historical charters in an appendix to his pamphlet. Claiming that histories are overgrown with "Legends of Miracles and Visions on the one hand, and larded with many Romantick Fables, and Traditions on the other" (p. 15), he maintains the verity of documentary evidence.

The claim for Scotland's historic independence also drew on the concept of the "community of the realm," which Colin Kidd has traced back to the struggles between John de Baliol, Robert the Bruce, and Edward I. The Declaration of Arbroath (1320), according to Kidd, stressed "the priority of the Scottish community over the authority of Scottish kingship" (p. 17). The Declaration stipulated that if ever the king should make Scotland subject to England, he should be driven out as an enemy. Scottish historians in the century leading up to the Union of Crowns drew on this idea of an antique Scottish government. George Buchanan's histories, *De Jure Regni Apud Scotos, Dialogus* (1579) and *Rerum Scoticarum Historia* (1582), also emphasized the sense of national constitution.[19] Such appeals to Scotland's nationness took on new life in the debates regarding the Union. In fact, a copy of the Declaration was rediscovered before the Revolution of 1688–89 (Kidd, p. 28).

What these representations of the nation—as mythic, filial community or historically independent constitutional body—have in common is the idea of similarity: both rely on the identicality of the nation's members, in blood and in historical experience. Both representations are employed by John Hamilton, the second Baron Belhaven, in his famous speeches against the Union in order to achieve an image of a homogeneous Scotland. Framing Defoe's debate with Belhaven, then, is a difference in ways of imagining the nation. Whereas Defoe, arguing for the Union, bases his ideal for a united Britain on the conjunctive power of written language, Belhaven stresses the myth of national belonging. It was not the immediate threat of Belhaven's speeches in Parliament that Defoe feared; the speeches were in truth politically ineffective, being delivered at a time when the Union was a fait accompli. Rather, Defoe was anxious about Belhaven's impact on the public sphere. Belhaven's speeches represented a threat to the future stability of the British nation, inasmuch as they embodied a myth of the pure nation that was anathema to Defoe's new construction of Britain. Belhaven's image of the Scottish nation, though an imagined construction itself, pointed out the incommensurable gaps over which the new Britain had to be forged.

Belhaven's interest in Scotland's prosperity as an independent nation goes back to the time before the Union. He supported William and Mary during the Glorious Revolution, participating in the battle of Killiecrankie in 1689 and then serving as a member of the Scottish privy council.[20] What we know of his activities and speeches, however, suggests that although he promoted the Williamite line, he was concerned with the improvement of his nation and the promotion of its industry. Under the pseudonym A. B. C., he wrote *The Countrey-man's Rudiments, or, An Advice to the Farmers of East Lothian to Labour and Improve their Grounds* (1699). He invested a thousand pounds in the South African Company, and he supported the unfortunate Darien scheme. His concern for historical recognition of his nation is evident in a speech he delivered to the Scottish Parliament on January 10, 1701, *On the Affair of the Indian and African Company, and its Colony of Caledonia*, where he elaborated on how the label "Scottish" had been erased from the annals of history. He argued that in the European wars, if the Scots distinguished themselves, their exploits were claimed in the name of England, and if they asserted themselves for individual honors, they were ignored: "If any Noble Action was performed by Scots-men, all was said to be done by the English; If we pretended to Precedency as Guards, Royal Regiments, or the like, we were then not *English*, that's in plain *English* nothing; For if *Scots*, we had as

Just a Pretence of competition with the *English*, as they had of Precedency over the Dutch" (pp. 6–7). Belhaven's pun on *"English"*—indicating both national origin and language—is a pointed comment on the political and linguistic hegemony of England. Not to be English is to be "no thing," or at least no thing of value. Moreover, Belhaven recognizes the relationship between words and national identity. Because the name Scotland is never associated with positive exploits, he suggests, it is not surprising that the English look unkindly upon the Scots: "It is no wonder, if some Blundering Bullies, in both Houses of the Parliament of England, give us Names of Poverty and worse" (p. 7). Scotland had been voiceless since the Union of Crowns, he argues: "we have neither been considered in Times of War, nor Treaties of Peace" (p. 7).

The speech also highlights Belhaven's concern with portraying a nation that is emotionally accessible to its members. In the middle of his speech, he stages a pause in midsentence: "Yea, indeed, *My Lord*, I must stop, for I find Old Caledonia-Blood too hot in my veins, my Pulse beats too quick for my Tongue, my Heart is too large for my Breast, and my Choler for my Reason" (p. 9). The cause of his distress is the relation of the misadventures of the Company of Scotland, which he offers to his audience: "Therefore, lest I offend this House by some indecent and angry Expressions, I shall come to the Application, only I must say, let any Scots-Man eat this Book that's in my Hand, and he shall find it as bitter as Gall in his Belly, as at present I find it in mine" (p. 9). The prop he offers to supplement his speech is *The Printed Collection of all the Publick Papers relating to the Company*.

In contrast to the bleak perspective found in the "Book," Belhaven says he will continue his speech with an oral narrative: "a Hopeful Paralel taken out of our own History," adding that he will leave the Application" to his listeners (p. 11). The story Belhaven tells is how the Scots were betrayed by the Picts and were forced to give up "old Caledonia" until finally their country was restored through the efforts of Kenneth III. The story ends with an assertion of the unique homogeneity of the Scottish nation: "The *Romans* and *Danes*, conquered the *Brittons*, the *Danes* arid *Normans* the Saxons, so that by the Providence of God, we are at this day the only *A-borigines* of great *Brittain*" (p. 11). As "A-borigines," the Scots have a unique inviolable bond, a bond of bloodlines. More important, Belhaven compels his contemporary audience to participate in imagining the nation by figuring out for themselves the analogy with the present situation in Scotland; the audience extends the historical bond of the past into the present. The burden of Belhaven's speech is to move away from the actual history presented in the "Book" to a more distant or mythic past. In a later speech, *Upon an Act for Security of the King-*

dom, in case of the Queen's death (1703), Belhaven again attempts to draw on a mythic idea of Scottish homogeneity, suggesting that the Scots were like the ancient Israelites wandering in the wilderness (p. 4).[21]

In 1704, Belhaven was accused of participating in the "Scotch Plot." He was found not guilty, and, if anything, the accusation established him further in the public sphere as an important representative of his nation. Belhaven had already achieved status as a "Noble Patriot" by the time he delivered his most famous speech during the Scottish Parliament's final debate on the twenty-five articles of the Act of Union. In his speech of November 2, 1706, Belhaven again constructs the nation through involving its members in shared experiences. David Macaree, in his article "The Flyting of Daniel Defoe and Lord Belhaven," calls the speech a "melodramatic" outburst of oratory (p. 72). Nevertheless, it is important to look at how Belhaven the orator actually contributes to the discourse on the nation. It is the rhetoric of this speech, rather than its actual effectiveness in deterring the Union, that determined its popularity as a representation of Scottish nationhood.

Employing symbolism and spectacle, Belhaven conveys his idea of mythic national belonging; accordingly, the operative action in the speech is prophetic vision. Belhaven begins with an unfolding dream-vision in which he portrays the Scottish nation's giving up its freedom: "I think I see a *Free and Independent Kingdom* delivering up That, which all the World hath been fighting for, since the days of Nimrod . . . *to wit*, A Power to manage their own Affairs by themselves, without the Assistance and Counsel of any other" (*Speech,* 2 November 1706, p. 3).[22] He goes on to portray dissolution on all levels of society. The National Church has become identical with "Jews, Papists, Socinians, Arminians, Anabaptists, etc." because it has lost the "Claim of Right," the rock on which it was secured. The speech continues as if describing a train of characters in a procession, including the Peers of Scotland, the Royal State of Burroughs, the Judges, the Soldiery, the Tradesmen, the "Laborious Ploughman," the Landed-men whose daughters are unable to find husbands, and the Mariners "earning their Bread as Underlings in the Royal *British* Navy" (pp. 3–4). All of the scenes Belhaven describes emphasize the way in which the people of a once proud and self-sufficient nation have become impoverished, dependent, and, worst of all, servile. The climax of the speech is the following striking image: "I think I see our *Ancient Mother* CALEDONIA, like *Cesar,* sitting in the midst of our Senate, ruefully looking round her, covering her self with her Royal Garment, attending the Fatal Blow, and breathing out her last with a *Et tu quoque mi fili*" (pp. 4–5). This part of the speech draws upon the masque or spectacle tradition used by Stewart monarchs to convey a sense of immediate national belonging.[23] The difference here, however, is that the monarch does not appear in this masque to restore peace to all; rather, this masque concludes with a vision of a defiled Scotland, presented as a combination of a ravaged woman and a betrayed Caesar. This hybrid symbol ensures both the moral outrage and sympathy of the members of the nation and suggests the sovereign claims of Scotland. Belhaven also builds a contemporary spectacle into his 1706 speech: "*My Lord*, I find my Heart so full of Grief and Indignation, That I must beg Pardon not to finish the last part of my Discourse, that I may drop a Tear, as the Prelude to so sad a Story" (p. 15). The actual figure of a weeping Belhaven replaces the metaphorical figure of a defiled Caledonia, focusing the national gaze literally on the betrayal of Scotland.

The reference to Caesar draws attention to the tradition of civic virtue and public participation that pre-Augustan Rome was believed to represent. Belhaven also includes another example of public spectacle from Roman history in his speech: "*My Lord Chancellor*, the greatest Honour that was done unto a *Roman*, was to allow him the Glory of a Triumph; the greatest and most dishonourable Punishment, was that of *Paricide*: He that was guilty of *Paricide*, was beaten with Rods upon his naked Body, till the Blood gush'd out of all the Veins of his Body; then he was sow'd up in a Leathern Sack . . . with a Cock, a Viper, and an Ape, and thrown headlong into the Sea" (p. 6). A worse crime than parricide, suggests Belhaven, is patricide—and that is what the Scottish Members of Parliament will be guilty of if they accept the Act of Union. The slippage in Belhaven's image is pertinent; as he draws on the tradition of the imperial Rome of Julius Caesar and the contemporary Scottish Parliament, he conflates the representations of Scotland's sovereign and constitutional history.

But even Belhaven's mythic image of the nation contains evidence of modern contingencies in its reference to written language. After "*some Discourses by other Members intervening*" (p. 15), Belhaven continues his speech, moving away from the tropes of vision and spectacle to comment more on the activity of writing. Belhaven cautions the members of Parliament to consider carefully before signing the first Article of Union, because to agree to one article will commit them to agreeing to the rest of the articles: "To say, You'll agree to the Union of the two Kingdoms, before you agree in the Terms upon which they are to be United, seems like *driving the Plough before the Oxen*: The Articles, which narrate the Conditions, seem to be the Premises, upon which the Conclusion is inferred" (p. 16). Belhaven advises the commissioners to look before they leap. As he has already indicated, the Scots themselves have power over their national identity, and that identity is contingent upon the act of not signing the Act of Union: "Nothing can destroy

Scotland, save Scotland's self; hold your hands from the Pen, you are secure" (p. 5). In fact, it is the threat of fixed language that Belhaven hurls at his parliamentary compeers, as he brings up the image of people in posterity having "a Recourse unto our Records" to "see who have been the Managers of that Treaty, by which they have suffer'd so much" (p. 14). Belhaven's speech merges representations of the Scottish nation as a filial association, a mythic "ancient kingdom of Caledonia" with an understanding of the nation as a written construct which is closer to Defoe's ideas.

Even though Belhaven's recollection of a past homogeneous nation was logically unstable and anachronistic, it nevertheless was of great concern to Defoe, who was well aware of the effect of discourse, however outmoded, on popular thought. Defoe labeled Belhaven's imaginings the "Cant of Old Times." He wrote to Harley describing his distress about the impact such "Cant" had when delivered by Scottish parliamentarians: "D[uke] Hamilton Rav'd, Fletcher of Saltoun, and the Earle of Belhaven, Made long speeches, the Latter of which Will be printed—The Clamour without was so great That a Rabble was feared tho' the Guard are Numerous and were Drawn Out in Readyness" (*Letters*, p. 142). His reference to the printing of Belhaven's speech suggests that Defoe considered the circulation of Belhaven's visionary speech enough of a threat to the future of the united nation that he took elaborate steps to counteract its influence.

Specifically, he countered fire with fire and produced his satirical poem *The Vision*, which he wrote on the night after Belhaven had delivered his speech so that it could be copied out and distributed on the following Monday (November 4), before the vote on the first Article of Union was due to be held. It was published soon after, and Defoe noted the effects with satisfaction in a letter to Harley dated November 14, 1706, commenting that his satire on Belhaven "has made Some sport here and perhaps Done More Service than a More Solid Discourse" (*Letters*, p. 148). *The Vision* initiated a direct debate between Defoe and Belhaven, which inspired two, or possibly three, subsequent poems.[24] The poetical debate between the opponents reinforced the fundamental difference between their different appeals to the members of the nation. Defoe recognized that in order to promote a new imagining of the nation, it was necessary to dispel residual notions of Scottish national identicality and mythical belonging. Belhaven reiterated his original visual metaphors and once again employed the emotional charge of betrayal.

Defoe sets out to devalue the mystical language of his opponent. In *The Vision*, Defoe describes Belhaven variously as a magician or conjurer, an "exorcist," and a "ghost in a circle." Accordingly, Belhaven's vision is discussed as a trick:

Come hither ye Dreamers of Dreams
Ye soothsayers, Vizards and Witches,
That puzzle the World with hard Names,
And without any meaning make Speeches.
   Here's a Lord in the North,
   Near Edinburgh Frith;
Tho little has been said of his Name or his Worth;
He's seen such a Vision, no Mortal can reach it,
I challenge the Clan of *Egyptians* to match it.

(ll. 1–9)

Defoe cancels out Belhaven's vision by suggesting that he is speaking "enchantments." Instead of Scotland's entering into abject slavery, as Belhaven would have it, Defoe maintains that Scotland would enjoy a situation of more freedom, peace, and plenty. According to Defoe, Belhaven presents things backward, as wizards often do. Such misinterpretation attempts to empty the meaning out of Belhaven's mythic vision: "Two hours he talk'd, and said nothing at all, / But let drop a few hypocritical tears" (ll. 105–6).

Later, in *A Reply to the Scots Answer to the British Vision*, Defoe shifts to a consideration of the readers of political pamphlets, indicating his concern with the impact that Belhaven's speech had on the public. This poem also reveals Defoe's own view of "The listning Crowd" as unreliable, unthinking, and awed by mere novelty:

What tho in mighty Parable 'twas spoke,
The listning Crowd thy Oracles invoke;
Charm'd with thy *Ciceronian* Eloquence,
They view the Language, thou alone the Sense,
Nor is it fit th'uncomprehending Age,
Should in abstrusest Meanings far engage.
So Latine Prayers implicitly thought Good,
Edified, tho never understood.

(ll. 31–37)

Defoe's final blow here is to link Belhaven with the Roman Catholic Church, which he represents as another practitioner of conjuring.

For his part, in *A Scots Answer to a British Vision*, Belhaven replays the powerful matricidal scene from his original speech as he comments despairingly: "let Squadrones go on / To Murder their Mother" (ll. 60–61). His reply attempts to distinguish between what is "*Scots*" and what is "*British.*" However, his own mistaking of Defoe's identity proves that this has already become impossible. Defoe had employed several scotticisms in *The Vision*, leading Belhaven to believe that *The Vision* was coauthored by a Scot and an Englishman. Belhaven mocks the national union of poetic wits that he imagines has produced the reply to his speech: "Thus *Thames* and *Tine*, / Without reason or rhime, / Do most fondly combine" (ll. 35–36). His antiheroic description of such a poetical collaboration has wider implications for the political Union:

> When *Highlands* and *London*
> Agree to make Druids,
> Then our Union is half done,
> It wants but some fluids.
>
> *(ll. 46–49)*

But for all Belhaven's ranting, his mistake in fact suggests something that is closer to Defoe's position: that the written word serves not to distinguish the two nations of Scotland and England but to make them indistinguishable.

The difference between the two perspectives can be understood further as involving opposite claims of national immediacy. The primal moment in Belhaven's representation of the nation, as I have suggested, is a dramatic allegory of a once independent nation brutalized by its own people. This is balanced by a signification in the present whereby his audience substitutes the weeping Belhaven for the distraught Scotland. Scotland appears to them immediately through myth and symbol. The primal moment in Defoe's representation of the nation, on the other hand, occurs through the immediacy of the acts of writing and reading. In the Saturday, March 29, issue of the *Review*, Defoe informs his readers of the happy occasion of the Union:

> I have a long Time dwelt on the Subject of a Union; I have happily seen it transacted in the kingdom of Scotland; I have seen it carried on there through innumerable Oppositions, both public and private, peaceable and unpeaceable; I have seen it perfected there, and ratify'd, sent up to *England*, debated, oppos'd, and at last pass'd in both Houses, and having obtained the Royal Assent, I have the Pleasure *just as I am writing these lines*, to hear the Guns proclaiming the happy Conjunction from Edinburgh Castle.
>
> And though it brings an unsatisfying childish Custom in Play, and exposes me to a vain and truly ridiculous Saying in England, *As the Fool thinks, &c*, yet 'tis impossible to put the lively Sound of the Cannon just

now firing, into any other Note to my Ear than the articulate Expression
of UNION, UNION.

Strange Power of Imagination, strange Incoherence of Circumstances
that fills the Mind so with the thing, that it makes even the Thunder of
Warlike Engines cry peace; and what is made to divide and destroy,
speaks out the Language of this Glorious Conjunction! [my italics]
(*Review* 4, no. 21, p. 81).

For Defoe, the ultimate act of union takes place in the encounter of words on
the page. It is, more than anything, the "strange power of imagination" acting on otherwise "incoherent" circumstances that constructs the union of the
two nations. Furthermore, this encounter would have been reproduced in the
imaginations of Defoe's readers in their particular coffeehouses. Defoe's *Review* makes the Act of Union a community experience of reading. Where
Belhaven appealed to his fellow Scots by asking them to visualize images of
the nation, Defoe encouraged all and sundry to participate in the unification
of the nation of Great Britain through the fiction of watching over his shoul-
der as he wrote the report for the *Review*: "just as I am writing these lines"
fixes his readers in the present. Both authors make claims for immediacy, despite the fact that both their representations of the nation are in fact highly
mediated by allegory and the printed word.

Moreover, Belhaven's plea for a homogeneous nation constituted through
immediate knowledge depends paradoxically on the effectiveness of print
culture, the new medium of heterogeneity being promoted by Defoe. Belhaven presents a nostalgic image of the nation as immediate, not filtered
through written language or constitutions, a nation that has existed in a pure
form since time out of mind; however, he relies on the medium of print to
convey that representation. He was in fact one of the few members of Parliament who made a point of publishing his speeches for popular distribution.[25]
We can see in an earlier speech his awareness of what translating from oral
performance to printed document actually means. In the speech of January
10, 1701, *On the Affair of the Indian and African Company, and its Colony of Caledonia,* Belhaven indicates his awareness of the discrepancy between the spo-
ken and written word:

Being obliged, at the desire of several Noble and worthy Members of
Parliament, to Print this Discourse, I hope those, who heard me, will not
be offended, if they find it not exactly in the very precise Words and
Sentences as I Spoke it; because I must acknowledge, I did not design it
for the Press, having never so much as taken Notes of the Heads thereof,

before I spake it in Parliament; Yet this I can say, it is materially the same,
without either Addition or Diminution, yea much the same words, if I
remember well. (Preface)

Here Belhaven wants to convey the idea of spontaneity that accompanies oral
performance; therefore, he emphasizes the fact that his speech was not written before it was delivered. But his observation also indicates that he realizes
the difference that exists between the spoken and the written word; hence, he
hastens to minimize it, assuring his readers that there is no "material" difference between the two. He wants both to draw attention to the uniqueness of
oral delivery—it was not designed for the press—and to capitalize on the
wider power of dissemination that is available through print culture.

Belhaven was concerned that his work circulate among the general population outside of the Parliament. William Law Mathieson notes that Belhaven's speeches were "circulated widely out of doors" (pp. 167–68). Although Belhaven's November 2, 1706, speech offered a representation of the
nation as an unwritten bond between people, established through shared history and tradition, the fact that he published the speech indicates his awareness that this was essentially a representation that was no longer appropriate.
Belhaven's portrayal of the homogeneous immediate nation is entirely dependent on the popularity of print culture.

Defoe and Belhaven's debate, then, was not solely a disagreement about
national identity; paradoxically, it constituted an agreement about a new
means of shaping the nation. Their controversy reflects the difference in perspectives between a Scot and an Englishman, a lord and a tradesman. Yet although Belhaven was a peer, his pamphlets circulated in the same social circles as those of Defoe. Their debate may be interpreted as indicative of a
larger shifting of the grounds of nation-building to the printed page—and a
consensus on the uneasiness surrounding that means of building: the printed
word.

For Defoe's appeal to national heterogeneity through the medium of language also had its limitations. Although he used the printed word as a medium of unification, Defoe also saw the problems involved with that medium,
namely that the nation united by reading and writing in the present had to
be continually read or written in the future.[26] If we look again at Defoe's description on the day of Union in the *Review*, we detect an element that suggests the darker side underlying Defoe's optimistic tone: "Strange Power of
Imagination, strange Incoherence of Circumstances that fills the Mind so
with the thing, that it makes even the Thunder of Warlike Engines cry peace;
and what is made to divide and destroy, speaks out the Language of this Glo-

rious Conjunction!" Even in this moment of national cohesion through language there exists the fear that the "thing" that unites (and the indeterminacy of "thing" here is pertinent) will slip away, that "the language of glorious conjunction" will once again become that which "divides and destroys." Indeed, Defoe soon found that it was not enough to write the Union into being once. He had to keep on writing it, chiefly because the reality of the situation did not measure up to his promised vision of a "Union of affection." Thus, he pledges his services: "I cannot quit the Subject, nor go on in the History of this Union, which, God willing, I propose to write, till I have, as I lately promised . . . undertaken to show these Nations their reciprocal Duty and Obligation one towards another" (*Review* vol. 4, no. 21, p. 82). Yet even as Defoe makes such an attempt, he still cannot guarantee the success of his effort. Ironically, according to Defoe, the *Review* lost its audience precisely because of his constantly writing about the Union. Defoe admits this in the preface to volume five:

> The author having been in *Scotland* at the time of finishing the Union
> there, the last *Volume* and this are taken up in many *Parts* of them with
> that Affair. At first the Novelty of the Union took up every Body's
> Thoughts, and the Town was delighted to hear of the disputed Points as
> they went on. But *Novelty*, the Age's *Whore*, debauching their Taste, as
> soon as they had fed on the Shell of the Union, they were satisfy'd, and
> the *Review* entering into the substance of it, they grew palled and
> tired . . . the People would take up the Paper, and read two or three
> Lines in it, and find it related to *Scotland* and the *Union*, and throw it
> away; *Union, Union*! this Fellow can talk of nothing but *Union*—I think,
> he will never have done with this *Union*; he's grown mighty dull of late.

The basic problem, then, that Defoe confronts in his efforts to imagine the nation is that the Act of Union must be repeated, but it must be repeated in novel ways in order to ensure the participation and interest of its citizens.

Defoe himself soon undertook a new rewriting with his *History of the Union Between England and Scotland*. His strategy is best understood in terms of the "double narrative movement," which Bhabha describes as characterizing the "complex rhetorical strategy of social reference" involved in writing the nation:

> the people are the historical "objects" of a nationalist pedagogy, giving
> the discourse an authority that is based on the pre-given or constituted
> historical origin *in the past*; the people are also the "subjects" of a process

of signification that must erase any prior or originary presence of the
nation-people to demonstrate the prodigious, living principles of the
people as contemporaneity. (*Location*, p. 145)

Belhaven uses his audience (and later, his readers) as both narrated objects—
members of a historic and mythic past—and performing subjects—participants in his contemporary national imagining. Defoe, however, in attempting to unite the communities of England and Scotland faces a different task.
His appeal to a "pre-given or constituted historic origin" in fact attempts to
dispel the myths of separate identities in the past. In order to do so, he concentrates on rewriting history so that the past appears as a series of feckless
attempts that prefigured the present success of the Union. Defoe's "double
time," then, involves his readers as performing subjects reading the nation
into being in the present and as objects of a history of the present.

This project culminates in the *History of the Union Between England and
Scotland*, which depicts the Union as an inevitable process, a "Threed of History to be imagined by readers," and a providential act (p. 45) that has determined their present circumstances. In the section entitled "A General History
of Unions in Britain," he describes the Union as a "wonderful Transaction"
and says that all the "various Turns the Island of Britain has had in the Com-
pass of a few past Years" have "had their direct Tendency to this great Event"
("General History," p. 1). British identity, then, according to Defoe, although
not historically constituted in the past, existed nonetheless as an idea waiting
to be born, just as Britain was a nation waiting to be narrated.

The *History of the Union* begins with the end of the story, emphasizing the
event as an act of creation:

> The Union took Place, as has been Noted the 1st of *May* 1707, The Man-
> agement of the Revenue, the Trials in the *Exchequer* and *Admiralty*, were
> all Settled on a New Foot, Commissioners of the *Customs*, *Excise*, and
> *Equivalent*, were appointed; Judges of the Court of Exchequer; a New
> *Admiralty*, and their respective Offices were all fix'd; the Coin was Re-
> formed, and entirely Reduc'd to the *English* Standard (*the small Copper
> Money only Excepted*). Weights and Measures were Regulated in part, and
> the respective Alterations and Models, whether in Government, or Com-
> merce, Enacted by the *Union*, began every where to be put in practice.
> (Preface, p. i)

Everything is new, everything is regulated, and everything goes according to
plan, suggests Defoe. (Significant for the general tenor of the work, however,

are his comments that the measures are "Reduc'd to the *English* Standard" and that some traces of the previous national affiliation still remain in "the small Copper Money.") The rest of the *History* narrates the events leading up to the Union, showing the macrocosmic history of previous attempts at union and the microcosmic history of the particular events determining the Union. In order not to disrupt the continuity of the story, Defoe places the authenticating documents in appendixes at the back. As in his earlier pamphlets and *Review*, in his *History* Defoe attempts to counteract arguments for Scottish independence based on its past history and its alleged homogeneity. He folds history into the present, conscripting characters from the past into approving of the Union. He claims, for example, that although Robert the Bruce opposed union with England in his own time, he would have encouraged it had he lived at the present time, "*Could he have seen what these Ages have been brought to know*" ("General History," p. 4). Defoe suggests that "never any rational prospect of Uniting these Kingdoms appeared in the World, but both the Nations unanimously agreed, that Union was for the mutual Advantage of both" ("General History," p. 6). He explains the failures of union in the past as being due variously to sins of both countries, party politicking, or intrusive enemies of both nations. The independence of the two nations is reinterpreted as an unnatural mistake.

Defoe also reinterprets the issue of national homogeneity in his rewriting of the past. "The General History" offers a definition of the two nations based on their differing degrees of ethnic purity. He notes that the Scottish "ancient Families seem to have been preserved, and Foreign Nations have only seemd to increase their Number" ("General History," p. 2). But he also promotes the advantages of heterogeneity, as he had done in "The True-Born Englishman":

> Tis true, *England* is much more mix't in Blood, and the Reason for this is Plain, in that being a Nation powerful in Wealth, Fruitful in Soil, and above all, increasing in Commerce, more Nations have sought to settle among them, numbers of People have flowed in upon them, from all Parts of the World, and blending their Blood with the most ancient Families, have destroyed all that can be called National, as to Antiquity among them, and they do not pretend to it. ("General History," p. 2)

At the same time, he suggests paradoxically that there is a homogeneity among all the inhabitants of Britain by virtue of their all being heterogeneous: "By frequent mutual invasions made upon them, by the same Foreign Nations, who have left their Race behind them, it is not at all an Excursion

to say, They are the same in Blood, of the same Off-spring, and became inhabitants the same way" ("General History," pp. 1–2). Ironically, Scotland and
England are united by being conquered by the same original races.

Throughout the work, Defoe makes a point of commenting on the written language in which the discussion regarding the Union was conducted. He
begins this preoccupation in the "General History" when he describes the
pamphlet debate, blaming the dissent among the two nations on works such
as those by Anderson and Hodges: "a Pen and Ink War made a daily Noise in
either Kingdom, and this served to Exasperate the People in such a manner,
one against another, that never have two Nations Run upon one another in
such a manner, and come off without Blows" ("General History," p. 43). The
last of the narrative sections of the *History* are notable for their increased attention to written language. On one hand, Defoe condemns writing that is
contentious and that inflames the tensions between the two sides. On the
other hand, he praises the redemptive power of truthful writing. The spate of
literature that resulted from the publication of the Articles of Union had a
detrimental effect, he suggests. Up until that point, says Defoe, "the People
were generally very desirous of the Union, as a thing which tended to the
putting an end to all former Animosities, burying the ancient Feuds between
the nations, and removing the Apprehensions good People on both sides had
justly entertain'd of a new Rupture, in case of the Queen's Demise." However, as soon as the Articles were ordered to be printed and delivered to
Members of Parliament, "the Gentlemen, who set themselves up against
them, began to Preach upon the general Heads, as their Humour and Talent
instructed them, in order to possess the people against the particulars"
("General History," p. 10). At this point, "the whole Nation fell into a general kind of Labour, in Canvassing, Banding, and Cavilling at the Conditions"
("General History," p. 13). In particular, there was a great deal of false information bandied about through the printed word. The *History* itself becomes
part of the process of rewriting the nation, as Defoe equates the new relationship between Scotland and England with a new relationship between
words and history.

The old style of history was a product of violence, but the new style of
history would reflect the peacefulness of the negotiations of the Union. In
the Dedication to Queensbury, Defoe writes:

> "*If* Triumphs *were allowed to those Generals who subdued by Force of* Arms
> *the Barbarous* Nations *to the Obedience of the* Roman *Empire, if their Victories*
> *which were Impres't with* Blood, *and which at best consisted in Devastation of*
> Kingdoms, *and destroying* Nations, *were the Subject of the flourishing* Ora-

tions, *and* Heroick Poems *of the Learned Men of that* Age; *How much more Just are the* Triumphs of Peace, *and the* Praises of such Victories *which prevent* Destructive Wars, *and lay solid Foundations for the lasting Tranquility of* Nations?" (Dedication)

His own narrative work, Defoe suggests, will be the modern nation's equivalent of the ancient's "flourishing Oration" and "Heroick Poem." Accordingly, there is a stylistic change after the first two sections of the *History*, as Defoe moves away from describing past failures to describing the circumstances of the Union and the sensitive issues separating Scotland and England. He makes his own presence as a participant in the events more apparent to the reader, beginning with "Of the Last Treaty Properly Called the Union," as he attests that he has "been Eye Witness to much of the General Transaction, and furnish'd by the best Hands with every most secret Affair in the Carrying it on" ("Last Treaty," p. 1). The last two sections of the book contrast with the former in their self-reflection. Defoe wants to associate the success of the Union with the success of a new style of narrative, one written as from the eye of an impartial observer. Defoe's gaze as eyewitness and narrator of the past trains the reader to see the falseness of "Cant" and the "Truth" of the inevitability of Union.

But the book does not simply end with the narrative account of the Union. In an effort to prove the impartiality of his eyewitness perspective, Defoe includes numerous appendixes at the back of the book, including the "Minutes of the Parliament of Scotland" with his own observations. And, most pointedly, Lord Belhaven's speech arises again; Belhaven's November 2 speech is one of the few speeches from Parliament that Defoe includes in its entirety in his *History of the Union of Great Britain*. In reprinting the speech, Defoe acknowledges its continuing fame; it is "so much talk'd of in the World" ("Minutes," p. 32). By including it, Defoe attempts to contain the speech's impact. He emphasizes again the fact that it is empty language. It failed to "answer what had been said by [the previous speaker] M. Seton," and was "premeditate" ("Minutes," p. 32). In addition, he says that the speech had been inconsistent in its focus: "The Reader may see, [it] was pointed directly against the Union, and in the first part of it argues against the Whole, in the last against the Parts—; but concludes to move against the immediate Proceedings" ("Minutes," p. 32). It goes against the "Threed" of debate as well as the "Threed" of history. Defoe also tries to reduce Belhaven's impact by citing the Earl of Marchmont's reply to him, which, Defoe notes, "occasioned some Laughter in the House . . . *viz. He had heard a long Speech and a very terrible one, but he was of Opinion, it required a short Answer . . . Behold*

[Belhaven] *Dream'd, but, lo! when he awoke, he found it was a Dream"* ("Minutes," p. 44). Nevertheless, by incorporating Belhaven into his own text, Defoe re-creates the lord's powerful rhetoric. Struggling with such a legacy, Defoe is forced to narrate not only the smooth "Threed of History," but also the knots that strained the fabric of the nation.[27]

Such knots took on different forms. The years directly after the Union saw another kind of challenge by Scots as political objections to the Union were expressed in the cultural realm. The first collections of Scottish literature, James Watson's *A Choice Collection of Comic and Serious Scots Poems both Ancient and Modern* (1706–11) and Allan Ramsay's *The Ever Green* (1724) and *The Tea-Table Miscellany* (1724–37), were published in response to the Union.[28] In addition, Belhaven himself was re-created in the course of time as a Scottish patriot, a lordly and more colorful equivalent of Fletcher of Saltoun. His epitaphs indicate his apotheosis into the role of true Scot. In an elegy entitled *On the never enough to be Lamented Death of Lord John Hamilton of Balhaven*, the author describes Belhaven:

> Yet he's not Dead in Heaven still Liveth He,
> From *English* Goal, and all Restraints he's free,
> This Clear Bright Star, his Fame on Earth shal shine,
> While Sun and Moon shines, for he was all Divine.
>
> (*ll. 12–15*)

An Elegy on the much Lamented Death of John Hamilton Lord Balhaven takes up a similar position, describing Belhaven as one "Who always Strove his Country to Uphold."

What is interesting for the purposes of this argument is how frequently Belhaven's November 2 speech was translated into different contexts after its initial publication.[29] William Donaldson notes that Belhaven's speech fostered "a heroic popular history" of Scotland (p. 10), and Murray Pittock suggests that the speech was "more popular on the streets than in the Scots Estates" (*Poetry and Jacobite Politics*, p. 153). With its emphasis on the ancient kingdom of Scotland, it was easily co-opted by the Jacobite cause. It is in this guise that we find it turned into a poem that was first published in London in 1729, but that was probably written earlier. *Belhaven's Vision, or His Speech in the Union-Parliament November 2, 1706* promotes immediate and continuous national connection through the "ancient Crown / Which their Ancestors Blood and Sweat / Had handed down" (p. 3). The Scottish nation is described in mythic terms:

> The Sun two thousand times did fly
> Round the twelve Chambers of the Sky,
> Since *Fergus* form'd our MONARCHY,
> And to this Hour,
> Our Laws have been controuled by,
> No foreign Pow'r.

> *(p. 7)*

The poem presents the Stewart monarchy as an integral part of this ancient nation and the ancient land:

> Our *Stewarts*, unto peaceful James,
> *Gordons, Kers, Campbels, Marrays, Grahams,*
> Hero's, from *Tyber* known to *Thames,*
> For Freedom stood;
> And dy'd the Fields, in purple Streams
> Of hostile Blood.

> *(p. 8)*

Thus incorporated into a politically dissident sector of popular culture, Belhaven's vision continued to assert its presence throughout the century, in negotiation with Cromartie's plea that the Union would eliminate those names of Scotland and England and with Defoe's bid for a nation united through writing and reading.

Both Defoe's and Belhaven's works were republished at points of tension between their respective countries, translated from the specific context of 1707 to become representative of the differences existing in the supposedly United Kingdom of Britain. Their debate also contributed to an image of Britain not as a stable nation, but as a concept created through dialogue, and therefore by nature ambiguous. Great Britain as it is commonly understood is in fact from its inception a bricolage of literary activity reflecting hegemonic struggles. What has emerged from this initial exploration, then, is a sense of the tensions and negotiations that went into creating the British nation in its earliest manifestation and an understanding of why those negotiations had to be continually repeated throughout the next century. As Defoe himself perceived, a nation united by reading and writing has to be constantly reread and rewritten in order to maintain its existence.

CHAPTER 2

Narrating the '45: Henry Fielding, Tobias Smollett, and the Pretense of Fiction

Born on shaky ground, British national consciousness was sorely tried in the years following the Union. In 1713 there was an unsuccessful attempt to have the Union dissolved. The year of George I's accession, 1714, saw rioting in Glasgow over an increase in the malt tax. Discontent culminated in the 1715 Rebellion, which was led by the Old Pretender, the son of the deposed James II. Little direct action had been taken to discipline the disaffected in the early years of the eighteenth century. After the rebellion in 1715, a Disarming Act was passed in the British Parliament requiring all Highlanders to give up their weapons voluntarily, but the law was almost wholly ignored except by those clans loyal from the outset to the Crown. The first effective efforts to control the northernmost region of Scotland did not occur until some years later. Then in 1724, General Wade was sent on a combined cartographic and military venture to map out the Highlands as British territory by building roads, bridges, and barracks throughout the area and establishing forts along the Highland frontier (Mitchison, p. 30).[1]

But it was the Rebellion of 1745–46 in particular that raised the specter of national dissolution. As Jeremy Black points out, the uprising was a threat to the entire British Constitution, inasmuch as Charles and his father, James, were challenging what they saw as a usurpation of their rightful throne (p. xiii). The Rebellion threatened the basis of British national unity not only because of its close success, but also because it generated suspicion in England toward anyone of Scottish origin and because the reprisals against the entire Highland population raised the indignation of many Scots.

This chapter examines the manner in which negotiations about nationhood were transferred from the political to the cultural realm at midcentury. Specifically, I focus on how the novel form in the hands of an Englishman, Henry Fielding, and a Scot, Tobias Smollett, functioned to represent the contradictions of British national identity during the years following the '45. I begin by considering how popular and political printed narratives (including pamphlets by Fielding himself) focus attention on the fictions surrounding the Rebellion. I then examine how Fielding and Smollett use the ambiguous space of the novel—which is related to but distinct from political discourse—in order to manipulate readers' perceptions of the '45 uprising in Britain. In his journal *The True Patriot*, Fielding hones the techniques he will employ in his novel *Tom Jones* to contain and reshape the '45 uprising by creating a structured, cohesive nation of readers. Tobias Smollett, too, responds through his writing to the shattering effects of the Rebellion. His early works, the "Tears of Scotland" and *The Regicide*, already suggest his sense of the tenuousness of national identity. In *Roderick Random* he finds an appropriate medium for representing this tenuousness so that it critiques but does not threaten British unity. Where many critics focus on the debate between Fielding and Samuel Richardson as a crucial moment in the development of the novel, in this chapter I draw attention to the less famous negotiation between Fielding and Smollett as also influential in the history of fiction.

To begin with, I want to explore the novel's close connection to the political realm by virtue of its shared origins with political narratives. J. A. Downie's *Robert Harley and the Press* argues for an evolutionary development between political writing and novels: "It would not be stretching the evidence to suggest that the political literature of the reign of Queen Anne laid the groundwork for the prose fiction of subsequent years" (p. 14). Downie identifies two reasons for this. First, he argues that "the fictional aspects of some political pamphlets are not far removed from genuine fiction" (p. 14). Second, he says that "the constant appearance of political literature whetted the contemporary appetite for reading matter" and produced a kind of "cult of 'pamphlet readers'" who "would buy and consume each tract as it came onto the bookstalls" (p. 14). Downie's observations suggest that the readers of the pamphlet wars of 1707 served to exercise and stretch the market for later readers of novels dealing with the '45 Rebellion. Following a similar argument in *Before Novels: The Cultural Contexts of Eighteenth-Century English Fiction*, J. Paul Hunter also situates the novel in "the context of cultural history," suggesting that "popular thought and materials of everyday print—journalism, didactic materials with all kinds of religious and ideological directions, and private papers and histories—need to be seen as contributors to the social and intellectual world in which the novel emerged" (p. 5).[2] Lennard

Davis, too, in *Factual Fictions: The Origins of the English Novel* contends that news and novels shared a common origin as prose narratives in print (chapter 3). As all of these critics have argued, the novel has its feet firmly planted in the political realm.

But the novel also situates itself as distinct from political narratives. Davis examines the pressures of print technology and legal restrictions that were brought to bear on printed works in an effort to separate truth from fiction. He argues that such pressures created in the news/novels discourse an "inherent doubleness," making it "both old, new, false, and true . . . by affirming that it is new and true, it denies those qualities at the same moment" (p. 56).[3] Building on Davis's comments, I want to argue that the '45 Rebellion constituted an important historical moment for the development of the novel. Fielding and Smollett capitalize on the ambiguous relationship between narration and the nation that is made apparent during the Rebellion, but they also move to contain the contradictions in both within the medium of the novel.

The interrelation between narrative and national identity can be seen in the contradictory claims concerning the identity of the real monarch in Britain. On August 3, 1745, Charles Edward Stewart landed on the Scottish mainland after a journey from France that twice brought him close to capture by government forces.[4] On August 19, 1745, he raised the standard of King James at Glenfinnan. The potential doubleness of the nation was now embodied in the two kings in Britain, each claiming legitimacy.[5] Now there were again two nations, for part of the Stewart plan included the revocation of the Act of Union, which was referred to as a "pretended union."[6] Furthermore, popular discourse on the Rebellion conflated the issue of national identity with the question of truth or fiction in narrative accounts. Reports on the Highland forces were varied. In *The True Patriot* W. B. Coley notes that "The first public notice of the [Young Pretender]'s landing to appear in the official *London Gazette* was in the issue of 13–17 August [1745], in the form of a report based on Edinburgh letters dated 11 August, which stated that seven persons had landed between Mull and Skye, one of whom, 'there is reason to believe', was the pretender's son" (p. xxxi). Coley adds that no further official mention of the Jacobites appears in the *Gazette* "until 10–14 September, barely a week before the battle of Prestonpans (21 September) when it was reported merely that the clans were gathering" (p. xxxi). Essentially, the majority of citizens in Britain experienced the Rebellion as a series of acts of narration whose credibility they either believed or doubted.

The epistemological uncertainty surrounding narratives concerning the Rebellion also became a political issue in Westminster. At first the government treated reports of an uprising as a false alarm, believing them to be a ploy by the opposition to force the return of troops from Flanders and to disgrace the government's policy on the European wars, as a letter written by Reverend Thomas Birch to Lord Hardwicke indicates: "Would you imagine that in this dangerous situation Lord Granville and his friends have taken no small pains to treat the affair of Scotland as a fiction or a mistake, and as of no other importance than to give a handle to their antagonists in the ministry to draw off our troops in Flanders, and by that means defeat the great schemes which might be executed on the Continent?"[7] The Pelhams saw a way to turn the situation to their advantage by taking the Rebellion seriously and calling for the retrieval of troops from Europe. Certain Scottish lairds also used the issue in their struggle for position. Tweeddale and the Earl Stair, for example, denied the seriousness of the Rebellion and urged against bringing troops back (Coley, p. xxxii).

The result of the political controversy over the reports of the uprising was apathy among the general public. On August 31, 1745, Hardwicke wrote Archbishop Herring, "There seems to be a certain indifference and deadness among many, and the spirit of the nation wants to be raised and animated to a right tone" (Coley, p. xxxi). Although little published commentary on the Rebellion appeared in the beginning, it soon attracted the concern of the nation.[8] What appears most prominently in the printed commentary on the Rebellion later is a concern regarding the response of the general public once reports of defeats for the government and of the progress of the rebels started to come in.

An example of this anxiety regarding reader response can be seen in the debate surrounding the defeat of Sir John Cope at Prestonpans. Rumors suggested that members of Cope's infantry had deserted in the midst of the battle. Up to that point, the disturbances in the Highlands had been treated, even by those who guessed at the full strength of the Highland forces, as a result of the lack of British vigilance. The Prestonpans defeat implied, however, that even when full government forces were deployed the Highlanders could still triumph. Accordingly, the representation of the event in the newspapers was a highly politicized act, one that could have immediate consequences for the success or failure of the Rebellion. On one hand, if the loyal citizens of Britain read about a rebel victory, they might lose faith in the government and prepare to switch allegiances. On the other hand, if they read about a government victory, their resulting apathy might also be advantageous for the rebels' cause. The effect of narrative was at this time directly aligned with the future of the nation.

The literary battle to write the history of the event, which was extensive, again suggests the dependence of the imagining of the nation on claims of truth versus fiction. The *Caledonian Mercury* of September 23, 1745, featured the journal of an officer who claimed to have been with Charles at Prestonpans. The account bore witness to the cowardliness of Cope's troops and the bravery of the forces of the Stewarts, and it defended itself against accusations of fictitiousness: "Tho' the following plain Journal may appear but the fictitious Dream of a luxuriant Fancy, yet as the minutest Circumstance thereof is Sterling Truth, therefore it is confidently presumed that the publishing the same will be highly acceptable to the Publick." Countering this thrust, the *London Evening Post* of October 17, 1745, featured "A Compleat Journal of Sir John Cope's Expedition in a Letter from an Officer to his Friend," which purported to be written by one of Cope's officers who was taken prisoner and was currently on parole in Edinburgh. The printing of the officer's letter was intended to assure the public that the officers at Prestonpans acted heroically, as British soldiers should.

On November 23, 1745, came a denunciation of Cope in the *London Courant*, taken from an earlier published pamphlet. This prompted an indignant reply on December 2, 1745, from a man who purported to have come to London soon after the battle of Prestonpans. He noted that he "was amazed to find, how much of the Publick was impos'd upon by an infinite Variety of Falshoods, industriously spread about in every Coffee-House," which, in the writer's opinion, were "altogether without Foundation, and a gross Misrepresentation of Facts." He professed to have no personal connection with any of the officers present at Preston, but, rather, claimed to have been reacting to a distortion of the truth. He explained the credulity of the many people who maligned Cope as having been due to national trauma: "the Shock which follow'd upon the News of this unhappy Affair's reaching *London*, affected the Interest of so many People in so strong a Manner, that it was no wonder they were exasperated, and greedily listened to any suggestion, true or false, which tended to load the Gentleman, who had the Honour to Command there, and in a Country more bias'd with Liberty than any other Nation in the World besides." Still, the writer indicated his trust that that "bias" would also cause Britons to "listen to Truth, and . . . think, as in Justice they ought, of the Persons who have misinform'd them." A reasoned assessment could come about only as a result of a government inquiry, and the public was urged to refrain from passing judgment until that time. The author claimed that he would correct misinformation only this once, while his antagonist might continue to publish: "if his Itch for Writing, or some such laudable Motive, should prevail with him to entertain the Publick with any more of his performance, I will not trouble them with any more of mine, because what I have said is Fact." According to this writer, truth need be told only once, whereas fiction needs constant repetition. For government supporters, handling the discourse surrounding Cope's defeat became almost more important than dealing with the defeat itself.

Writing in the midst of this debate, Fielding also reflects concern about readers' responses to narratives about the Rebellion, inasmuch as he was becoming more sympathetic toward the government. Looking back on the early stages of the Rebellion in his *History of the Present Rebellion in Scotland From the Departure of the Pretender's Son from Rome, down to the present time*, Fielding recalls that "few, except the most credulous, gave any Belief to it, imagining it was rather a Story devised by some Persons for particular Purposes which need not be mentioned" (Coley, p. 42). He himself saw the serious consequences of reader apathy: "This Infidelity was of very pernicious Consequence, especially as it prevailed in some measure even among the greater People: Nay, so accustomed were they to treat this Rebellion as imaginary, that even when it was impossible to doubt longer of its Reality, they made it still the Subject of Contempt and Ridicule; saying it was only a Company of wild Highlanders got together, whom the very Sight of a Body of Troops, however small, would infallibly disperse: Nay, one great Man is reported to have asked, with a contemptuous Air, Why they did not read the Proclamation to them?" (Coley, p. 42). Brian McCrea suggests that the '45 was "the definitive event in [Fielding's] political life," forcing him to articulate "the old Whig principles" in reaction to the political apathy around him (Coley, p. 112). Without doubt, Fielding set to work quickly to remedy the situation of the public's ignorance. In October 1745 he presented the public with three anonymous pamphlets to warn them of the danger of the Rebellion.

Although the pamphlets are typical of anti-Jacobite propaganda at the time, they foreshadow a later interest in the political uses of fiction. *A Serious Address to the People of Britain in Which the Certain Consequences of the Present Rebellion, Are Fully Demonstrated. Necessary to be Perused by Every Lover of His Country, at this Juncture* begins with an admonishment for people to take the threats to the country seriously: "The Rebellion lately begun in *Scotland . . .* is no longer an Object of your Derision" (Coley, p. 3). The *Serious Address* warns citizens of the civil, religious, and national threat that the Pretender poses. *The History of the Present Rebellion in Scotland* bears an elaborate subtitle that indicates the author's concern to chart everything meticulously: "In which is a full Account of the Conduct of this Young Invader, from his first Arrival in *Scotland*; with the several Progresses he made there; and likewise a very particular Relation of the Battle of *Preston*, with an exact List of the Slain, Wounded, and Prisoners, on both Sides" (Coley, p. 34). Like the *Serious Address*, the *History of the Present Rebellion* wants to supply the facts in order to convince the readers of the seriousness of the cause: "The present Rebellion is a Matter of such Consequence to this Country, and must so seriously engage the Attention of every *Briton* who hath the least Regard either to his own real Good, or the Welfare of his Posterity, that I shall make no Apology for the present Undertaking; in which my Reader may be assured, that as the utmost Pains have been taken to procure the best Intelligence, so he may safely rely on the Truth of the Facts related" (p. 35). Yet there is an underlying fiction to this claim of truth. The subtitle claims that the work was "Taken from the Relation of Mr. James Macpherson, who was an Eye-Witness of the Whole, and who took the first Opportunity of leaving the Rebels, into whose Service he was forced, and in which he had a Captain's Commission" (p. 34). The *Caledonian Mercury* of October 28, 1745, claimed, however, that "there never was an officer of the Name of Macpherson in the Prince's Army" (p. xlviii). Fielding's last pamphlet, *The Dialogue Between the Pope, the Devil and the Pretender*, fictionalizes the dangers of the Rebellion more overtly as a discussion between what he presents as three contemporary allegorical characters.

However, it was in the *True Patriot*, begun later in November 1745, that Fielding first systematized his response to the public confusion regarding the narration of the Rebellion. Instead of working to convince readers of the truth of his facts in order to direct their opinions, he turns rather to making use of fiction to manipulate his readers' perceptions of the Rebellion. Like Defoe's *Review*, the *True Patriot* has an agenda of achieving consensus through weekly contact with the reading public. Unlike the *Review*, however, Fielding's journal does not seek to achieve consensus through persuading the reader of the truth of the words it employs. Rather, in the *True Patriot*, Fielding seeks to devalue the idea of accurate truth, concentrating instead on getting the reader to develop the right attitudes, which, he implies, lie beyond the facts of the words. Fielding is concerned with using narrative to shape readers' attitudes even while he points out the unreliability of claims for truth. In the *True Patriot*, Fielding suggests that news that purports to be factual is dangerous, but that fiction can train the reader to develop accurate perceptions.

The *True Patriot* is divided into several sections: an editorial commentary, foreign news, and domestic news. In addition, the first seventeen editions, those in which Fielding was most involved, contain a section called the "Apocrypha," which includes items taken from the London papers with Fielding's editorial comments added. The "Apocrypha," described as "a curious Collection of certain true and important WE HEARS from the News-Papers," takes as its model Defoe's "Mercure Scandale" section of the *Review*. Fielding ferrets out the inconsistencies and misinformation in the newspapers. In number 3 (November 19, 1745), for example, he disputes mortality

statistics by putting together the accounts given by the papers and concluding that the number of dead reported are equivalent to the number of men
in the entire Highland force: "By these Accounts put together, it is most certain, that the whole Army of Rebels which came from Scotland is destroyed,
and consequently those before Carlisle can be no other than GHOSTS"
(Locke, p. 54).[9] He suggests that the papers present an impossible version of
the truth. Number 4 also questions the objectivity of alleged facts by quoting several papers' comments on the movements of General Ligonier: "General Ligonier is recover'd. G.A. He is judged in a fair way of recovery. D.A.
He is perfectly recover'd G.A. He is to set out To-morrow, being Thursday.
He set out to Day, being Thursday. He set out Yesterday, being Thursday. *Several papers*" (Locke, p. 62). The words say the same things, yet mean nothing.
Words are, after all, just words, Fielding implies, and can be arranged in any
particular fashion to suit a writer's purpose.

By presenting selected absurdities from newspapers and providing his own
editorial comments on news events, Fielding lays open readers' doubts about
the truth of what they read. He suggests that what has been seen as objective
truth is not very truthful at all. But in the first section of the *True Patriot*, containing editorial commentary, Fielding also musters the power of fiction. He
employs a number of fictional devices to manipulate the reader's sympathies,
including letters from imagined people and deliberately fictionalized accounts. Number 12 (January 21, 1746) includes a letter from the Old Pretender to his son: "The following Letter having been found at Penrith, in a
Room which the Pretender's Son had just left in a Hurry on the Alarm of the
Duke's Approach, there can be no doubt of its being genuine" (p. 192).
Other letters appear from miscellaneous people: Prince Charles, a footman,
even an Italian opera star.[10] Number 7 is attributed to a fictional character,
Abraham Adams, from Fielding's own novel *Joseph Andrews*.

Two issues of the *True Patriot* contain fictional visions of the future, alarming the readers with the possibility of a Jacobite victory. In number 3 (November 19, 1745), for example, the narrator relates a vision he has had of being arrested for writing the journal by "several Men, who were in Highland
Dresses, with broad Swords by their Sides" (p. 128). He is charged with trea-
son and appeals to British law, but "the Chief Justice told me in broken *English*, that if I had no other Plea, they should presently over-rule that; for that
his Majesty was resolved to make an Example of all who had any ways distinguished themselves, in Opposition to his Cause" (p. 130). He is found
guilty by the court, delivered to the executioner, but just as the executioner is
putting a rope around his neck, his little girl enters, and he awakes to find
that a celebration in honor of the king's birthday is proceeding.

A similar fictitious account is provided in number 10 (January 7, 1746). Fielding says he has "framed an imaginary Journal of Events, with which I here present you, as with a waking Dream" (p. 171). The imaginary journal lists events taking place after a Jacobite success, including the repeal of the Act of Habeas Corpus, the restoration of abbey lands, and the execution of Protestants at Smithfield. Fielding even includes a gibe at the Highlanders' hygiene: "March 9: My little Boy *Jacky* taken ill of the Itch. He had been on the Parade with his Godfather the Day before, to see the Life-Guards, and had just touched one of their Plaids" (p. 178). The journal ends on March 17, 1746, with rumors of a plot that will include "a Riot in the City—a Rising in the North—a Descent in the West—Confusions, Uproars, Commitments, Hangings, Burnings, &c. &c." (p. 180). The fictions are designed to frighten the reader with the drastic consequences of the dissolution of the nation if the Jacobite forces prevail. The *True Patriot* employs a double strategy: in the "History of the Present" and the "Apocrypha," Fielding destabilizes the truth of factual language; in the editorial sections, he molds his reader's attitudes through the use of fiction.

Fielding takes pains to persuade his readers of the underlying integrity of the British nation, being careful to point out that the entire Scottish nation is not culpable for the crime of rebellion. In the first issue he condemns the "indiscriminate Censure which some over-hot Men are at this Season too apt to vent on the whole Body of the *Scottish* Nation" (p. 113), confining the blame for the uprising instead to a certain faction. He emphasizes that "The common People of the Lowlands in *Scotland* are as well affected to his Majesty as any of his Subjects" (p. 115). He suggests that the people who did join the rebellion were "the savage Inhabitants of Wilds and Mountains, who are almost a distinct Body from the rest of their Country. Some Thousands of them are Outlaws, Robbers, and Cut-throats who live in a constant State of War, or rather Robbery, with the civilized Part of *Scotland*" (p. 113). Especially after the defeat of the Rebellion, Fielding is anxious to present a united national front, as his commentary on the restoration of peace to the nation indicates:

> By this Victory we see an End put to the Rebellion, and which is much
> more, the Spirit of Rebellion either extinguish'd or turn'd to Despair. For
> it is now evident, not only that such Attempts are vain and fruitless, but
> that they are rash and ridiculous. It is now clear, that a Highland War can
> end only in Destruction, and which is what the Disaffected never appre-
> hended, cannot be protracted by removing it beyond the Highlands."
> (Locke, p. 300)

The *True Patriot* ends with a vision of the restoration of peace and unity: "His Highness's Valour has subdued the Highlanders, and the Highlands themselves will soon be civilized" (Locke, 300). Fielding suggests that the aftermath of the Rebellion will serve to subdue the Highlanders by assimilating them into the British nation.

In fact, this process of civilization involved the slaughter of Highland troops, the destruction of the clan system, the forced resettlement of the Highlanders, and the execution of captured rebels, all of which created huge rifts between the English and the Scottish populations. The government reacted swiftly and brutally. Duncan Forbes's memorandum drawn up for Cumberland suggests the attitude of the top-ranking officers: "No severity that is necessary ought to be dispensed with, the omitting such severities is cruelty to the king and kingdom" (Speck, p. 168);[11] the lower-ranking officers carrying out the orders showed even less restraint. Roderick Watson notes the statistics of the aftermath: "In the savage aftermath of the battle more than 3000 men women and children were imprisoned and shipped to the south, where 120 were executed and over a thousand more banished and transported" (p. 163). Many of those who were incarcerated died of fever or starvation. In addition, the government confiscated land from those chiefs involved in the uprising. Highlanders were forbidden to wear kilts or play the bagpipes, and, most catastrophic of all for the clans, the Highland justice system, under which each chief had the right to act as judge over the affairs of his clanspeople, was abolished and replaced by a uniform public legal system. In short, the cultural and material ties that bound Highland communities together were deliberately severed.[12]

In his discussion of the Jacobite paper war of 1747–48, Thomas Cleary suggests that the effectiveness of harsh retribution against the rebels can be seen by the fact that Fielding's next journalistic project, the *Jacobite's Journal*, aimed at the Tories, does not seriously consider the possibility of another Jacobite threat: the "Jacobite-Tory theme survived to be used by Fielding and his opponents, not as a real threat, but as an obvious slur or rough political jest" ("Jacobite Paper War," p. 2). Cleary describes the ideological watershed after the '45 Rebellion, arguing that Jacobitism changed from being a threat to the nation to being material for political satire by government and opposition writers. But although there was little chance of another Jacobite rebellion, the nation was still suffering from the consequences of the recent one. National affiliations and resentments came back into the forefront as even those Scots who had not been on the rebels' side were outraged at the treatment of their fellow countrymen (Speck, p. 187). In addition to writing the *Jacobite's Journal*, which was read only by certain citizens, Fielding sought to respond to the more general fracturing of national interests. He turned to a form with which he had experimented previously and that he recognized as capable of affecting a more general readership: the novel. J. Paul Hunter points out that "unlike older literary forms, the novel does not depend upon an established community of readers"; rather it is concerned with "developing a new kind of relationship with new combinations of readers" (*Before Novels*, 39). Moreover, although the novel was related to political discourse, as we have already seen, it claimed membership in a separate sphere: the cultural realm. Fielding was concerned to forge a new community of disparate readers who become a united national body through the act of reading. The novel's ambiguous identity, existing in the interstices of truth and fiction, allowed him to do so. *Tom Jones* is at once connected to the same discourse as the political pamphlets examined so far in this chapter, and distinguished from it as a fictional work.

Scholars unanimously agree that Fielding is unique in the previous history of novelists in making "the political commentary in his work an integral part of the structure of his own novel" (Lennard Davis, p. 196). They disagree, however, about when Fielding made the momentous decision to set the novel during the Rebellion. Wilbur L. Cross says he began the novel in summer 1746 (2: 10). Martin Battestin has argued convincingly that Fielding had begun working on the novel at an earlier date, but that he reordered the whole work when the Rebellion became common knowledge (1: xxvii–xlii). Similarly, diverse critical assumptions have been made about the novel's treatment of the Rebellion. Cleary attributes the setting of the novel to Fielding's involvement in the Jacobite paper war during its last stages ("Great Jacobite Paper War," p. 10). Peter J. Carlton argues that "Between Partridge and Western, the novel implies that the Jacobites—and by extension the ruler they support—are unfit for authority 'by nature'" (p. 366). Lennard Davis suggests that Tom's rebellion against Allworthy and Sophia's against her father parallel the rebellion of the Pretender, although their rebellion turns out to be just "because it conforms to human nature and eventually satisfied tradition and authority" (p. 203).[13]

Rather than see the novel as a direct analogy to the events of the Rebellion, however, I want to read it as a more general attempt to create a homogeneous readership in the nation. Whether it was begun before, during, or after the Rebellion, it nonetheless registers Fielding's concern about national discord. Fielding acknowledges the differences which exist within the nation, but he reframes these differences in the cultural realm by using the medium of the novel, thereby defusing their direct political threat.

Tom Jones seeks to reimagine the nation as a community of readers and to demonstrate the proper relationship between the individual and the nation. As in the *True Patriot*, Fielding works on several levels to achieve his purpose. On the plot level, he shows the reader how the activities of the characters run parallel to the events of the nation, suggesting the unconscious but integral part each individual plays in the life of the nation. On the narrative level, he trains the reader, as he did in the *True Patriot*, to read properly by questioning the truth of narration presented as fact. But he also trains readers to think similarly, thereby becoming a nation of assimilated individuals. Despite its attempt to knit the nation together, however, Fielding's fictional rereading of the Rebellion also records the ambivalences that call the cohesive nation into question.

The first part of the novel introduces characters and situations applicable to what Fielding calls "domestic Government" (1: 81) or "Domestic History" (1: 85). The action takes place within the parish. Allworthy serves as a domestic head of government, as the description of Paradise Hall indicates. The Hall combines the best features of English architecture, "*Gothick*" and "*Grecian*" (1: 42), and commands a view of sublime and beautiful nature, ranging from "wild Mountains" to "a fine Park" (1: 43). The "Grove of old Oaks" (1: 42) suggests the antiquity of the site. At the start, then, *Tom Jones* promises to be a novel about property, propriety, and love matches, and the characters themselves look no farther than their immediate circumstances. Apprising Squire Western of Jenny Jones's pregnancy, the parson is taken to task for bothering with trivial matters. He replies, "As to National Matters, your Worship knows them best. My Concerns extend no farther than my own Parish" (1: 189). What becomes apparent as the novel progresses, however, is how the concerns of the parish are in fact deeply intertwined with "National Matters."

The introduction of the Rebellion in the novel strikes the reader as a surprise. This monumental event is first raised as Tom is buying drinks for some soldiers in order to avoid a dispute among them. The sergeant of the troops informs Tom that they are marching "against the Rebels, and expect to be commanded by the glorious Duke of Cumberland" (1: 367). Fielding adds a coy aside to the reader that this was "a Circumstance which we have not thought necessary to communicate before" (1: 367). Although the characters themselves have not been interested by the events outside the parish, then, serious national conflict is taking place. In fact, says the narrator, "this was the very Time when the late rebellion was at the highest; and indeed the Banditti were now marched into England, intending, as it was thought, to fight the King's Forces, and to attempt pushing forward to the Metropolis" (1: 368). Fielding presents the rebels as doubly foreign here; not only are they outside England, but they are described as Italian thieves. Fielding suggests that even though characters may not perceive the circumstances beyond their own parish, they are nonetheless implicated in those circumstances.

Fielding writes the personal and the political together in the novel. He says he eschews writing a dry account, like a "painful and voluminous Historian" (1: 75), but rather chooses to write history from the perspective of an individual. Accordingly, national events are reflected in the lives of the characters. When Tom is unable to find a horse at a crucial point in the novel, Fielding explains that this is a circumstance that "the reader will not wonder at, when he considers the hurry in which the whole nation, and especially this part of it, was at this time engaged, when expresses were passing and repassing every hour of day and night" (2: 654). The connection between individual circumstances and national events is also seen in the episodes in which Sophia is mistaken for Jenny Cameron. The landlady delivers an encoded message to Sophia: "A Gentleman who was here just now brought excellent News; and perhaps some Folks who have given other Folks the Slip, may get to London before they are overtaken" (2: 591). The relevance of the message to both Sophia's personal circumstances and national events suggests the connection Fielding is trying to draw between the private and public spheres. Furthermore, political inclinations are presented as a part of the characters themselves. Lennard Davis suggests that Fielding introduces a "new kind of political manipulation by virtue of the fact that so many admirable characters were Hanoverians, and so many foolish ones were Jacobites" (pp. 202–3). Tom, for example, "had some heroic ingredients in his composition, and was a hearty well-wisher to the glorious cause of liberty, and of the Protestant religion" (1: 368). He later delivers a speech extolling the virtues of fighting for religion as well as king and country (1: 374). The Jacobite Partridge, however, is a superstitious coward and a boaster. Squire Western, also a Jacobite, acts tyrannically toward his daughter. We are led to judge characters by their political affiliations.

Fielding situates his novel squarely in the contemporary discourse (such as that concerning Prestonpans) regarding the truth or fiction of narratives about the Rebellion. The story of the Man of the Hill comments on the political danger of false accounts. In the Man of the Hill's account, set during an earlier national disturbance, the Monmouth Rebellion, the apothecary was used to giving out falsehoods to persuade others to join his cause: "He would swallow almost anything as a Truth, a Humour which many made use of to impose upon him" (1: 476). The example of Partridge also demonstrates the consequences of misperceiving. Partridge believes the words of a Catholic priest who told him, "The Catholicks did not expect to be any Gainers by the Change . . . and that nothing but Regard to Right made him and the rest of the Popish party to be *Jacobites*" (1: 439). Fielding suggests that people must be on guard against false information. They must intuit the truth behind language.

Partridge also serves as a negative example for the reader when he mistakes Tom's political affiliations: "Indeed, had the Words been less ambiguous, *Partridge* might very well have construed them as he did; being persuaded as he was, that the whole Nation were of the same Inclination in their hearts: nor did it stagger him that *Jones* had travelled in the Company of Soldiers; for he had the same Opinion of the Army which he had of the rest of the People" (1: 441). When he does realize his mistake, he changes sides, for "however well affected he might be to *James* or *Charles*, he was still much more attached to *Little Benjamin* than to either; for which Reason he no sooner discovered the Principles of his fellow-traveller, than he thought proper to conceal, and outwardly to give up his own to the Man on whom he depended for the making his Fortune" (1: 441–42). Not only is Partridge an example of a bad reader, he is also a bad citizen, not realizing the proper connection between the individual and the nation.[14] For Fielding, prudence on an individual level is equated with order on a national level. He draws an analogy between the national disruption and personal development: "As a conquered rebellion strengthens a government, or as health is more perfectly established by recovery from some diseases; so anger, when removed, often gives new life to affection" (2: 933).

But Fielding does not merely illustrate this lesson with examples for his readers to observe. He is also concerned with educating his readers into good reading and, as a result, good citizenship. Glenn Hatfield notes the connection between Fielding's political concerns and his concerns regarding language: "It is significant that the form this political concern takes [i.e., the political tracts of 1745, the *True Patriot*, *A Dialogue between a Gentleman of London and an Honest Alderman*, and the *Jacobite's Journal*], whatever Fielding's immediate ends of larger purposes, is so often one which represents the political rhetoric of persuasion and equivocation as a corruptive perversion of language" (p. 90). Hatfield suggests that Fielding associated Jacobitism particularly with the corruption of language: "The covert nature of Jacobitism, its refusal to declare itself openly, its hypocritical way of mouthing the very principles (according to Fielding) that i[t] sought to overthrow, made it especially insidious as a perverter of language" (p. 97). However, it is not just the language of the Jacobites that is shown to be misleading. All language in *Tom Jones* is shown to be suspect. What Fielding implies is that learning proper discernment of language is the only way to be a good citizen. The novel becomes the training ground for the readers of the nation.

The narrator reinforces the connection between citizenship and reading when he assures us that he is "the Founder of a new Province of Writing" (1: 77). But the domain of the narrator is essentially tyrannical, as is evident in his assertion that in his new province he is "at liberty to make what Laws I please therein. And these Laws, my Readers, whom I consider as my subjects, are bound to believe in and to obey" (1: 77). He continues the metaphor of sovereignty, assuring us that he does not practice a *jure divino* type of tyranny, but rather has been set over the readers "for their own Good only, and was created for their Use, and not they for mine" (1: 78). However, his attitude suggests otherwise.

The narrator asserts his authority often in the novel. Early on he tells us about his intention to digress:

> Reader, I think proper, before we proceed any farther together, to ac-
> quaint thee, that I intend to digress, through this whole History, as often
> as I see Occasion: Of which I am myself a better Judge than any pitiful
> Critic whatever; and here I must desire all those Critics to mind their
> own Business, and not to intermeddle with Affairs, or Works, which no
> ways concern them: For, till they produce the Authority by which they
> are constituted Judges, I shall plead to their Jurisdiction. (1: 37)

The end of the novel, in which the truth of Tom's origins is revealed, appears to be the culmination of the narrator's authority, as he requests the reader to "refresh his Memory, by turning to the scene at *Upton* in the Ninth Book. . . . Instances of this Kind we may frequently observe in Life, where the greatest Events are produced by a nice Train of little Circumstances; and more than one Example of this may be discovered by the accurate Eye, in this our History" (2: 916). The narrator depicts himself frequently as an all-knowing paternal guide to the landscape of the novel, pointing out the worthy prospects.

However, the idea of narrative authority proves to be a false guide because as the novel progresses, the reader perceives the necessity of subjecting the narrator's comments to scrutiny, too. The narrator withholds information from the readers by stating, for example, that he does not know what kept Allworthy so long in London (1: 38) or who touched the pin that fell to reveal Square in Molly's bedroom (1: 229). And although he indicates at moments that something important has occurred and the truth will be revealed to us, he also refrains from giving us hints about what will be important. He proves to be essentially unreliable.

The narrator himself, then, serves to make us aware of the instability of language. He constantly reminds us of the materiality of writing and reading by foregrounding the novel's "bookishness." He provides prefaces, or "bills of fare," to each of the books, all of which are given self-reflective titles like that of Book Four, Chapter One, "Containing five Pages of Paper" (1: 150). In the first paragraph of the novel, he draws an analogy between the novel and a public-house meal, where "Men who pay for what they eat, will insist on gratifying their Palates, however nice and even whimsical these may prove; and if every Thing is not agreeable to their Taste, will challenge a Right to censure, to abuse, and to d—n their Dinner without Controul" (1: 31). The irony here is that, as Timothy O'Brien points out, it is the author who is writing because he needs to eat, not the reader (p. 616). From beginning to end, readers are aware of an author who is in the business of using language. Furthermore, Fielding suggests that it is not the content of what is written but the style in which it is dressed that counts. And he is adept at employing language as ornament. He can describe Sophia "in the Sublime" (1: 154) or paint a battle scene between jealous women "in the Homerican Style" (1: 177).

The reader dismisses Fielding's ironic comments about grumbling being a more impressive sign of obedience than silent acceptance, even though they are accompanied by assurances of sincerity: "As this is one of those deep observations which very few readers can be supposed capable of making themselves, I have thought proper to lend them my assistance; but this is a favour rarely to be expected in the course of my work. Indeed I shall seldom or never so indulge him, unless in such instances as this, where nothing but the inspiration with which we writers are gifted, can possibly enable any one to make the discovery" (1: 47). The narrator proves to be a negative example of authority. What becomes apparent, then, is that the reader has to decide on each occasion whether to take his comments seriously or not. In fact, using the persona of the narrator, Fielding the author aims to instruct his readers about the nature of authority and the problem of basing judgment on language. He makes the reader judge the narrator as well as the characters by representing the unreliability of authority.[15]

Yet at the same time, Fielding wants the reader to come away from the novel with a sense that there is a purpose behind it. He assures his reader that this purpose is essentially moral, explaining in his dedication to George Lyttleton that "to recommend goodness and innocence hath been my sincere endeavor in this history" (1: 7). He has done this, he suggests, by painting a picture: "for an example is a kind of picture, in which virtue becomes as it were an object of sight, and strikes us with an idea of that loveliness, which Plato asserts there is in her naked charms" (1: 7). Finally, at the end of the process of reading, the readers are encouraged both to share an awareness of the power of words to shape our views and to reflect on the relationship between writer and reader, but still to have a sense of meaning and purpose in life and in reading. Ultimately, readers are all trained to think identically, not with the narrator, but with each other. Fielding builds the nation through the consensus of fiction.

What also becomes apparent, however, is his awareness of the tenuousness of this consensus, which, even as it is suggested, also hints at a multiplicity of differences which have to be brought into union. Unable to ignore the contradictions within the homogeneous nation, Fielding uses the novel to reconfigure political differences. His general project to build a cohesive British nation is structured around an episode of absolute difference that is separated from the rest of the narrative, but that nevertheless comments on it: the encounter with the gypsies. The Gypsy King episode raises the most crucial of the wider concerns of the novel: the nature of good government. The episode allows for the existence of a contradictory stance on the question, but also attempts to diminish the impact of that contradictory stance.

Fielding's presentation of the gypsies has generated much critical debate on whether the episode is either a critique or a celebration of monarchical authority.[16] His description of the gypsies can be seen as advocating this latter position, inasmuch as he presents the gypsies as existing in complete happiness. The narrator seems to suggest without irony that "Mankind have never been so happy, as when the greatest Part of the then known World was under the Dominion of a single Master" (2: 671). But lest some advocate of arbitrary power should "hereafter quote the Case of those People, as an Instance of the great Advantages which attend that Government above all others" (2: 671), he also includes a qualification; he warns that such an arrangement is made difficult by the fact that ideal monarchs are few and far between, and that absolute power vested in the wrong person is certain to lead to disastrous trouble (2: 671). In fact, the ambiguity of this passage in the novel replicates the ambiguity that exists within the nation. The episode with the gypsies shows Fielding's awareness of the contradictory positions that continue to be unresolved within the nation.

But the impact of these contradictory positions is also minimized. The gypsies are meant to suggest the Jacobites insofar as they represent difference within the nation of Britain, including desire for a different form of government. As Fielding shows us, the gypsies' law and their society operate according to a completely different set of rules: they "differ from all other people" (2: 673). Unlike the Jacobites, however, the gypsies do not represent a political threat to the prevailing order. Instead, they are shown as being quite separate from that order; indeed they provide an alternative positioning of difference as compared to the proximity of the Jacobites. Existing in the forest and presented at first as supernatural beings, they constitute a realm which is beyond the pale of everyday life. As Tom, Partridge, and their guide approach the camp of the gypsies, they hear "singing, laughing, and hallowing, together with a strange Noise that seemed to proceed from some Instruments; but could hardly be allowed the Name of Music" (1: 664). Indeed, to Partridge it sounds like "Music bewitched" (1: 664). The language the gypsies speak also distinguishes them from other groups of characters within the text of Fielding's novel. Ricardo Ortiz discusses the "profound alterity" of the gypsies' language (p. 613), maintaining that the dialectical idiosyncrasies manage "a kind of ventriloquy or dummy effect" (p. 618). He notes that the King even refers to himself in the objective tense, as "me." Although the gypsies "differ from all other people" (2: 673), then, they do not threaten other people. They can be happily acknowledged and left aside while the narration (and the nation) continues.

As Fielding deflects the Jacobite theme onto this isolated episode, so he also steers attention away from the actual Jacobitism which does threaten the nation. The novel shifts from the events of the Jacobite Rebellion as abruptly as it first raised them. The last third of the book centers on London, a London that, as readers would no doubt have been aware, would have been in a state of panic at this historical juncture. Yet there are no further references to the political troubles of the nation. Instead, events are focused on the working out of individual lives in the metropolis. In *Natural Masques: Gender and Identity in Fielding's Plays and Novels,* Jill Campbell notes that *Tom Jones* switches from the Rebellion to the pursuit of Sophia, a pursuit "of female virtue, of heterosexual union, and of personal happiness" (p. 163). For Campbell, this switch suggests "the interconnections between historically specific political purposes and this experience of private pursuits" (p. 163). I want to extend this analysis a little further to suggest that Fielding uses the disappearance of the Rebellion as a correlative to its introduction in the first part of the book. If the introduction of the Rebellion encourages the reader to think that the experiences of private individuals are actually dependent on the wider events of the nation, then the erasure of the Rebellion leads the reader to conclude that the stability of the nation is related to finding satisfactory solutions to private problems. Fielding's *Tom Jones* reinforces the connection between narration and political events seen in earlier prose works concerning the Rebellion. But by drawing readers together in the common act of reading and by turning attention to the private realm, the novel also minimizes contradictions within the nation.

Fielding's contemporary Tobias Smollett was also eventually to turn to the novel form to confront the political contradictions he perceived within a sup-

posedly united Britain. As a Scottish writer in London in the aftermath of
the Rebellion, Smollett had a firsthand understanding of the contradictions
within the nation. He was educated as a surgeon at Glasgow but headed
south to London, more intent on being a writer than on being a physician.
He was with Dr. Alexander Carlyle in a coffeehouse when the news of Culloden was delivered. Carlyle writes of that experience: "London all over was
in a perfect uproar of joy. . . . I asked Smollett if he was ready to go, as he
lived at Mayfair; he said he was, and would conduct me. The mob were so ri-
otous, and the squibs so numerous and incessant that we were glad to go into
a narrow entry to put our wigs in our pockets, and to take our swords from
our belts and walk with them in our hands, as everybody then wore swords"
(Kelly, p. 32). Smollett's warning to Carlyle suggests his realization of the
danger of being identified as Scottish. He cautioned Carlyle "against speaking a word, lest the mob should discover my country and become insolent,
'for John Bull,' says he, 'is as haughty and valiant to-night as he was abject and
cowardly on the Black Wednesday when the Highlanders were at Derby'" (p.
32). This episode indicates Smollett's awareness of his own peripheral position
in an allegedly united Great Britain.

Recent criticism has attempted to understand Smollett as a Scottish writer
working in an essentially English market. Damien Grant suggests that "As a
Scotsman [Smollett] shared the sense of grievance against a Whig, Hanoverian England . . . that had betrayed Scottish interests both before and after
the Act of Union in 1707" (p. 129). More sensitive to the ambivalences in
Smollett's work are James G. Basker and Kenneth Simpson. Basker comments
on the "anxiety that Scottish writers felt perhaps more acutely than any others in the mid-eighteenth century: that is, a sense of cultural ambivalence, of
trying to participate and distinguish themselves in what was, essentially, an
English world of letters, while still bearing in their speech and writing telltale traces of their Scottish origins" (p. 81). Basker argues that Smollett was
extreme in his manifestation of this ambivalence: "It was probably Tobias
Smollett who suffered more than any other writer of his time from the clash
between the Scottish and English cultures" (p. 86). In a similar vein, Simpson describes Smollett's "Protean" position in eighteenth-century Scotland.[17]
According to Simpson, his style shows readiness to experiment, "but it is also
the response of a creative talent that has suffered enforced dislocation from its
cultural roots" (*Protean Scot*, pp. 15–16). I suggest that Smollett's ambivalence
not only has implications for his portrayal of Scottish identity, but also that it
indicates his awareness of the ambiguity that exists within the whole of Britain. In the novel *Roderick Random*, he attempts to contain that ambiguity,
which he perceived in his early work, within the confines of the novel.

Smollett's sense of the ambiguity of national identity can be seen in his first published work, a poem called "The Tears of Scotland" (1746), which, while expressing anger at the "pacification" of the Highlands by the Duke of Cumberland, also contains an indictment of Scotland itself. The poem was written as a response to the government treatment of the Highlands and to the kind of prejudices being hurled at Scots. Damien Grant observes that Smollett wrote "The Tears of Scotland" "against the advice of his friends" and "in sympathy for the failure of the Scottish cause in the rising of 1745 and in protest against the atrocities committed by the English after Culloden" (p. 129). Alexander Carlyle, who was shown the manuscript of the poem, commented that "Smollett, though a Tory, was not a Jacobite but he had the feelings of a Scotch gentleman on the reported cruelties that were said to be exercised after the battle of Culloden" (Kelly, p. 32). The poem describes the drastic changes that have occurred in Scotland as a result of Culloden. Caledonia, personified, as in Lord Belhaven's speech, as a disconsolate woman, is seen lamenting her losses. The events are presented as a betrayal of the "peace" of the Union:

> Mourn, hapless Caledonia, mourn
> Thy banish'd peace, thy laurels torn!
> Thy sons, for valour long renown'd,
> Lie slaughtered on their native ground.
>
> *(ll. 1–4)*[18]

Smollett portrays a rural Scotland of swains and flocks, whose peaceful innocence has been destroyed. He blames England, indicating that the atrocities that occurred after the war were worse than the carnage of the battle: "Yet, when the rage of battle ceas'd / The victor's soul was not appeas'd" (ll. 39–40). Then, in the final stanza, the narrator assumes his role of articulating the sorrows of his nation:

> While the warm blood bedews my veins,
> And unimpair'd remembrance reigns,
> Resentment of my country's fate
> Within my filial breast shall beat;
> And, spite of her insulting foe,
> My sympathetic verse shall flow:
> "Mourn, hapless Caledonia, mourn
> Thy banish'd peace, thy laurels torn."
>
> *(ll. 49–56)*

Inscribing his own verse back into the poem, the phrase, "Mourn, hapless Caledonia, mourn," becomes a refrain indicating Smollett's assumption of the position of national bard.[19]

"The Tears of Scotland" attempts to gain sympathy for the Scottish nation by showing how the nation has come apart. But Smollett's poem does not paint a straightforward picture of English oppressors and Scottish victims; it complicates the issue by suggesting that the Scots have been party to their own downfall. The Rebellion, which began in Scotland, has caused a split between families as "The sons against their father stood" and "The parent shed his children's blood" (ll. 35–36). Smollett notes that the martial spirit for which Scotland is famous has been extinguished, not by foreign invasion but through civil war: "What foreign arms could never quell, / By civil rage and rancour fell" (ll. 23–24). Smollett seems to call into question the identity of the Scots even as he tries to preserve it.

A similar ambiguity of national affiliation can be seen in Smollett's play *The Regicide*, a retelling of the assassination of James I in 1437. The play centers on a rebellion against lawful authority. The resolution of the play encourages us to support the cause of James I, the legitimate ruler, but the circumstances surrounding the resolution raise the issue of whether or not rebellion is legitimate. Although the play was begun six years before the '45, it can be seen as offering a perspective on earlier post-Union rebellions. *The Regicide* does not just offer an analogy of the Stewart versus the Hanover wars, however. It concerns the assassination of a Scottish king, and both protagonists and antagonists are Scottish. Paradoxically, both sides of the warring factions embody aspects of the fallen Stewart regime. The legitimate king, James I, shares the same nomenclature as the monarch dispossessed at the time of the Revolution. In addition, loyalty to James I is expressed in terms of absolute obedience: *jure divino*. Dunbar rails against Athol betraying both country and personal friendship: "Against a Prince with ev'ry Virtue grac'd / That dignifies the Throne" (p. 96). James is indeed a predecessor of later believers in the divine right of kings.

However, James's opponents also elicit the audience's sympathy and demonstrate a certain affiliation with the Stewarts. The chief character from the opposite side is referred to by the name "Stuart." Furthermore, while the play is sympathetic to the legitimate king, it also expresses elements which can be interpreted as supporting the deposition of the regime. Stuart's expostulation against James—"Curse on his arts!—his aim was to enslave" (p. 103) can also be seen as relating to the Hanoverian usurpation of the throne against the "native rights" of Britain's Stewart king. References to the Jacobite hope (and culpability) are thus embedded in the play on both sides.

The Regicide also presents the difficulty of deciding what makes a cause just. The rebels and the king have different sides of the story. The king accuses Grime of being a three-time traitor, "a rugged Rebel still, Unaw'd and unreclaim'd!" (p. 123), while Grime replies that he owes his life, "Not to thy mercy but thy Dread . . . Wrong'd as I was" (p. 123). The audience is made to feel that there is some justice in both their remarks. The final outcome of the play directs audience sympathy to the king, while the language of the play directs sympathy away from the rebels; their speeches, like those of Shakespeare's Iago, are full of dark imagery: carcasses, rot, revenge, and gore feature predominantly. However, the ambiguity in the play remains unresolved, complicating the audience response as it complicates national identity in the past and, by extension, in the present.

Smollett experienced great difficulty in getting *The Regicide* produced, and eventually he resorted to publishing it by subscription in 1749. By that time, he had successfully published his first novel, *Roderick Random*. The connection between the two works can be seen in the fact that they both address the tension between center and periphery in an ostensibly united nation.

Roderick Random expands on the portrayal of the ambiguity of national identity seen in the earlier "Tears of Scotland" and *The Regicide*. The novel traces the adventures of a young man, a Scot, who attempts to make his way in England and who is forced to leave Britain for the West Indies before he can reenter and integrate into British society. Like *Tom Jones*, *Roderick Random* is situated within and draws upon contemporary political discourse concerning fact and fiction. It also focuses on a critical issue in the post-Rebellion years: the role of Scots in British politics and culture. Robert Crawford suggests that "Smollett produced the first important novel in the English language to have a Scot as hero" (*Devolving*, p. 60). For Crawford, *Roderick Random* is an attempt to redress the bias against the Scots: "Schooled in Scotophobia, Smollett's triumph was to write the eighteenth century's greatest novel on the theme of prejudice" (p. 57). Crawford says that it "pushes strongly to win sympathy for the young Scot and for other social outsiders" (p. 60). But the case is not that simple. Although reading about the national contradictions in the form of a novel provides a temporary kind of integration, *Roderick Random* suggests the impossibility of any attempt to identify a cohesive nation in post-'45 Britain.

The preface to the novel illustrates the ambiguous perspectives regarding national affiliation and narration that will characterize the rest of the book, as Smollett explains why he chose a Scot as a main character. First, he says that by doing so he could provide his main character with a level of education not available in England for a person of his "birth and character" (p. xxxv). He promotes the image of the Scots, even the most poor, as being well educated.

Second, he can "represent the simplicity of manners in a remote part of the
kingdom, with more propriety, than in any place near the capital" (p. xxxv).
Third, he points out that the "disposition of the Scots, addicted to travelling"
adds credibility to the nature of Roderick's wanderings (p. xxxv). His explanation is a subtle comment on the confusion of British national identity.
The first two remarks suggest positive aspects of Scottish identity, but the last
comment focuses on a less pleasant feature: Scots are such extensive travelers
because they have had to go south to find work. Within the nation of Britain,
Scotland is both privileged and discriminated against. The preface also calls
attention to the possible unreliability of the writer: is he being ironic or
merely disingenuous? Smollett himself hints at the ambiguous nature of his
work, explaining that the kind of satiric fiction he is writing has "a double
force on the imagination" (p. xxxiii).

The novel begins with Roderick noting the fact that he is from North
Britain. His place of birth is "in the northern part of this united kingdom" (p.
1), and, as the book progresses, the irony of description becomes clear; the
phrase, "united kingdom," is simply a construction of language, as problematic
in 1748 as it had been in Defoe's time. As the novel continues, and Roderick
leaves Scotland for London, the actual difference between the diverse parts of
the nation is made evident. The carman curses Roderick and Strap "for a
lousy Scotch guard," and they are taunted by other Londoners (pp. 62–63).
Someone "understanding by our dialect who we were, came up to me, and,
with a very grave countenance, asked me, how long I had been caught? . . .
and he went on, saying, it could not be a great while, for my tail was not yet
cut; at the same time taking hold of my hair, and tipping the wink to the rest
of the company, which seemed highly entertained with his wit" (p. 63). The
same man asks Strap what he carries in his knapsack: "Is it oat-meal or brim-
stone, Sawney?" (p. 63). Again and again, Roderick is subject to abuse merely
for being born "in the northern part of this united kingdom."

Roderick notes the pains some Scots go to counteract anti-Scottish prejudice. A fellow countryman has taken lessons to disguise the accent that so
often betrays Roderick and Strap. This man "had come from Scotland three
or four years ago" and taught French, Latin, and Italian in a school, "but what
he chiefly professed was the pronunciation of the English tongue, after a
method more speedy and uncommon than any practised before" (p. 66). But,
as Roderick suggests, he is still marked as different: "For although I could
easily understand every word of what I had heard hitherto since I entered
England, three parts in four of his dialect were as unintelligible to me, as if
he had spoke in Arabick or Irish" (p. 67). The man can change his accent, but
he cannot change the fact that he is foreign.

Roderick's uniqueness, however, lies in his ability to erase the signs that betray his difference. After he leaves the ship, Roderick becomes more integrated into London society at the same time that he begins to conceal his story. Eventually he learns also to disguise his accent, so that by the end of the book his origins are unclear. His identity is mistaken by Mr. Medlar, who asks if he is an Englishman, or from Ireland, or one of the "settlements abroad" (p. 266). Mr. Banter informs Roderick of similar confusions about his character: "One suspects you to be Jesuit in disguise; another believes you are an agent from the Pretender; a third believes you to be an upstart gamester, because no body knows any thing of your family or fortune; a fourth is of opinion, that you are an Irish fortune-hunter" (p. 284). Roderick's language no longer gives him away. Smollett suggests that one answer to anti-Scottish prejudice is to assimilate.

Roderick Random finishes with a wedding which provides a symbol of such assimilation. Roderick's final act of integration into British society is his marriage to Narcissa. Robert Crawford argues that *Roderick Random* represents a vision of British unity: "The acceptance of Roderick's continuing Scottishness within a British union is emblematized in the novel's final chapter in a way that anticipates the Scott of *Waverley* . . . *Roderick Random* concludes with a vindication of the young immigrant with whom, in the face of prejudice, the reader has been brought to sympathize and who has established his place in British society" (*Devolving*, p. 61). In fact, by reversing the gender roles commonly associated with each country—Sister Peg and John Bull, Fergusia and Heptarchus—Smollett is presenting Scotland as in the stronger position. Nevertheless, there is a troubling qualification at the end of the novel in the description of Narcissa's delight with Scotland: she is "so well pleased with the situation of the place, and the company round, that she has not *as yet* discovered the last desire of changing her habitation" (p. 434, my italics). Whereas Crawford says that this phrase "might promise something to the cynical English reader," it seems also to indicate the fragility of the fictional union, echoing the instability that was hinted at in the very first line of the novel: "North Britain" will always be considered different.

The novel also suggests the universality of prejudice toward an identified Other. Even when Roderick leaves England, prejudices abound on board the ship. There, however, it is not the English who are the oppressors, but the Irish, as seen in the captain, Mackshane. In scenes in which Mackshane persecutes Roderick and others, the novel suggests that those subjected to prejudice internalize the violence and practice it themselves when given a chance. At the same time, Smollett himself perpetuates prejudices against the Irish in his narrative. Both Roderick and Thompson have been keeping a journal in Greek, which is mistaken for a secret code by the captain. Several sailors who have visited a Greek port are brought forward to testify against Roderick's plea of innocence. Roderick protests that they speak "an imperfect Gothic dialect that rose on the ruins of the former" pure Greek language. Roderick then challenges Mackshane to speak to the seamen in Greek. Instead, Mackshane addresses one of them in Irish, which he claims is Greek. Smollett makes Roderick and Thompson, both Scots, the representatives of classical learning, in contrast to the ignorant Irish who speak a language described as mere "gibberish" (pp. 172–76). The episodes on the ship suggest the universality of prejudice and the impossibility of achieving unity either in the microcosm of the individual ship or the larger context of the ship of state.

On the level of style, too, the novel reinforces the contradictions that exist within the nation. *Roderick Random* is narrated by Roderick, who, as suggested by his various adventures, has a prominent Scottish accent. Yet, the actual writing of the novel in standard English belies this. The reader is left in the position of being completely aware of the differences in speech throughout the British Isles, yet having no signification of those differences; difference is both indicated and denied in *Roderick Random*. Smollett's writing and his representation of the nation turn out to be very much a product of "double impressions."

Fielding's post-'45 novelistic effort goes to great lengths to provide a sense of historical accuracy with details about the Rebellion. What is interesting, of course, is how Smollett bypasses the historical incident most crucial to Roderick's treatment as a Scot: the Rebellion itself. He presents episodes that encompass the time period between 1739 to "about 1747" (Beasley, p. 164). Yet the only reference to the Rebellion here is a comment about Roderick's being mistaken for one of the Pretender's men. Smollett avoids direct mention of the Rebellion, preferring to focus attention on European wars or colonial battles. However, by omitting to comment on this event, Smollett also draws attention to it, for the '45 would have been the political event most recent in his contemporary audience's consciousness. The missing '45 Rebellion in *Roderick Random* acts as an absence whose presence is palpable and disturbing.

Like Fielding and the pamphlet writers around the time of the '45, Smollett is concerned with the use of narrative to shape readers' responses to political events. He addresses these issues in *Roderick Random* in two episodes drawn from events in his own life: the battle at Cartagena and the story of Melopoyn. The relation of the battle of Cartagena stands apart in the text as an extended passage of biting irony, quite uncharacteristic of Smollett's narration up to that point. He imitates the rhetoric of government officials attempting to explain away what was a military and a human disaster. Like

Fielding in the *True Patriot*, Smollett undermines official accounts. In explaining why the British ships lie in wait at Port-Royal, he speculates: "I would ascribe this delay to the generosity of our chiefs, who scorned to take any advantage that fortune might give them, even over an enemy" (p. 179). Smollett utilizes a language of chivalry which rings hollow considering the actual circumstances of the carnage. Yet, despite the smooth veneer of the official language, there comes out a clear note of bitterness. It starts with a slight hesitation, as Smollett describes the starvation that is imposed upon the troops: "This fast must (I suppose) have been injoined by way of penance on the ship's company for their sins; or rather with a view to mortify them into a contempt of life, that they might thereby become more resolute and regardless of danger" (p. 186). But what follows is Smollett's own descent into the grotesque: he finishes this description with a vulgar analogy of the dispute between the two commanding officers which precipitated the slaughter: "Between two stools the backside falls to the ground" (p. 187). Smollett ends this chapter with a description of the bodies floating in the water and the rain that begins to flash, so "that one can see to read a very small print by the illumination" (p. 189). The message to which he wants to draw attention is the way narrative can be manipulative. The reader is never told a true version of what happens at the battle. Instead, Smollett suggests that when language is involved there are multiple truths. Perhaps the only true way of expressing the horror of the scene is Roderick's primal "bellowing" as he lies chained to the deck and is spattered with the brains and entrails of his shipmates.

The episode involving Melopoyn, like the Cartagena passage, also explores the manipulations of narrative, conveying to the reader how writing creates multiple truths. Melopoyn is a victim of official language. In trying to make his way as a writer, he faces an ever-expanding number of barriers or rejections. He is told that his play has been accidentally destroyed, but even though he is willing to rewrite his work, he is refused the opportunity. As he finds out later, this is because one of the patentees rejected his play in order to produce the work of a friend. In addition, the Melopoyn incident implies that writing is a business. Written works are market commodities, and each genre comes with particular political and commercial expectations. Melopoyn is offered the chance to work at a journal, but, because it was "calculated to foment divisions in the commonwealth" (p. 383), he refuses. He tries poetry, which is rejected by a bookseller. Another bookseller tells him that the town was "cloyed with pastorals" and advises him, if he intends "to profit by my talents, to write something satirical or luscious" (p. 383), but he refuses to prostitute his pen. Still another bookseller inquires about the possibility of his writing novels and asks if he "had got never a piece of secret history, thrown into a series of letters, or a volume of adventures, such as those of Robinson Crusoe, and Colonel Jack, or a collection of conundrums, wherewith to entertain the plantations" (p. 383). At last, Melopoyn considers translation, even though a bookseller tells him "that translation [is] a meer drug" (p. 383), a worthless commodity. Melopoyn's adventures, like Fielding's narrative comments, emphasize the material considerations that go into the creation of published texts. Smollett asks his readers to question the novel they are reading even as he uses it to shape their impressions of the world.

Smollett's representation of national contradictions is distinctly more disturbing than Fielding's. In his later novel, *Humphry Clinker* (1771), Smollett would present a more settled resolution of differences within the nation (in part because he displaces the difference between Scotland and England by concentrating on a character to whom both nations seem both familiar and different: Matthew Bramble, a Welshman). *Roderick Random*, however, operates more on a level of pointing out rather than healing the rifts within Britain. Still, by choosing to represent those contradictions in novel form, Smollett, too, draws on the unifying possibilities of culture.

In this discussion, I have been suggesting ways in which Fielding's and Smollett's novels both represent and reframe the political discourse of the '45. Although the two writers themselves were to engage in a debate in the 1750s centering on particular similarities between their work (Smollett accused Fielding of plagiarism),[20] it took Samuel Johnson to realize the more general affinities between them. Johnson saw them as perpetrators of a new and dangerous kind of fiction and considered both of them a threat to the literary realm. Johnson's essay in the *Rambler* (March 31, 1750) condemns them both, pointing out instead what he considers to be the proper purpose of fiction. Writers of old romances had an easy task, he offers. They could just invent out of their heads, but:

> The task of our present writers is very different; it requires, together with that learning which is to be gained from books, that experience which can never be attained by solitary diligence, but must arise from general converse, and accurate observation of the living world. . . . They are engaged in portraits of which every one knows the original, and can detect any deviation from exactness of resemblance. Other writings are safe, except from the malice of learning, but these are in danger from every . common reader. (*Works of Samuel Johnson*, 2: 16)

Johnson wants the new variety of novel writers to guard the "young, the ignorant, and the idle, to whom they serve as lectures of conduct, and introductions into life" (3: 21). Young readers' minds, he suggests, are "unfurnished with ideas, and therefore easily susceptible of impressions; not fixed by principles, and therefore easily following the current of fancy; not informed by experience, and consequently open to every false suggestion and partial account" (3: 21). Like the political writers during the '45 Rebellion, Johnson is chiefly concerned with readers' responses. Ironically, Fielding and Smollett wrote their novels with precisely this susceptibility of readers in mind. Intent on addressing the political contradictions within the nation, they moved away from fiction that presents abstract models of behavior to fiction that molds readers' impressions of the dynamic relationship between moral behavior and political events.

In this chapter, I have examined the '45 Rebellion as a crucial point in the history of the novel and of the British nation precisely because it brought to the forefront the connection between narrative and nationhood. The novel, as employed by Fielding and Smollett, served to address political issues in the nation because it was itself related to political discourse. But at the same time, the novel also began to help isolate the realm of culture from that of politics. By centering readers' sensibilities on contemporary issues, Fielding's and Smollett's midcentury novels produced citizens who felt rather than merely contemplated their society and who extended their thoughts to "National Matters" beyond their own parish, even when they least expected it: in their leisure time. National differences are raised in the pages of the novel. But political sensibilities are worked back into the cultural realm through the resolutions of plots. The Rebellion can be upstaged by the marriage of Tom and Sophia; anti-Scottish prejudice can be put aside (although temporarily) in the nuptial ceremony between Roderick and Narcissa. Fielding's and Smollett's renegotiation of the Union signals a shift from the fiction of politics introduced by the discourse on the Rebellion in 1745 to the politics of fiction represented in the midcentury novel.[21]

We should bear in mind, however, that the realm of culture is never completely separate from the political realm. The cultural realm serves to change the focus on political events, but those events remain repressed, not resolved, and they eventually return to affect the possibilities of cultural realm. As we will see in the next chapter, the realm of culture that allowed for the temporary containment of political contradictions after the Rebellion was to become itself the new battleground for defining British national identity. Culloden may have ended the threat of Jacobite political power in Britain, but it did not settle the underlying national tensions on both sides of the Tweed.

CHAPTER 3

Origin of the Specious:
James Macpherson, Samuel Johnson, and
the Forging of the Nation

The threat of another Jacobite invasion was essentially laid to rest after the defeat of the Jacobite army. Moreover, in the decades following the Rebellion, there was considerable change in the dynamics of the relationship between the Scots, both Highlanders and Lowlanders, and the English.[1] J. Mackinnon suggests that the aftermath of the Jacobite Rebellion actually brought the two nations closer together: "The rebellion of 1745 is not merely a striking landmark in Scottish political history. It is memorable as marking the beginning of a closer and more sympathetic intercourse between Scot and Englishman" (p. 461). The Rebellion in Scotland further encouraged a Scottish Enlightenment, already underway, as Scots sought both agricultural and cultural progress. While landlords busied themselves with finding out the best way to improve their farming techniques, members of the literati in their turn addressed the improvement of society.[2] As I suggested in the Introduction to this book, in this process Scottish writers like James Beattie also attempted to become more English than the English, instructing their fellow Scots on how to eliminate all scotticisms from their vocabulary.[3]

The emphasis on improvement at home was both a reaction to and an action to encourage further Scottish participation in a United Kingdom. Scots began to play a bigger part in the British military, despite being denied their own militia.[4] Linda Colley points out how during the Seven Years War, "For the first time ever, the British army had been able to recruit men on a massive scale from the Scottish Highlands" (p. 103). Such changes were due to the work both of the Scots, who were anxious to present a more positive view of Scotland to ensure their participation in the British economic market, and of the English, who were equally anxious to create a united national identity in the face of international unrest and competition in Europe and North America.[5] But the search for national unity in Britain was more complicated than some citizens liked to admit. The complications came out in a renewed antagonism between the two nations that occurred as a result of the ascension of a Scot, Lord Bute, to a position of power and influence over King George III in the early 1760s.[6]

Bute was given an English earldom and was subsequently made secretary of state in 1761, then prime minister in 1762. He was a close friend of the king, and for that reason his rise to power was viewed suspiciously. Bute's detractors argued that Bute favored his fellow Scots and implied that his position constituted as much of a Scottish conquest of England as a successful Jacobite invasion would have achieved. Particularly relevant for this discussion are the stereotypes of Scotland that were successfully employed against Bute; his enemies focus on his Scottishness as evidence of his unscrupulousness. The discourse regarding Bute and the danger of his political power turned on the fear of the assimilation of the Scots into England.[7]

The issue of assimilation is also behind the journalistic battle between Tobias Smollett and John Wilkes. Smollett, continuing his efforts to knit the nation together, had taken on the task of defending Bute in the *Briton* (May 29, 1762–February 13, 1763), a journal intended to promote the union between the two nations. Smollett said that the *Briton's* principles were "not to alarm, but to appease; not to puzzle but explain; not to inflame but to allay," and that it aimed "to detect the falsehood of malice; to expose and refute the insinuations of calumny; to pluck the mask of patriotism from the front of faction, and the torch of discord from the hand of sedition" (p. 239). Smollett draws on a sense of an imagined community of Britain when he claims the "undoubted privilege of every Briton" to "speak his opinion freely" (p. 241). As it turned out, he enjoyed that right, but he was also severely taken to task for it when he was attacked by his erstwhile friend, John Wilkes, who launched his opposing journal on June 5, 1762. The *North Briton* returns to the difference between the two nations, a return that seems to have been welcome, inasmuch as Wilkes proved much more successful in using propaganda to turn opinion against Bute than Smollett had been in defending his fellow Scot. In the *North Briton*, Wilkes confirms the worst fears of anti-Scottish readers by pretending to be a Scot who is scheming to take over Britain. He mimics Smollett's claim for free speech in the unified nation, twisting his words so that they imply an intrusion rather than a right: "And I will exert the undoubted privilege of every North Briton, that of speaking my opinion freely on every subject that concerns the community, of which I am a member" (p. 8). Wilkes plays on English xenophobia, not just of Scottish culture but of Scottish economic power. The second issue begins, "I Cannot conceal the joy I feel as a *North Briton*, and I heartily congratulate my dear country-men on our having at length accomplished the great, long fought, and uni-versally national object of all our wishes, the planting a *Scotsman* at the head of the *English* Treasury" (p. 10). He refers to the money that Bute is directing to the Highland chiefs and the four thousand pounds of public money re-cently given to construct a bridge over the Tweed, suggesting that this will enable more Scots to make their way to England. Wilkes's argument appeals to the English fear of Scottish infiltration of everything English, even the lan-guage: "Though I am a NORTH BRITON, I will endeavor to write *plain English*, and to avoid the numerous *Scotticisms* the BRITON abounds with; and then, as the world is apt to mistake, he may be taken for a *Scotsman*, and I shall pass for an *Englishman*" (p. 8). Plagued with such virulent and xenophobic attacks, Bute finally resigned on April 8, 1763, after the riots that occurred after he introduced a cider tax (Owen, p. 175).

This chapter will examine how the work of James Macpherson and Sam-uel Johnson reflects and restages contemporary struggles between Scots and English for political and cultural hegemony in a debate concerning the ori-gin of culture of Britain. In his Ossianic poetry and his later historical work, Macpherson presented a positive image of the Scottish people in the years shortly after the smear campaign against Bute. But this positive image oper-ates by conflating Lowlanders and Highlanders and by constructing a history of British culture which could include English subjects as well. Situating the origins of British culture in a mythic Caledonia, Macpherson creates what is in effect a historical narrative of a homogenized nation that prefigures the homogenization he desires in the present. In contrast, in *A Journey to the West-ern Isles of Scotland* (1773), Samuel Johnson articulates the distinction between the oral Highland and the literate English cultures. He places England on a higher level of civilization, but he also values the Highland culture for the difference it represents within Britain. Like Defoe, Johnson values the het-erogeneous history of Britain, although for Johnson the value of heterogene-ity lies not only in economic but also in cultural strength. Where Macpher-son presents a historical narrative that begins with homogeneity, evolves into difference, and then resolves in a renewed union, Johnson's Britain is consti-tuted by heterogeneity and a hegemonic relation between the constituent parts.[8]

I conclude this chapter by examining how Boswell's *Journal of a Tour to the Hebrides*, by rewriting Johnson's account, also contributes to the negotiation of the relationship between Scotland and England in the last quarter of the eighteenth century. Boswell conscripts aspects of both Macpherson's and Johnson's imagined communities, but emphasizes in his account the importance of the Lowland Scots as the arbiters of contemporary British culture.

To begin with, I examine Macpherson's position in the debate on national identity. From the 1761 publication date of *Fingal, An Ancient Epic Poem* onward, studies of Macpherson have concentrated on the authenticity of his alleged Gaelic translations and the motivation of their fabricator, to the exclusion of other considerations. Only recently have critics begun to read Macpherson in the context of Scottish politics, suggesting that he provided a focus for Highland and Lowland cultural national sentiment after the shattering defeat of Culloden.[9] Macpherson was born in the Highlands, seven years before the Jacobites' last stand, and was a direct witness to the English reprisals. The government barracks at his birthplace, Ruthven, Invernesshire, were occupied for thirty years, during which time they were twice attacked by the local inhabitants. Ruthven was also the site at which the remaining Jacobite soldiers gathered after their bloody defeat at Culloden. John Macqueen emphasizes the impact of Macpherson's early years on his writing, suggesting that Macpherson "resented the Union of 1707" and the "destruction of the Highland way of life" and that he wrote "to preserve as much of the old way of life as was possible" (p. 89). But Macpherson's project also needs to be seen in the context of the more recent rhetorical attacks against Bute and the Scots regarding cultural miscegenation.

Macpherson's poems and later prose works became common cultural property that helped construct the imagined community of Britain, reflecting and reinforcing the changing hegemonic relationship between England and Scotland. Howard Weinbrot suggests that Macpherson's Ossianic poems "almost succeeded in again unifying Europe beneath the Celtic banner and mocking the Anglo-Saxons beneath the Tweed" (p. 524). I want to read Macpherson's work in a different vein, suggesting that rather than merely promoting "the Celtic banner" and condemning Anglo-Saxons, Macpherson problematized the distinction between the two ethnic categories. The poems of Ossian were forgeries in a different sense than is usually applied to them; they forged a common identity for Highland, Lowland, and English readers alike, silencing in this process the existing voice of Gaelic Scotland.

Macpherson's work reflects the dilemma of a writer caught between different worlds, between the Highland village of Ruthven, where he spent his early years, and anglicized Aberdeen, where he attended university—between the stark rural settlement and the stimulating city of the Enlightenment that boasted the presence of such philosophers as Thomas Reid. The eroding Highland society represented for Macpherson the Scottish past, whereas the busy anglophone city suggested a future of commerce and industrialization. Macpherson's work registers the tension between what Christopher Harvie calls the values of "the simplicity and purity (real or imagined) of nativism" and "cosmopolitan sophistication," as Macpherson interweaves praise for and dissatisfaction with his native land (p. 112).

This ambivalence is reflected in an early poem of Macpherson's, "The Hunter." In "The Hunter," written at a time when Macpherson was working as a teacher at Ruthven after leaving Aberdeen, he combines an insider's perspective on his native area with a knowledge of English and classical works. "The Hunter" both accepts the demise of Highland society as the way to prosperity and laments its passing. The protagonist, Donald, shoots a deer beloved by a fairy. Her father subsequently arranges a revenge that involves putting Donald under a spell and making him suddenly dissatisfied with his Highland life, which up to this point has been full enough with just "a gun, a plaid, [and] a dog" (*Poems of Ossian*, Laing, ed., 2.i.7). Now, when Donald surveys the wilderness before him, he takes no delight in the "rough-browed rocks" and the "sloping hills and plains" of his home. Instead, he compares his hard life to that of the citizens of Edinburgh, who live comfortably "in stately halls" while he forces "poor sustenance from barren land" (2.ii.1–17).[10] The difference between the barren hill exposed to "the north-descended cold" and the "deluges of joy" that exist in Edinburgh persuades Donald to undertake the journey between the Highlands and the Lowlands in order to gain riches.

Donald arrives at Edinburgh just in time to take part in a battle against the invading Saxon hordes. Although the Scots bravely defeat the Saxons, the poem predicts an ultimate defeat for Scotland, not through martial conquest but through commerce. On his deathbed the Saxon leader, Henry, prophesies a grim future for the Scots:

> a race, deep-versed in policies,
> Shall sprout from Saxon trunk, and schemes unfold,
> To change their steely points to fusil gold;
> Then shackled on his heath the hill-born swain
> Shall crawl along, and move his hard-bound lips
>   with pain.
> Fair liberty to them shall lose her charms,
> And Scots shall tremble at the sight of arms.
>
> *(2.iv.182–88)*

Macpherson suggests that English "policies" turn the once fearsome Scots into base slaves, dependent on monetary gain. But he makes it clear that the Scots are responsible for their downfall. Significantly, the main ingredient in the spell the fairy puts on Donald is the "black humour" (1.i.115) of desire for power taken from a courtier in Edinburgh. Edinburgh itself has already fallen because its citizens have been chasing after that humor. It was "Once the proud seat of royalty and state," but it is now the home of "fops and scriveners, and English'd whores" (1.i.139–42). The poem indicts the Lowlanders of the present day for adopting English ways, and it suggests that their greed has also infected the Highlanders, making them discontent with their old way of life. Avarice and effeminacy have spread to the Highlanders, causing them to sacrifice their independence for worldly goods. The main character, Donald, delivers a speech reviling the future actions of the Scots and calling them "more than slaves," "mean debasers of our blood," and "the gold-deluded brood" (2.v.13–14). But the poem remains ambivalent. Donald himself is revealed to be a Lowlander taken away at birth to be raised in the Highlands. Most important, the narrator of the poem occupies an indeterminate space. "The Hunter" relates the adventures of a Highlander and praises the old way of life, but the poem is told in heroic couplets, the standard Augustan English form.

"The Hunter" was brought to the public's attention only after Macpherson started publishing the poems of Ossian, but it prefigures contradictions discernible in the later works. Macpherson's actual career as a popular writer began in 1759 when he was working as a tutor in Dumfriesshire. There he was introduced to John Home, the renowned author of *Douglas*. Home had read a translation of an old Gaelic poem, "Albin and the Daughter of Mey," published by Jeremy Stone in the January 1756 issue of the *Scots Magazine*, in which Stone commented that the "sublimity of sentiment, nervousness of expression, and high-spirited metaphors" of the ancient Gaelic poems are "hardly to be equaled among the most cultivated nation" (Leneman, pp. 14–15). In questioning Macpherson about what remained of the literature and the manners of the Highlands, Home pressed his companion to produce a translation of what fragments he could remember. Macpherson obliged Home with some reluctance and several days later presented him with "The Death of Oscur," a tract expressing the bard Ossian's lament for his son.

"The Death of Oscur" was included in a small volume of more "translations" that Macpherson published with the support of Home and Hugh Blair in 1760, entitled *Fragments of Ancient Poetry collected in the Highlands of Scotland and translated from the Galic or Erse*. In the preface to this work, Macpherson makes a claim for his poems' authenticity: "The public may depend on the following fragments as genuine remains of ancient Scottish poetry" (*Poems of Ossian*, Gaskill, ed., p. 5). Ossian again features as narrator, relating the death of both his father, Fingal, and son, Oscur (or, at times, Oscar), who have been killed in battle. Ossian laments the unnatural circumstances by which the past and the future generations have been cut off from him. His position as the only one of his tribe left to tell the story parallels Macpherson's similarly solitary literary endeavors. In choosing to tell the story through the character of Ossian, Macpherson suggests an analogy between himself and Ossian, inasmuch as both poets are the last of their tribe and the preservers of the spirit of their people. Macpherson also alludes in his *Fragments* to a larger work of Scottish poetry:

> It is believed, that, by a careful inquiry, many more remains of ancient genius, no less valuable than those now given to the world, might be · found in the same country where these have been collected. In particular there is reason to hope that one work of considerable length, and which deserves to be styled an heroic poem, might be recovered and translated, if encouragement were given to such an undertaking. (p. 6)

The community of Scottish literati did give their encouragement to the undertaking. Hugh Blair sent the *Fragments* to various friends of his, such as Sir David Dalrymple and Horace Walpole, to solicit subscriptions for the publication of further material. Home, William Robertson, Adam Ferguson, and others, including James Boswell and various members of Parliament House, paid for Macpherson to spend the summer of 1760 in the Highlands, salvaging what he later described as "what remained of the works of the old bards, especially those of Ossian, the son of Fingal, who was the best, as well as most ancient, of those who are celebrated in tradition for their poetical genius" (p. 36). Macpherson returned to Edinburgh in January 1761 and set to translating his poems, consulting with several gentlemen "skilled in Gaelic literature on the fidelity of his translation." He moved to London with a letter of introduction from David Hume to a Scots publisher who was living in that city and who published *Fingal* in 1762, closely followed in 1763 by *Temora*.

Richard Sher points out that one reason the Edinburgh literati were so anxious to support Macpherson was that they relied on him to present a vision of a chivalric Highland past to contest the decision against allowing a Scottish militia.[11] But another crucial reason for Macpherson's popularity in Scotland is that the campaign to discover the works of the ancient Highland civilization also took place at the same time as the smear campaign against Lord Bute. The members of the literati also would have recognized the use of such a narrative to counteract the mounting protest against their fellow

Scot, to whom Macpherson had probably been introduced by John Home.
The advertisement preceding the first edition of *Fingal* connects that work
with Bute; the translator notes that he is "deeply sensible" of the generosity
of "a certain noble person," yet he avoids naming him, "as his exalted station
as well as merit has raised him above the panegyric of one so little known"
(Gaskill, p. 33). In the dedication to "The Earl of Bute, Knight of the most
Noble Order of the Garter, &c. &c." in *The Works of Ossian* (1765), Macpherson draws a direct parallel between Bute and Ossian:

> I throw no reflections on this age, but there is a great debt of fame owing
> to the EARL OF BUTE, which hereafter will be amply paid: there is also
> some share of reputation with-held from Ossian, which less prejudiced
> times may bestow. This similarity between the Statesman and the Poet,
> gives propriety to this dedication. (Gaskill, p. 41)

The two-volume collection of the *Poems of Ossian* was published two years
after Bute left office. By relating the "Statesman and the Poet," Macpherson
suggests that Bute, like Ossian, is suffering from the effect of prejudice, but
that time will restore to him his proper reputation. Contrary to such expectations, however, as Fiona Stafford notes, "Bute's patronage of Macpherson
made *Fingal* the perfect butt for any writer bent on exposing the unpopular
Minister" (p. 166). Certainly, Wilkes had a gibe at the popularity of Ossian,
commenting in the *North Briton* that "The most rude of our bards are admired; and I know some choice wits here, who have thrown aside *Shakespear*,
and taken up *Fingal*, charmed with the variety of character, and richness
of imagery" (p. 10). Macpherson's plan to counteract contemporary anti-
Scottish prejudice paradoxically drew forth that same prejudice.

It is worth examining further the complexities of the image of the nation
which Macpherson offered in order to counteract such prejudice. Like
Wilkes's persona in the *North Briton*, Macpherson both asserts and denies
Scottish difference, although not, like Wilkes, satirically. On the surface, Macpherson's poems attempt to present a sympathetic image of the Highlanders
by providing them with a past of glorious battles and noble deeds. Like the
earlier "The Hunter," *Fingal* highlights the bravery of the Caledonian warriors. The poem is narrated by Fingal's son, the bard Ossian. It begins with an
imminent invasion of Ireland by Swaran, King of Scandinavia. Cuchullin,
guardian to the young king of Ireland, Cormac, sends for help from Fingal,
"king of those Caledonians who inhabited the western coast of Scotland" (p.
37). In the meantime, Cuchullin fights against Swaran but is defeated. The
six day-long episodes that constitute the cantos of the poem describe how

Fingal arrives with his fleet and repels the Scandinavians. Swaran is bound and delivered as a prisoner, but out of pity Fingal lets him go back to Denmark after Swaran promises not to return to Ireland. The conclusion of the poem emphasizes the chivalric nature of the Highlanders. Grateful for his release, Swaran effuses to Fingal, "In peace thou art the gale of spring. In war the mountain storm. Take my hand now in friendship, king of echoing Selma" (p. 101). Fingal also graciously returns Cuchullin's kingdom to him with words of encouragement: "The fame of Cuchullin," he says, "shall grow, like the branchy tree of Cromla" (p. 104). Fingal's generosity earns him as much respect and admiration as does his military prowess. Macpherson is intent on supplying the Highlanders with elegant manners as well as brave deeds.

Temora continues the exploits of Fingal and the Highlanders. It pits two races against each other: the Firbolgs, the original inhabitants of Ireland, and the Gaels, of Caledonian descent. When the poem opens, Cairbar, of the Firbolg race, has murdered Cormac, the young Gaelic king of Ireland, and usurped the throne. Fingal decides to help reestablish the Gaelic royal family on the throne. Cairbar is killed in battle by Fingal's grandson, Oscur, and Cathmor, Cairbar's brother, takes his place as leader of the Firbolgs. In the ensuing action, Oscur is killed, as is Fillon, Fingal's son and Ossian's brother. Finally, Fingal slays Cathmor. The poem ends with a feast at Temora, the royal palace.

As well as presenting a positive image of Highland society, Macpherson says that he also seeks to restore the morale of the Highlanders. In "A Dissertation Concerning the Antiquity, &c. of the Poems of Ossian the Son of Fingal," he elaborates on the necessity for the Highlanders to maintain their traditions:

> The genius of the highlanders has suffered a great change within these
> few years. . . . Many have now learned to leave their mountains, and seek
> their fortunes in a milder climate; and though a certain *amor patriae* may
> sometimes bring them back, they have, during their absence, imbibed
> enough of foreign manners to despise the customs of their ancestors.
> (Gaskill, p. 51)

But the effect of Macpherson's work was much more complicated than his stated purpose. His poetry actually redirected public interest toward an ancient Highland tradition instead of contemporary indigenous Gaelic culture at a time when, in fact, there was a renaissance in Gaelic poetry, a rejuvenation of Gaelic culture in the midst of political and economic changes. The old bardic system had all but disappeared, and a new, more colloquial poetry, on diverse subjects and with looser rhyme schemes, was being composed. The first book published in Gaelic appeared in 1751, called pointedly, *Aiseiridh na Sean Chánain Albannaich* (The resurrection of the ancient Scottish language). The author, Alasdair Mac Mhaighstir Alasdair (Alexander MacDonald), imagines the Highlands marching once again under the Stewarts, freed from association with the Lowland Scots (Watson, pp. 194–99). But people investigating the existence of Gaelic poetry looked only for poems about Ossian and the heroes. *Fingal* erased, then presented anew the rich tradition of Scots Gaelic literature with a single opus.[12]

Furthermore, although Macpherson claims to do justice to Gaelic poetry by bringing it to the attention of more British people, he appears to be just as concerned with his English-speaking audience's reaction to the Ossianic poems as with restoring the morale of the Gaels. He notes that until the popularity of his own *Fragments*, he was not convinced that the poems would be acceptable to an English-speaking audience: "The manner of these compositions is so different from other poems, and the ideas so confined to the most early state of society, that is was thought they had not enough of variety to please a polished age" (Gaskill, p. 50). Macpherson also notes in the "Dissertation" that it is strange that the Ossianic poems, so popular in "one part of the kingdom," were unknown in another, and that "the British, who have carefully traced out the works of genius in other nations, should so long remain strangers to their own" (p. 50). He suggests that his role is to render these compositions "agreeable to an English reader" (p. 50), and, accordingly, keeping the English-speaking public's predilections in mind, he styled *Fingal* and *Temora* as Homeric epics. The phrase accompanying the etching on the cover of *Fingal*, "*Fortia facta patrum*," is drawn from Virgil, further suggesting Macpherson's eagerness to make his poems acceptable to an audience with a classical education.

Finally, Macpherson's poems encouraged an assimilation of Highland, Lowland, and English subjects. Leah Leneman argues that *Ossian* played a crucial role in the time after the '45 rebellion, as Lowlanders struggled with finding themselves dismissed by the English as Highland rebels. The poems encouraged Lowland Scots, who were generally more inclined to want to assimilate to England, to identify with the Highlanders whom they had previously regarded as quite distinct. Leneman notes that "much of the eagerness to believe in Fingal was because this epic enabled Lowlanders not only to accept the Highlands as part of their Scottish nation, but to do so with pride and honour" (p. 24). But the Highlands they accepted were an imagined conception, not the actual culture that existed north of Edinburgh.

Just as Macpherson provided the Lowlanders with an imagined vision of their common origins with the Highlanders, he also provided English readers with an image of their common cultural origins with the Scots. For what is most striking about Macpherson's "forgeries" is that they present the people of the British Isles as homogeneous. *Fingal* and, even more so, *Temora*, presents Scotland as the cradle of civilization from which all the inhabitants of Britain emerged. The Highlanders Macpherson depicts in his poems are *not* his contemporaries living in the north of Scotland; they can be, and were, viewed as the mythical warriors of a British past. The Ossianic poems portray a Britain that both the English and Scots can identify with. When Macpherson refers to Fingal fighting the "King of the World," the Roman emperor Severus, he presents a homogeneous Britain united in the face of an external assailant (Smart, p. 103). The poems of Ossian gloss over the distinction between the Scots, both Highlanders and Lowlanders, and the English.

After the success of *Fingal* and *Temora*, Macpherson was granted a government post and accompanied Governor George Johnstone to Florida as secretary, president of the council, and surveyor-general, posts he was no doubt given as a result of Bute's patronage. He returned to England in 1765 and was allowed to retain his three hundred pounds per annum on the understanding that he would continue to serve the government. His later work continues his project of writing the Scottish and English together.

The *Introduction to the History of Great Britain and Ireland* (1771) serves as another example of how Macpherson provides the Scots with a rich past, again by inventing a Celtic culture, while gesturing toward their ultimate assimilation. The *Introduction* clearly asserts the superiority of the Celts over the Anglo-Saxons. The ancient Celts in Britain were, says Macpherson, "fierce, passionate, and impetuous. . . . This vehemence of temperament proceeded, according to the ancients, from the full habit of their bodies, and the abundance of their blood" (p. 198). They were plain and honest though quick-tempered, curious and hospitable, clean and neat. Proof of this may be given, Macpherson says, by any man who has encountered the present-day Highlanders.

Macpherson points out the aesthetic sensibilities of the ancient Celts. Song played an important role in their diversions and daily life: "The moral character of our ancestors owed more to the compositions of the Bard than to the precepts of the Druid" (p. 210). They listened to the poems "with such rapture that their character and manners were modeled on the virtues the Bards sang about" (p. 212). Ironically, Macpherson refers to his own *Fingal* for proof of this. Furthermore, he suggests that the government of the Celts was also enlightened. They practiced a kind of democracy which led to representative government: "It is certain that the ancient Britons . . . had their general assemblies of the people, in which all affairs of public concern were decided by the plurality of voices" (p. 248). Then when the state grew, not all the members could convene in the general assembly: "The expedient of delegation was obvious, and was naturally adopted; and length of time polished into what is called a convention of the states the democratical meetings of the Celtic nations" (p. 249). Macpherson draws a parallel between Celtic government and the British government of his own day, both being a mixture of aristocracy and monarchy.

In contrast, the manner of life of Macpherson's Anglo-Saxons, or Sarmatae, was "as opposite to those of the Celtae as the barbarism common to both could permit" (p. 284). The history of the Saxons before they conquered Europe has been lost, he says, but this is not to be regretted because they contributed no model of virtue. They were warlike, drinking ale from the skulls of their enemies and worshiping a God who delighted in human blood. They accepted a king in times of war, but they persecuted him later because they were so keen on their own freedom. The Celts were clearly the more advanced society, according to Macpherson.

Yet in the process of praising the Celts over the Anglo-Saxons, Macpherson also lays the groundwork for their union by suggesting that they share a common origin. He identifies three nations that populated Great Britain. The first group to settle in Britain from the Continent were the Gaels, who eventually took up residence in the north and who were of pure Celtic origin. Second were the Cimbri, the ancestors of the modern Welsh people. They were actually a mixture of Celtic and Teutonic, or Sarmatic, races: "An unavoidable mixture with the Sarmatae beyond the Vistula and the Baltic had an effect on the genius of the Celtae of Germany; and they departed . . . from the purity of the language and from some of the manners of their ancestors" (p. 11). The third migration to Britain, which was from Belgium, occurred considerably later. The Belgae were more versed in "civil arts" than the other two groups, having left the Continent at a later period. Like the Cimbri, the Belgae were a mixture of Celtic and Sarmatic blood. Macpherson emphasizes that although these three groups spoke distinct languages, they descended from the same origin. Moreover, we learn that the Anglo-Saxons, who invaded Britain after the Roman dominion failed, shared in part the ancestry of the three British groups, for Macpherson notes that the region around the Baltic and modern Germany was the border country between the Celtic and the Sarmatic races. Although "The Saxons [who] settled in Britain are the most unmixed of the Sarmatae who first settled on the southern shore of the Baltic," they, too, were partially Celtic (p. 15). In fact, Macpherson suggests that "scarce any one people from the pillars of Hercules to the Tanais" are free from intermixture (p. 19). His *Introduction* suggests the consanguinity of Scots and English. The two nations share common blood. Their historical union in fact prefigures for Macpherson their contemporary union in Britain, effected as a result of the market system. Although they had taken different evolutionary paths, he says, the Celts and the Saxons started to mix again once they began trading goods. Macpherson creates a basis for the contemporary union of Scotland and England by presenting a common culture of origin for both nations.

Macpherson's contradictory stance of both asserting and assimilating Scottish culture is also apparent in the *Introduction*'s theories concerning language. On several occasions Macpherson notes the purity of the Celtic language in Scotland. He appears to defend the integrity of language: "Nations are not so tenacious of their customs and manners as they are of their aboriginal tongues. The first may gradually vanish in the growing improvements of civil life; the latter can only be buried in the same grave with the people themselves" (p. 255). But he goes on to show how the language loses its integrity: "Conquest may confine the bounds of a language; commerce may corrupt it; new inventions, by introducing new words, may throw the old into disuse; a change in the mode of thinking may alter idiom: but . . . [language] retires from invasion into rocks and desarts; it subsists with the remains of a people; even mountains and rivers in part retain it when the people are no more" (pp. 255–56). He portrays a language gradually changing until there is nothing left of the original tongue but place names on a map. In the picture Macpherson draws, the native speakers disappear; there is nothing left but an ephemeral spirit over the land. As I discuss in the Conclusion, this idea proved extremely appealing a century later to Matthew Arnold in his effort to integrate a Celtic spirit with Saxon practicality.[13]

Macpherson's interest in the Union in his own day is more explicit in *The History of Great Britain, from the Restoration to the Accession of the House of Hanover*, written in 1775. Here he undertakes to write the history of a period "hitherto very imperfectly known," in particular, the intrigues of the Glorious Revolution, the negotiations of James II in France, and Scottish affairs after the Union. He claims to have made "intense inquiry into what has been advanced on all sides" with the design of producing a narrative in which all the little known affairs "have been carefully connected to the great line of history" (1: 15). Like Defoe, Macpherson weaves the Act of Union into this "great line of history" as an inevitable event. He writes that the common people were enraged at the idea of uniting with England, but they were powerless to prevent it: "The interval of the adjournment [during the debate of the Act of Union in the Scottish Parliament] was filled with tumults, clamour, and confusion, without doors. But, within, a determined resolution was formed to adhere to the articles of the treaty" (2: 353). The Scottish peers were either too greedy for the English government's bribes or too weak in spirit to protest the Union. In either event, suggests Macpherson, they should have bargained better for Scotland: "the Union had become much more necessary for England than for that kingdom" (2: 357). He continues, "Had, therefore, the parliament of Scotland regarded their own future interest more than a trivial advantage at present, there is scarce any doubt but they could have commanded terms more consonant to the independence which they claimed in the name of their country" (2: 358).

In his summary reflections, however, Macpherson expresses relief at the Union: "Though the terms of the Union were by no means calculated to flatter the pride of the Scots, as an independent people, no expedient could be deemed unfortunate, that put an end to their own government, as it then stood" (2: 360). The previous Scottish parliament, he claims "could not fail to be productive of perpetual evils to the nation" (2: 360). He dates the shiftlessness of the Scottish parliamentary system to the Revolution of 1688, when "The parliament were placed in a situation to make the most for themselves, at the hands of the King, while the people felt nothing from the alteration in government, but a change in tyrants . . . in the animosity of parties, all regard for the public was lost; and a kind of mean selfishness . . . took possession of every breast, and marked the age with indelible infamy" (2: 361).

Macpherson protests the same kind of internal divisiveness in his pamphlet *The Rights of Great Britain Asserted against the Claims of America, being an Answer to the Declaration of the General Congress.* He begins by asserting the need for cohesiveness in any state: "No maxim in policy is more universally admitted, than that a supreme and uncontrollable power must exist somewhere in every State" (p. 1). He continues, "His majesty owes his Throne to the Laws of England; and, as King, he can have no subject that is not bound by law" (p. 38). The American colonies are questioning the authority that works in their best interest. Their behavior toward the British is unnatural: "Did not the Mother-country, with more than a mother's fondness, upon all occasions, nourish, cherish, and support this prodigal child?" (p. 12). Furthermore, by demanding no taxation without representation, they are asking for special privileges, for under this rule, "scarce one in twenty-five of the people of Great Britain is represented" (p. 5). Macpherson asserts that the colonies "speak no longer as subjects. They assume the language of rivals and they act as enemies" (p. 6). And as long as they pretend weakness, they will "inspire her enemies with a confidence of success" (p. 4). He acknowledges the importance of having an opposition to counteract the "charm of authority," but only when the opposition acts in the best interests of the state.[14] Unfortunately, this has not always been the case. Macpherson writes, "the Author of the following Essay has long entertained an opinion, that the most formidable foes of Great Britain were nursed in her own bosom" (p. 2). His remark is peculiarly resonant considering his own participation in the assimilation of one group of England's erstwhile "foes," the Highlanders, into the rest of Great Britain.

The later events in Macpherson's life can also be read as illustrative of his promotion of the integration of Scotland into Britain. He bought a seat in Parliament, thus becoming a political representative in Britain as well as a cultural one, but he represented not Scotland but a small town in Cornwall. Toward the end of his life, when he returned to the country of his youth, he built for himself a palatial residence that he called after the very un-Scottish name of Bellevue. Macpherson's move from his birthplace in Ruthven to a position in Westminster confirms the idea that a Scotsman could indeed "pass for an *Englishman*" of sorts by the end of eighteenth century. The tacit argument of the poems of Ossian and the later prose works, then, are similar: they promote an image of a homogeneous nation. Macpherson's idealized version of Highland Scotland counteracted the negative image of the Scots that had been promoted after the battle of Culloden and during the ascendance of Lord Bute to power—but only by forging a fictitious Great Britain, one that was the subject of much critical scrutiny.

In his study *James Macpherson*, Paul DeGategno arranges the controversy surrounding the *Poems of Ossian* into three periods: an initial stage in the period five years after the publication of the works; a time of renewed conflict, which includes Macpherson and Samuel Johnson's vituperative exchange; and a final period involving the special investigation by the Highland Society (pp. 99–111).[15] The debate on the authenticity of Macpherson's work was officially settled in 1805. After Macpherson's death, the Highland Society called for a report on the authenticity of Macpherson's poems. They selected the novelist Henry Mackenzie to oversee the efforts. Macpherson himself had encouraged the belief that the poems were passed down orally for ages and continued to be recited, but that he had access to ancient written sources. Society members were sent to the Highlands to question anyone who had provided Macpherson with information and to receive statements before a justice of the peace. Witnesses were asked to determine if the poems of Macpherson corresponded with any such poems in Gaelic. The committee found that Macpherson had at one time had access to a book of Gaelic verse and a number of written ballads, but that for the most part his sources were oral.

He had transcribed what he heard from storytellers with the help of a kins-
man, Lachlan Macpherson (Smart, p. 142). The committee's final ruling was
that Ossianic poetry did exist in the Highland tradition, but they had not
been able "to obtain any one poem the same in title and tenor with the poems published by [Macpherson]" (p. 151).[16] The *Report of the Committee of the
Highland Society of Scotland Appointed to Inquire into the Nature and Authenticity
of the Poems of Ossian* conjectures that Macpherson

> was in use to supply chasms, and to give connection, by inserting passages
> which he did not find, and to add what he conceived to be dignity and
> delicacy to the original composition, by striking out passages, by soften-
> ing incidents, by refining the language, in short by changing what he
> considered as too simple or too rude for a modern ear, and elevating
> what in his opinion was below the standard of good poetry. (p. 152)

The report refrains from discussing the extent of Macpherson's alterations,
however: "To what degree . . . he exercised these liberties, it is impossible for
the Committee to determine" (p. 152).

Despite this refutation of their authenticity, however, the Ossianic poems
remained popular. Fiona Stafford argues that the poems' continuing popularity was due to the fact that they appealed to the current vogue for the sublime while providing "a reassuring sense" of the permanence of classicism (p.
178). Adam Potkay concurs with this analysis, suggesting further that the poems also help "bridge the gap separating the emerging 'feminism' of polite
society from the male 'chauvinism' of both the ancient polis and its modern
apologists" (p. 121). In addition, I contend that the poems and the controversy surrounding them, particularly as represented by Samuel Johnson,
served as a public focus for the continuing negotiation of the relationship between Scotland and England after the Bute affair.

Thirty years before the Highland Commission met to discuss the problem
of the Ossianic poems' authenticity, Macpherson's claims for his poems had
been soundly dismissed by none other than Samuel Johnson. The Doctor's
Journey to the Western Isles of Scotland (1773) unequivocally denied the Ossianic poems' authenticity:

> I believe [the poems of Ossian] never existed in any other form than that
> which we have seen. The editor, or author, never could shew the original;
> not can it be shewn by any other . . . to revenge reasonable incredulity, by
> refusing evidence, is a degree of insolence with which the world is not
> yet acquainted; and stubborn audacity is the last refuge of guilt. (9: 118)

Macpherson tried to convince William Strahan, the publisher of the *Journey*, to remove the words "insolence," "audacity," and "guilt" from the manuscript. Failing in this, he himself submitted an advertisement that he wanted Johnson to approve, saying that although it was too late to make any alterations at the time, passages such as those printed above would be struck. This was to assure the public that there was "no personal reflection" intended. When Johnson refused to sanction this advertisement, Macpherson wrote him an indignant letter that unfortunately has been lost but that may have contained a challenge to a duel, for Johnson refused to retract anything, noting he would defend himself against "the menaces of a Ruffian" (*Letters*, 2: 3).[17]

Johnson presents his written debate with Macpherson as a matter of "reverencing" truth. He suggests that Macpherson had lied in telling the public that he had manuscripts of the Ossianic poems. However, there is more than the question of ocular proof behind their debate. Johnson was antagonized most by the implications of Macpherson's claims regarding the relationship between the English and the Scots. As we have seen, Macpherson's poems and prose worked to erode the historical and contemporary difference between the Scots and the English by constructing a mythic Caledonian race that appealed to both nations. In contrast, Johnson promoted a vision of a contemporary Great Britain consisting of a historically heterogeneous but now unified mixture of peoples.[18] Katie Trumpener has argued that Johnson's "repudiation of Macpherson . . . becomes a repudiation of Scottish nationalism itself" (p. 78), but it is equally true to say that it is a repudiation of Macpherson's construction of Britain as well.

Johnson's image of the nation is more accurately understood when we look at that most national of projects, the *Dictionary of the English Language*. John Cannon comments that "in the *Dictionary*, on which Johnson began work in 1746, a national purpose was clear from the outset. Indeed, the whole enterprise seems to have been conceived—and was certainly publicized—in terms of national literary competition" (p. 237). Johnson himself suggests his concern with national literature when he says that he undertook the *Dictionary* project to bring order to a language "which, while it was employed in the cultivation of every species of literature, has itself been hitherto neglected; suffered to spread, under the direction of chance, into wild exuberance; resigned to the tyranny of time and fashion; and exposed to the corruptions of ignorance, and caprices of innovation" (5: 23).[19] But the order Johnson wants to establish does not set out to erase the wildness within the language or the nation. The predominant image that arises in the *Dictionary* is the heterogeneous nature of the dominant language used in Britain, and, by implication, of the nation itself. In his "Plan of an English Dictionary," Johnson discusses words in terms of their national origin, as if they were actual subjects of the nation. Of scientific words, he notes,

> all are not equally to be considered as parts of our language; for some of
> them are naturalized and incorporated; but others still continue aliens,
> and are rather auxiliaries than subjects. This naturalization is produced ei-
> ther by an admission into common speech, in some metaphorical signifi-
> cation, which is the acquisition of a kind of property among us . . . or it is
> the consequence of long intermixture and frequent use, by which the ear
> is accustomed to the sound of words, till their original is forgotten . . . or
> of the change of a foreign to an English termination, and a conformity to
> the laws of the speech into which they are adopted. (5: 4)

But although Johnson seemingly approves the assimilation or "naturalization" of foreign words, he is also concerned that their alien origins should be understood: "Every word will have its history, and the reader will be informed of the gradual changes of the language, and have before his eyes the rise of some words, and the fall of others" (5: 20). Marks of foreignness need to continue to be visible, even if the foreigners themselves conform to all the laws of the nation "into which they are adopted" (5: 4). The preface suggests that the British past conceals a barbarous mixture of conquerors; the resulting "genius" of the language is a mongrel, a Defoean "Het'rogeneous Thing."[20] Johnson implies that change happens by conquest and subjection, not by cultural erasure. The heterogeneity of the nation should not be lost in a homogenizing impulse.

When he made his journey to Scotland, Johnson was in the midst of revising the *Dictionary* for a fourth edition and was growing even more concerned that the *Dictionary* be used to create a proper national perspective. Allen Reddick has detailed the substantial changes in the fourth edition that Johnson made in the face of political and theological challenges to the connection between the Anglican Church and the state. At this time, then, he would have been peculiarly sensitive to the implications of Macpherson's claims for a competing history of Britain.

Johnson denies remembering "how the wish to visit the Hebrides was excited" (*Works*, 9: 3), but Boswell notes in his account of the tour that Johnson first spoke of journeying to Scotland in 1763 after recalling how he had been "much pleased" with Martin Martin's *Description of the Western Islands of Scotland* (1703), which he had read as a child (*Life*, 5: 13). The year 1763 also saw the publication of *Temora*, and it is possible that the debate surrounding the poems helped remind Johnson of the earlier travelogue. It took Johnson a decade to decide to undertake the journey. According to Boswell, "in spring, 1773," Johnson "talked of coming to Scotland . . . with so much firmness, that I hoped he was at last in earnest." Johnson finally embarked on his journey to the Highlands in 1773, the year Macpherson returned to England and released another edition of the *Poems of Ossian*. Paul DeGategno notes, "If Johnson's major intention in taking the trip was to research the question of [the Ossianic poems'] authenticity, the results of his inquiries were disappointing and inadequate" (p. 103). However, Johnson's project was larger than merely disputing the poems' veracity. He set out to provide a more accurate picture of the north of Britain than Macpherson presented, one sensitive to the distinction between Highlanders and Lowlanders, one that rebutted Macpherson's British myth. As Johnson himself noted, "If we know little of the ancient Highlanders, let us not fill the vacuity with Ossian. If we have not searched the Magellanick regions, let us however forbear to people them with Patagons" (*Works*, 9: 119).

Like Defoe in his *A Tour Thro' the Whole Island of Great Britain*, Johnson subjects Scotland to elaborate surveying. In this effort, Johnson is both individual focal point and objective narrator. For his northern tour, Johnson circumnavigates and contains Scotland in outline, omitting the inland areas and instead mapping out a route from Edinburgh up the east coast of Scotland, across to Skye via Inverness, then down the west coast and back to Edinburgh via Glasgow. He seeks to encompass, not to penetrate, Scotland, to view it from the four corners, not to traverse it. *A Journey* is an outsider's view of the edges of Scotland. Johnson glosses over the Lowlands because they are too similar to England. He comments only briefly on Edinburgh, noting that it is "a city too well known to admit description" (*Works*, 9: 3). Instead, he focuses from the beginning on matters of "curiosity" (9: 3). He understands his project in the *Journey* as writing "of the cities of our own island with the solemnity of geographical description, as if we had been cast upon a newly discovered coast" (9: 13).

The *Journey* abounds with Johnson's assessments of evidence of Scotland's historical and contemporary backwardness. Commenting on house windows that must be pushed up and down instead of moving on hinges, and that are not equipped with pulleys of any kind, Johnson says, "He that would have his window open must hold it with his hand. . . . What cannot be done without some uncommon trouble or particular expedient, will not often be done at all" (9: 22). He views the Scots as lazy natives, incapable of reasonable foresight. Johnson blames this native laxity for what he sees as the lack of agricultural improvement in the Scottish countryside. Time after time he remarks on the barrenness of the land:

The roads of Scotland afford little diversion to the traveller, who . . . has
nothing to contemplate but grounds that have no visible boundaries, or
are separated by walls of loose stone. . . . There is no tree for either
shelter or timber . . . and the whole country is extended in uniform
nakedness. . . . A tree might be a show in Scotland as a horse in Venice.
(9: 9–10)

And again: "Few regions have been denuded like this, where many centuries
must have passed in waste without the least thought of future supply" (9: 10).
Comparing Scotland's situation with that of Ireland, similarly bare, Johnson
finds no excuse for the Scots, for they have enjoyed settlement and security of
property for quite some time: "Of this improvidence no other account can be
given than that it probably began in times of tumult, and continued because
it had begun. . . . That before the union the Scots had little trade and little
money, is no valid apology; for plantation is the least expensive of all methods
of improvement" (9: 10). Johnson describes both the dimensions of a Highland hut and the manners of the Highlanders in the same matter-of-fact
tone, attempting to ascertain the essence of both. He uses the evidence
around him to support his generalizations on nature and civilization.[21]

One of the main points of Johnson's topographical survey is to demonstrate that Macpherson's elaborate depiction of Highland culture is inaccurate.[22] Johnson comments on the men, manners, and materials he encounters
on his journey as empirical evidence, believing, as he says, that "the true state
of every nation is the state of common life" (9: 22). Moreover, he implies that
the sense of what is "common life" can be ascertained only from one unfamiliar with the common. He notes that Martin failed by not describing the
things around him, thinking that they were common everywhere. If he had
described them, then "he might therefore have displayed a series of subordination and a form of government, which, in more luminous and improved
regions, have been long forgotten, and have delighted his readers with many
uncouth customs that are now disused, and wild opinions that prevail no
longer" (9: 65). Conversely, Macpherson, according to Johnson, fabricated the
"common life" he attempts to convey. Johnson presents himself as capable of
properly representing the Highlands because he is an outsider.

Johnson is particularly adamant to confirm the primitiveness of the Gaelic
language. He cannot accept the concept of Scotland having a legitimate literate past, for this would threaten his idea that England had civilized the
Scots when it introduced them to literature: "Literature soon after its revival
found its way to Scotland, and from the middle of the sixteenth century, almost to the middle of the seventeenth, the politer studies were pursued"

(9: 28). To him the Scots could not have been civilized because they had no writing with which to record their history. Johnson notes that "neither bards nor *senachies* could read or write. . . . Where the Chiefs of the Highlands have found the histories of their descent is difficult to tell for no Earse genealogy was ever written" (9: 112). He concludes, "Thus hopeless are all attempts to find any trace of Highland learning" (9: 112). Whereas Macpherson claimed an elaborate poetic tradition for the Highlanders, Johnson asserts that Gaelic ("Earse") is "the rude speech of a barbarous people, who had few thoughts to express, and were content, as they conceived grossly, to be grossly understood" (9: 114). In an indirect reference to Macpherson, he notes: "After what has been lately talked of Highland bards, and Highland genius, many will startle when they are told, that the Earse never was a written language" (9: 114). According to Johnson, it is only when a language "begins to teem with books," that "it is tending to refinement . . . diction, merely vocal, is always in its childhood" (9: 115). It becomes of the utmost importance to Johnson to deny that Macpherson could provide evidence of a fixed past. He asserts, "I believe there cannot be recovered in the whole Earse language, five hundred lines of which there is any evidence to prove them a hundred years old. Yet I hear that the father of *Ossian* boasts of two chests more of ancient poetry, which he suppresses, because they are too good for the English" (9: 117). In Johnson's imperial vision, culture did not grow naturally on Scottish soil; it had to be imported from south of the border. It was the duty of the English to impose literacy, as well as law, on the Scots.

Macpherson had commented that the Scots' oral tradition was meticulously accurate. Johnson is willing to accept the concept of an oral tradition, but not its accuracy, as he makes clear when describing an evening of bagpipe music to which he and Boswell are treated. When an old man explains to them the gruesome story behind the song, Johnson comments: "Narrations like this, however uncertain, deserve the notice of a traveller because they are the only records of a nation that has no historians, and afford the most genuine representation of the life and character of the ancient highlanders" (9: 50). However, having conceded that point, he hastily discusses the unreliability of the Highlanders' conversation, which he attributes to either "the sport of negligence, or the refuge of ignorance" (9: 51). At any rate, this allows him to conclude: "If individuals are thus at variance with themselves, it can be no wonder that the accounts of different men are contradictory. The traditions of an ignorant and savage people have been for ages negligently heard, and unskilfully related" (9: 51). He offers direct proof of the "laxity" of the Highlanders' speech against Macpherson's general assertions of the reliability of oral narratives.

At the same time, Johnson is not just promoting English superiority over Scottish ignorance. Although he refuses to allow the notion that Highlanders had a literate past, it is just this aspect of Highland life that also fascinates Johnson, as it represents an absolute difference of life from England's civilization. As Katie Trumpener points out, Johnson seems particularly intrigued with an alternative to ocular proof that the Highlands does offer: "second sight," which represents another mode of knowledge which is quite foreign to English reason (pp. 96–100). Throughout the *Journey*, Johnson attempts to ascertain the existence of such a phenomenon, noting, "Our desire of information [about "second sight"] was keen, and our inquiry frequent"(9: 108). Although he comments that there are "strong reasons for incredulity" (9: 109), Johnson yet professes himself "willing to believe" (9: 110). The Highlands remain interesting for their representation of cultural difference, in particular the cultural difference of superstition.

It is the desire to witness absolute difference which takes Johnson to Scotland in the first place. In *Johnson and Boswell: The Transit of Caledonia*, Pat Rogers notes that whereas usually "tourists went south to see the home of civilization in its pristine purity," "Johnson went north to see savage culture in its clearest expression" (p. 57). He argues further that "the rhetoric of his *Journey* is designed to play down contact with educated society and with 'civilized' values" (p. 65). Boswell had encouraged Johnson's northern journey for a long time: "Dr Johnson had for many years given me the hope that we should go together, and visit the Hebrides. Martin's *Account* of those islands had impressed us with a notion that we might there contemplate a system of life almost totally different from what we had been accustomed to see; and, to find simplicity and wildness, and all the circumstances of remote time or place, so near to our native great island" (5: 161). He notes that Johnson declines visiting the grounds and gardens of Lord Findlater because "he was not come to Scotland to see fine places, of which there were enough in England; but wild objects—mountains, waterfalls, peculiar manners, things which he had not seen before" (5: 219). Johnson regrets heartily that they have arrived too late to experience the true sense of Highland culture.

Significantly, Johnson makes his decision to write his *Journey* directly after he has reached the Highland line, just after he realizes he is reaching the most alien part of the country. Johnson describes the scene in which he first thought of writing his narrative:

> I sat down on a bank, such as a writer of romance might have delighted
> to feign. I had indeed no trees to whisper over my head, but a clear
> rivulet streamed at my feet. The day was calm, the air soft, and all was

rudeness, silence, and solitude. Before me, on either side, were high hills, which by hindering the eye from ranging, forced the mind to find enter- tainment for itself. Whether I spent the hour well I know not; for here I first conceived the thought of this narration. (9: 40)

The thoughts that came to him in this "unknown and untravelled wilder- ness" were not "such as arise in the artificial solitude of parks and gardens, a flattering notion of self-sufficiency," but a feeling of danger and vulnerability, a manifestation of the sublime (9: 41). Such thoughts of narration did not oc- cur to him in the Lowlands. It took a journey to the Highlands and the ex- perience of a completely different culture to inspire Johnson's desire to bear witness to the heterogeneities in his own nation.

Johnson's account suggests that his affinity for Highlanders is greater than that he has for the Lowlanders. He notes, even as they enter the "verge of the Highlands" and begin "to leave fertility and culture behind us," they come across a familiar scene: an orchard, which, says Johnson, "in Scotland I had never seen before, with some timber trees, and a plantation of oaks" (9: 25). Just as this representation of agriculture appears, so does Johnson find traces of culture with which he can identify. They travel to Forres, "the town to which Macbeth was traveling, when he met the weird sisters in his way" (9: 25). Johnson remarks "This to an Englishman is classic ground" (9: 25). He also remarks on the civility of the Highlanders, a result of the feudal system under which they had lived for so long: "Civility seems part of the national character of Highlanders. Every chieftain is a monarch, and politeness, the natural product of royal government, is diffused from the laird through the whole clan" (9: 29–30).

This affinity is reflected in the language of the Highlanders, too. "Those Highlanders that can speak English, commonly speak it well, with few of the words, and little of the tone by which a Scotchman is distinguished. . . . By their Lowland neighbours they would not willingly be taught; for they have long considered them as a mean and degenerate race. These prejudices are wearing fast away; but so much of them still remains, that when I asked a very learned minister in the islands, which they considered as their most sav- age clans: 'Those,' said he, 'that live next the Lowlands'" (9: 36). Johnson him- self seems to hold this same estimation of the Lowlanders' degeneration. The problem with the Lowland Scots is that they are too much affected by En- gland, he suggests. Johnson criticizes the insularity of the Lowland Scots dur- ing the Reformation: they then experienced "no dilution of their zeal from the gradual influx of new opinions" (9: 6). But what has occurred as a result of "trade and intercourse with England" is almost worse: "that laxity of practice and indifference of opinion, in which men, not sufficiently instructed to find the middle point, too easily shelter themselves from rigour and constraint" (9: 6).

Although Johnson is concerned to acknowledge the differences within Britain, he also notes how those differences are disappearing. In particular, he presents how change happened through conquest. Johnson justifies English involvement in the Highlands, though sometimes brutal, as being necessary to pull that region along the road to civilization: "What the Romans did to other nations, was in a great degree done by Cromwell to the Scots; he civilized them by conquest, and introduced by useful violence the arts of peace" (9: 27). Cromwell's soldiers taught the people to plant kale and to make shoes, the Highlanders themselves, as Johnson observed, being naturally inept at the "manual arts." Furthermore, "Till the Union made them acquainted with English manners, the culture of their lands was unskilful, and their domestick life unformed; their tables were coarse as the feasts of Eskimeaux, and their houses filthy as the cottages of Hottentots" (9: 28).

According to the *Journey*, one of the most useful things to occur as a result of Culloden was the centralization of power. Previously, because the Highlands were so "unconnected with the system of justice" in England, they were hard to keep under control of the law. The lairds had jurisdiction over counties, "till the final conquest of the Highlands afforded an opportunity of crushing all the local courts, and of extending the general benefits of equal law to the low and the high, in the deep recesses of obscurest corners" (9: 46). The destruction of their own legal system, which was actually protected in the Articles of Union, is presented as a democratic gain for the Highland people. Similarly, Johnson praises their change of dress as a civilizing influence. "The fillibeg, or lower garment, is still very common, and the bonnet almost universal; but their attire is such as produces, in a sufficient degree, the effect intended by the law, of abolishing the dissimilitude of appearance between the highlanders and the other inhabitants of Britain; and, if dress be supposed to have much influence, facilitates their coalition with their fellow subjects" (9: 52). Johnson comments that the Scots' "ignorance grows every day less, but their knowledge is yet of little other use than to shew them their wants. They are now in the period of education, and feel the uneasiness of discipline, without yet perceiving the benefit of instruction" (9: 90). He promotes this civilizing turn of events.

Johnson is eager to represent how both the Lowlanders and the Highlanders are conforming to English standards. He comments: "The conversation of the Scots grows every day less unpleasing to the English; their peculiarities wear fast away; their dialect is likely to become in half a century provincial and rustic, even to themselves. The great, the learned, the ambitious, and the vain, all cultivate the English phrase, and the English pronunciation, and in splendid companies Scotch is not much heard, except now and then from an old lady" (9: 162). Back in Edinburgh, he visits a school where the deaf and dumb are taught "to speak, to read to write, and to practice arithmetick" (9: 162) and is particularly entranced by the way the pupils can tell what a speaker is saying to them without actually hearing: "It was pleasing to see one of the most desperate of human calamities capable of so much help" (9: 164). Johnson's imaginative leap upon viewing this site of education takes him back to the primitive country through which he has just passed: "after having seen the deaf taught arithmetic, who would be afraid to cultivate the Hebrides?" (9: 164).

Yet at the same time, in the process of writing his account of assimilation, Johnson himself elegizes the passing of the old ways:

> There was perhaps never any change of national manners so quick, so
> great, and so general as that which has operated in the Highlands, by the
> last conquest, and the subsequent laws. We came thither too late to see
> what we expected, a people of peculiar appearance, and a system of anti-
> quated life. The clans retain little now of their original character, their
> ferocity of temper is softened, their military ardour is extinguished, their
> dignity of independence is depressed, their contempt of government
> subdued, and their reverence for their chiefs abated. Of what they had
> before the late conquest of their country, there remain only their lan-
> guage and their poverty. (9: 57)

Johnson betrays a feeling of regret for the changes that have happened in the Highlands, if only because he has not been able to observe them in their pure form. By the end of his journey, he exhibits more of an understanding about the circumstances of the Scots.

Moreover, Johnson writes with concern of "the general dissatisfaction, which is now driving the highlanders into the other hemisphere" (9: 38). His comments on emigration from the Highlands are particularly poignant. In part this is due to his sympathy for the Highland peoples whom he has been visiting. But his anxiety is also connected to his understanding that the Highlanders' dissatisfaction, a result of "the world" being "let in on them," can have dangerous effects on the British empire at home and abroad. He remarks:

> The great business of insular policy is how to keep the people in their
> own country. As the world has been let in on them, they have heard of

happier climates, and less arbitrary government; and if they are disgusted,
have emissaries among them ready to offer them land and houses, as a
reward for deserting their chief and clan. Many have departed both from
the main of Scotland, and from the islands; and all that go may be considered as subjects lost to the British crown; for a nation scattered in the
boundless regions of America resembles rays diverging from a focus. All
the rays remain, but the heat is gone. Their power consisted in their con-
centration: when they are dispersed, they have no effect. (9: 131)

Johnson suggests in this passage his conception of Britain as a series of rays
which need to be united on a focus.

Johnson's imagining of the nation, then, is ambiguous. Like Macpherson,
he raises interest in the Highlands as a romantic site, commenting that such
areas have been "in many countries, the last shelters of national distress, and
are every where the scenes of adventures, stratagems, surprises and escapes"
(9: 38). He finds the Highland area most interesting for its cultural difference
in the past, including its oral tradition, and refuses to entertain the idea that
the Highlanders enjoyed a cultural tradition similar to current English ideals.
In the process of exploring the Highlands, Johnson cannot help wistfully
commenting on certain aspects of what the old Highland life represented, including a feudal system which he admires.[23] Johnson's imagined Britain involves positive representations of Highland culture and of the English culture
which has asserted its hegemonic force over the region. However, he is dis-
paraging of the Lowlanders for belonging to neither one nor the other of
these nations with distinct cultures. The Lowlanders do not speak English
well enough to be English, yet they are "at least as ignorant" of "the past and
present state of the whole Earse nation" (9: 119). Johnson presents the inevitability of assimilation and heterogeneity in Britain, yet he mourns the loss
of the more original national identity of the Highlanders.

Johnson's *Journey* raised the ire of a number of Scottish writers. Rogers
notes that "When the *Journey* was published in 1775, journalists in both London and Edinburgh launched into a more sustained attack on Johnson. The
principal objects of their criticism were his attack on James Macpherson . . .
and his ingratitude in abusing Scottish hospitality" (p. 208). It is in part to
counteract the "remarks" "unworthy of my countrymen" (5: 3) that Boswell
undertook to publish his *Journal of a Tour to the Hebrides* nine years after Johnson's account. Boswell's account differs from Johnson's in a number of ways.
Where Johnson marks the journey to Scotland spatially, noting the peculiarities of each location and attempting to knit experiences together in a linear
narrative, Boswell gives an account across time that jumps between history,

dialogue, and personal anecdote, the entirety being punctuated with copious footnotes. More important, however, as well as amend the form of Johnson's *Journey*, Boswell also adjusts Johnson's representation of Britain, combining it in some ways with Macpherson's, but also providing his own perspective. Like Macpherson, Boswell makes a romantic story out of the Highlanders, one that overshadows their actual culture; where Macpherson concentrated on third-century Caledonian warriors, Boswell glorifies the lost Jacobite cause. On the other hand, like Johnson, Boswell is concerned to represent Britain as a historically heterogeneous nation. Part of his reason for delineating the differences between, in particular, the Highlands and England, I will argue, is to perform his own act of union through narration. In this process, Boswell redeems the Lowland Scots from their degraded position in Johnson's *Journey*, bringing them into focus as privileged middlemen between the English and Highland cultures. He himself embodies this role in his ability to observe the two cultures and to draw comparisons between them.

Much of Boswell's account is concerned with the suppressed Jacobite Rebellion. Pat Rogers suggests that Boswell utilizes Jacobitism to "cement his dream" of "engaging Johnson's vicarious participation" in his quest for adventure (p. 164). According to Rogers, Boswell tries to re-create much of Bonnie Prince Charlie's journey after the battle of Culloden, using Johnson as a representative of the prince. Boswell's interest in Charles Edward, suggests Rogers, "was a way of expiating Boswell's guilty awareness that he was regarded by his real father as a renegade Scot who attached himself to southern and cosmopolitan values" (p. 141). I want to examine Boswell's mythologizing of Jacobitism further, not as a reflection of his complex character, but as a strategy through which he conveys his ideal of the imagined community of the British nation in response to that of Johnson.

Stories about and references to the '45 haunt Boswell's narrative, appearing every few pages or so. Most notably, they are connected with the people whom he and Johnson are visiting. On Tuesday, August 24, for example, while staying with Lord Errol, he notes, "I saw, in imagination, Lord Errol's father, Lord Kilmarnock, (who was beheaded on Tower-hill in 1746,) and I was somewhat dreary" (5: 105). Similarly, describing the family at Raasay, he notes that Mr. Macleod of Muiravenside "was long in exile on account of the part which he took in 1745" (5: 165). His references suggest that involvement in the Rebellion was synonymous with Highland life. He expresses himself as very interested in learning as much as he can about the Rebellion, in particular, about the details of Charles Edward Stewart's flight after Culloden, and the results of his inquiry form a significant interruption in his account of his own travels. Boswell says that he includes the story of Charles because he thinks it will be "not uninteresting to my readers and, even, perhaps be of some use to future historians" (5: 187), but Boswell's is not primarily a historic account; it is a romanticized adventure of a lost but noble cause.[24]

Boswell makes the romanticization of his account clear, referring to Charles Edward with the mythic epithet "the Wanderer" and noting that Flora Macdonald exhibited "the magnanimity of a Heroine" (5: 188). Moreover, "the Wanderer"'s journey becomes a kind of saint's tale, as his various subjects collect relics of his journey. Kingsburgh saved "as long as he lived" the shoes Charles wore while posing as Flora Macdonald's maid, and they were subsequently bought by "a zealous Jacobite gentleman" (5: 189). Mrs. Macdonald wills that the sheets Charles Edward slept in should be kept "unwashed" and used "as a winding sheet" upon her death (5: 190). A number of Highlanders prepare themselves to lose their lives for the prince, and Malcolm Macleod swears that he would even kill his brother if he suspected him of treachery (5: 193). It is the wild geography of Scotland that inspires Johnson to see himself "as a writer of romance," but for Boswell it is Scottish history. Boswell's account of the Highland Jacobites recalls Macpherson's Fingalians: both demonstrate loyalty, chivalry, and bravery. Boswell's description of how Highland gentlemen describing their lord are "all so much affected as to shed tears" (5: 149) suggests, like Macpherson, the extreme sensibility of Highlanders. But, unlike Macpherson, Boswell situates his Highlanders in history. By focusing his account on conversations with actual living beings who participated in the Rebellion, Boswell gives his characters the authenticity that Macpherson's never enjoyed.

Despite his obvious interest in the lost cause of the Jacobites, however, Boswell is quick to suggest his, and the Highlanders', loyalty to the Hanoverian crown:

> Having related so many particulars concerning the grandson of the unfortunate King James the Second; having given due praise to fidelity and generous attachment, which however erroneous the judgement may be, are honourable for the heart; I must do the Highlanders the justice to attest, that I found every where amongst them a high opinion of the virtues of the King now upon the throne, and an honest disposition to be faithful subjects to his majesty, whose family has possessed the sovereignty of this country so long, that a change, even for the abdicated family, would now hurt the best feelings of all his subjects. (5: 202)

In following these remarks, Boswell evades the question of the "*abstract* point of *right*," noting that the 1688 rebellion, which created "a breach in the suc-

cession of our kings," took place "from political necessity" (5: 202). While offering reconciliation in the present, then, he also emphasizes the differences
within the nation that might have led to a victory for the Jacobites. Boswell's
Tour takes account of the alternative histories in Britain.

Boswell's emphasis on the romantic Jacobite history of Britain is part of
his overall project to show the Highland society as distinct in order, like
Johnson, to suggest the heterogeneous nature of the island. In addition to
foregrounding the Rebellion, he draws attention to the different customs and
traditions practiced in the areas in which they travel. Johnson plays an important part in Boswell's narrative of British heterogeneity. Rogers notes that
Boswell uses Johnson as a symbol of Englishness against which Highland life
can be compared: "Boswell textualizes Johnson's otherness: the life and landscape of Scotland become a norm against which the existential differences of
the visitor show up clearly. He emerges as a vector of social forces, the embodiment of his own civilization in a foreign clime" (p. 90). Boswell himself
suggests the basis for the identification of Johnson with Englishness, noting at
the beginning of his *Tour* that Johnson was "much of a *John Bull*; much of a
true-born Englishman" (5: 20). Boswell is keen to put Johnson in situations that
accentuate Johnson's difference and therefore Britain's heterogeneity: "To see
Dr Johnson in any new situation is always an interesting object to me; and, as
I saw him now for the first time on horseback, jaunting about at his ease in
quest of pleasure and novelty, the very different occupations of his former laborious life, his admirable productions, his *London*, his *Rambler*, &c. &c. immediately presented themselves to my mind, and the contrast made a strong
impression on my imagination" (5: 132).

In pointing out the differences between Johnson and the Highlanders and
between London and the Hebrides, Boswell betrays his desire to perform his
own act of union through the narration of his journal. Gordon Turnbull reads
Boswell's journals, including the *Tour*, as registers of the "complex interaction
of the question of Boswell's relation to Scotland, and his authorial ambition
as a literary Scot wanting to make his way in London."[25] He argues that
Boswell's "acquisition of Johnson as a biographical subject" serves his own
"psychopolitical needs" (p. 158), helping him to feel more connected to the
British nation. Turnbull suggests that "Boswell traces in 'the transit of Johnson over the Caledonian Hemisphere' (5 November 1773) the outline of one
contained and unified island, beginning and ending where Johnson begins
and ends, in London" (p. 165). Turnbull's reading of the relationship between
Boswell and Johnson is astute. I would like to look more carefully at the details of how Boswell represents this "unified island," however. In particular,
we will see that Boswell focuses on creating a union through rhetorical

means between the English Johnson and the Highland people. In the process, he puts Lowland Scotland in the position of privileged third party, embodying this role in his own process of narration.

Boswell is careful to draw parallels between seemingly distinct symbols of English and Highland culture. One of the most striking of these instances is his description of Johnson's conversation with Mrs. M'Kinnon regarding Charles Edward Stewart's escape: "Upon that subject there was a warm union between the soul of Mr Samuel Johnson and that of an Isle of Skye farmer's wife. It is curious to see people, though ever so much removed from each other in the general system of their lives, come close together on a particular point which is common to each" (5: 264). This "union of souls" is conveyed even more strongly when Boswell describes a transmutation of Johnson into a Highlander: "One night, in Col, he strutted about the room with a broadsword and target, and made a formidable appearance; and, another night, I took the liberty to put a large blue bonnet on his head" (5: 324). Boswell turns Johnson into a representation of Highland culture, a "*Senachi*," noting that "however unfavourable to the Lowland Scots, he seemed much pleased to assume the appearance of an ancient Caledonian" (5: 324–25).

Boswell here makes a point of acknowledging Johnson's antipathy to the Lowland Scots, a consequence, he suggests, of Johnson's resentment of their celebration of "that nationality which I believe no liberal-minded Scotsman will deny" (5: 20). Yet even as he acknowledges this, he shows the "union of souls" between Johnson and the Highlanders, and metaphorically the union of the nation, to be dependent on a Lowland Scot, himself. It is after all Boswell who observes the affinity between the Englishman and the culture with which he interacts. Boswell dresses Johnson up both in the flesh and in his narrative. His narrative confirms his own role as middleman, facilitating understanding between Johnson and the people around him. He notes that while breakfasting with Mr. Keith, "Dr Johnson expatiated rather too strongly upon the benefits derived to Scotland from the Union, and the bad state of our people before it. I am entertained with his copious exaggeration upon that subject; but I am uneasy when people are by, who do not know him as well as I do, and may be apt to think him narrow-minded. I therefore diverted the subject" (5: 128).

Boswell represents himself as a mixture of English and Highland traits. His participation as a Lowland Scot in English culture is established when he identifies in a footnote a scotticism that he made (5: 15). Instead of erasing it, he draws attention to the fact that he knows better than to use it, but he chooses to use it to establish his North British identity. But in a later footnote, he equally draws attention to his familiarity with the "Highland mode of expression" as he uses the phrase "a M'Queen" instead of "one M'Queen" (5: 135). He embodies the combination of rational knowledge, which he associates with Johnson and England, and emotional attachment, which is associated with the Highland clans. Unable to hold back tears on being told particulars concerning the battle of Culloden by M'Queen, he notes:

> There is a certain association of ideas in my mind upon that subject, by which I am strongly affected. The very Highland names, or the sound of a bagpipe, will stir my blood, and fill me with a mixture of melancholy and respect for courage; with pity for an unfortunate and superstitious regard for antiquity, and thoughtless inclination for war; in short, with a crowd of sensations with which sober rationality has nothing to do. (5: 140)

Understanding the different languages and possessing the different character traits of the two cultures, Boswell is, by his own account, equally at ease with Johnson in London and with Highlanders in the Hebrides. At the feast in Corrichatachin, Boswell notes that although Johnson "seemed to be forgotten" at moments, he himself, "though but a *Lowlander*, having picked up a few words of the language . . . presumed to mingle in their mirth, and joined in the choruses with as much glee as any of the company" (5: 157). Boswell seems more diverted with Johnson's being left out than Johnson was, the latter professing to have genuinely enjoyed the festivities.

In fact, Boswell is intent on writing his importance to Johnson into his account. On several occasions he remarks how much Johnson approves his writing of the journal. In a significant passage, he also records Johnson's fear about being left alone on the road to Glenelg when Boswell rides ahead of him. In his account of the episode, Boswell comments:

> It grew dusky; and we had a very tedious ride for what was called five miles; but I am sure would measure ten. We had no conversation. I was riding forward to the inn at Glenelg, on the shore opposite to Sky, that I might take proper measures, before Dr. Johnson, who was now advancing in dreary silence, Hay leading his horse, should arrive. Vass also walked by the side of his horse, and Joseph followed behind: as therefore he was attended, and seemed to be in deep meditation, I thought there could be no harm in leaving him for a little while. He called me back with a tremendous shout, and was really in a passion with me for leaving him. (5: 144–45)

According to Boswell, Johnson exclaims: "Do you know, I should as soon have thought of picking a pocket, as [of leaving you]" (5: 145). Yet in his own narrative Johnson makes no mention of this episode. Instead, he explains the fear Boswell describes as the result of his horse's having stumbled (*Works*, 9: 48). Boswell's elaboration suggests his intent on showing his necessity to Johnson. The subtext to the passage, and to the rest of Boswell's account, is how important Lowland Scotland is as a mediating force between the English and the Highlanders. Johnson is "a *John Bull*; much of a *true-born Englishman*," and the Highlanders belong to a lost feudal society, but Boswell identifies himself as "completely a citizen of the world" (5: 20), always at home anywhere he travels.

In this chapter, I have been examining the negotiation of the history of culture in Britain toward the end of the eighteenth century. Howard Weinbrot comments on the phenomenon of Ossian's popularity, suggesting that it indicates the integration of Scotland and England: "Much of Ossian's Scottish patriotism was consistent with English patriotism, for now each was indigenously 'British' and shared overlapping values, whatever the ongoing strains in competitive and often unpleasant regionalism and contests for power" (p. 555). According to Weinbrot, Ossian suggests how "Britannia's issue and Scotia's issue could at least be blended in cacaphonous harmony" (p. 556). But it is important to look at how Macpherson configures this blending—and how that configuration is contested. Macpherson creates a history that attributes the beginning of British culture to mythic Caledonians who represent not only Highlanders, but also Lowlanders and English.

Repudiating Macpherson's account, Johnson wants to preserve the idea of cultural heterogeneity in Britain's history, showing the Highland oral and the English literate cultures to be antithetical to each other. Although Johnson advocates "civilizing" the Highlands by making them more similar to England, he also values the region for the difference it represents: the trace of a primitive culture within Britain and of a Celtic romantic strain that is complementary to English reason.[26]

Boswell, however, gets the final word on culture in Britain. He historicizes the romantic chivalry of the Highlands by concentrating on the Jacobite Rebellion while promoting the values of English "civilization," but he also writes for the Lowland Scots an important role as the cultural mediators of the Union, not in the past but in the present. This is seen best in his account of a visit to the holy island of Iona.[27] After a moving experience viewing the ruins, Sir Allan M'Lean, Johnson, and Boswell spend the night on portmanteaus in a barn. Boswell notes, "When I awaked in the morning, and looked round me, I could not help smiling at the idea of the chief of the M'Leans, the great English Moralist, and myself, lying thus extended in such a situation" (5: 335). Representatives of the three heterogeneous parts of the island are thus united under the same roof; but it takes Boswell's observation to formalize the union. The three men are "extended" in the same "situation," but only one of them, Boswell, records the event. Boswell suggests that regardless of the past political and cultural record, it is the Lowland Scots, combining aspects of both Highland and English culture, who have the important task of consolidating the Union in the present through writing. This is a position that, as the next chapter will suggest, was revisited both by another Scottish writer, Robert Burns, and by his English counterpart, William Wordsworth.

CHAPTER 4

The Poetry of Nature and
the Nature of Poetry: Robert Burns
and William Wordsworth

Boswell's vision of the Lowland Scots as cultural mediators within a united Britain was soon to be contested by a Lowland Scottish writer whose poetry highlighted the ambiguities inherent in the attempt to write the nation. Robert Burns positioned himself partway between critiquing the cultural hegemony and participating in it. His poetry draws attention to the differences within the nation as well as indicating the acts of poetic and readerly imagination which are necessary to create a sense of national identity. In addition to troubling British national and cultural hegemony, Burns's poetry also questions the image of Scotland that writers like Boswell took for granted— "that nationality which . . . no liberal-minded Scotsman will deny" (5: 20). Burns was subsequently subjected to much repackaging by Scottish literati anxious to promote their own vision of a strong Scottish cultural nationalism within a united Britain.

It was the English poet William Wordsworth, however, who was responsible for the most enduring popular image of Burns in the nineteenth century. Wordsworth developed many of his poetic ideas in dialogue with Burns and continued to grapple with him throughout his career. Wordsworth's incorporation and marginalization of the Scottish poet, whom he re-created as an inspired but flawed poet of nature, demonstrates his concern to overwrite the national differences that Burns represented and to create an assimilated nation of participants in the British cultural realm. This chapter argues that the discourse regarding Burns, the "poet ploughman," during and after his death, illustrates the renegotiation of the relationship between England and Scotland in process in the cultural sphere at the time: a renegotiation that centered

around the competing definitions of Scottishness that were being offered by
Scottish and English writers alike.

Burns's interrogation of British culture—and Wordsworth's concern about
that interrogation—must be seen in the context of general political concerns
raised by the revolutions in America (1776) and France (1789). Scottish opinion generally supported the Westminster government's position on the American colonies, but the war with America opened up debates on the subject of
political representation in Scotland. As Bruce Lenman suggests, "the discom-
fiture and discrediting of government in the latter stages of the American
War . . . helped to provoke a movement for reform in that most indefensible
and corrupt part of the Scottish political power structure: burghal government" (*Integration*, p. 75).[1] The French Revolution also had considerable impact on the Scottish political scene.[2] Notably, much of the attention paid to
events in France was by "groups well below those social levels which were
traditionally expected to take an interest in politics" (Lenman, *Integration*, p.
102), in other words, by the class of people to which Burns belonged. Part of
this was due to differences in the structures of societies sympathetic to the
French Revolution. Membership subscription costs in the Society of Friends
of the People, for example, were lower in Scotland than in England, encouraging membership in the lower classes. Whereas previously the movement for
reform had been led chiefly by members of the professional classes north of
the Tweed, now it was skilled craftsmen who were marrying their economic
concerns with political principles. In *Memorials of His Time*, Henry Cockburn
writes about the pervasiveness of the debate on political events; the French
Revolution, he asserts, "was, or was made the all in all. Everything, not this
thing or that thing but literally everything was soaked in this one event"
(Fry, *Patronage*, p. 12).[3] Burns's poetry needs to be considered in terms of this
soaking. His career was launched a decade after the American War of Independence, and his *Poems, Chiefly in the Scottish Dialect* was published three years
before the French Revolution. Burns's writing questions the power relations
between center and periphery, a theme also prevalent in republican discourse
in both Scotland and the rest of Britain. In particular, Burns's poetry attempts
to include geographical peripheries (Scotland) and economic peripheries (the
laboring classes) in the cultural realm of the British nation. Burns's career was
forged during this tumultuous time; however, Wordsworth's first book of poems was not published until a decade after the French Revolution. His poetic
reflections on the events in France came already mediated by personal and
political disappointment. On his return from France, Wordsworth embraced
England and the English countryside with poetic passion, marking a turn in
his poetic career as well as his political affiliation.[4] Burns proved to be both a

model for Wordsworth of how poetry could extend its concerns to the "common man" and a representative of the national difference that Wordsworth sought to overcome.

In his poetry and songs, Burns seeks to expand the definition of British literature in such a way so as to include Scottish and laboring-class elements within it. From his position on the geographical and economic periphery of England, Burns, like Smollett, was only too aware of the unacknowledged gaps in the national fabric. Burns's criticism of hegemonic British values, although developed most fully in his published work, is seen in embryonic form in his first writings as he juxtaposes English and Scottish, cosmopolitan and rural, and literary and oral elements. In his *Commonplace Book*, Burns keeps notes about his reflections on turning his hand to writing poetry. He presents himself as "but little indebted to scholastic education, and bred at a plough-tail" and claims that his poems may be "strongly tinctured with his unpolished, rustic way of life" (*Poems and Songs*, 3: 968). Burns asserts the values of his local Ayrshire community, the labor of working in the fields, and unrefined taste. His inclusion of two quotations from Shenstone in the same preface, however, contradicts those values and suggests that he has at least some knowledge, if not of scholastic education, then at least of the contemporary literary field as well as the cornfield. Commenting on the "psychological and metaphorical" distance from London which Scots (and Americans) perceived, Susan Manning observes that citizens of those nations believed "the word—to be at once the source and the manifestation of their predestined passivity and distance from the heart of experience" (p. 51).[5] According to Manning, these citizens felt they had been "dispossessed" of their inheritance, "the language of the centre" (p. 51). Burns, however, seems intent not only on repossessing the language of the center, but also on questioning its centrality by exposing the competing traditions that exist within it. This split identity reflects Burns's own experience of heteroglossia, living as a Scot in Great Britain.[6] His education was conducted in English, which he spoke and wrote well. His tutor, John Murdoch, wrote that Burns studied the *Spelling Book*, the New Testament, the Bible, Arthur Masson's *Collection of Prose and Verse*, and *Fisher's English Grammar*, none of which included any Scottish writers at all (Daiches, *Burns*, p. 41). Burns discovered the Scots literary tradition of Allan Ramsay and Robert Fergusson only when he was twenty-three, after he had begun to write poetry in the Scots dialect himself. The two traditions, Scottish and English, rustic and genteel, inform each other in Burns's poetry.

The preface to the *Poems, Chiefly in the Scottish Dialect*, published in Kilmarnock in 1786, offers similar juxtapositions to those found in the *Com-*

monplace Book, as Burns introduces himself as both a member of the literary community of Britain and part of a community of Ayrshire "rustic com-peers." He starts his preface by apologizing for the "trifles" he is presenting to the public. He is, he suggests, "unacquainted with the necessary requisites for commencing Poet by rule," and he begs his readers, "particularly the learned and the Polite . . . that they will make every allowance for Education and Circumstances of Life" (*Poems and Songs*, 3: 972). Yet, far from confirm-ing his affinity for the plough-tail, his introduction suggests his literary dis-cernment.[7] Presenting himself as a British citizen of letters, Burns comments that the elegies of "that celebrated Poet," Shenstone, "do honour to our lan-guage, our nation, and our species" (3: 971). Among his reasons for "courting the Muses" is "to find some kind of counterpoise to the struggles of a world, always an alien scene, a task uncouth to the poetical mind" (3: 971). His nar-rative sensibility aligns him with "the Poet . . . with all the advantages of learned art," so much so that he can adopt the language of the outraged critic reading the *Poems* to condemn himself as "an impertinent blockhead, ob-truding his nonsense on the world; and because he can make a shift to jingle a few doggerel, Scotch rhymes together, looks upon himself as a Poet of no small consequence forsooth" (3: 971–72). This same indication of literary knowledge occurs in the texts of the *Poems* as Burns employs epigraphs from standard English poems at the beginning of a number of his own verses. His quotations—from Milton ("Address to the Devil"), Goldsmith ("Halloween"), Blair ("To J. S****" [James Smith]), Gray ("The Cotter's Saturday Night"), and John Home ("The Lament")—demonstrate his familiarity with the tra-dition of anglicized *belles lettres*.[8] In his writerly apparatus, then, Burns repre-sents himself both as worldly, knowledgeable critic and as rustic, unlearned bard, the latter being associated in particular with his Scottish identity.

Rather than just promote the Scottish language and identity, however, Burns commingles English and Scottish elements to suggest the contradic-tions that exist within the Union of Great Britain, contradictions that can be seen in the title of his first publication itself, *Poems, Chiefly in the Scottish Di-alect*. "Poems" connotes the literary world of English letters into which Burns would insert himself. "Scottish," on the other hand, draws attention to the lo-cal medium at his disposal, a medium that would prevent his entry into the lofty realms of poetry. Poems like the "Epistle to John Lapraik, An Auld Scots Bard," for example, similarly juxtapose the English and the Scottish literary traditions. "Epistle to Lapraik" begins with the narrator's comments regard-ing a song he had heard that pleased him. His attribution of the song to the likes of Pope, Steele, or Beattie gestures toward the aesthetic supremacy of the *belles lettres* tradition of English literature. Correspondingly, he seems to

depreciate the aesthetics of Scottish tradition, presenting his own work in the
Scots dialect not as "poetry" but as "rhymes":

> I am nae Poet, in a sense,
> But just a Rhymer, like by chance,
> An' hae to Learning nae pretence,
> > Yet, what the matter?
> Whene'er my Muse does on me glance,
> > I jingle at her.
>
> > > *(ll. 49–54)*

But Burns goes on to eliminate this hierarchy by depicting the Scottish tradition as being as valuable as the English tradition. He recalls the rich Scots
tradition to which he and Lapraik are heirs, suggesting that a "spunk o' Allan's glee, / Or Ferguson's" would be "lear eneugh" for him (ll. 79–83). The
form of the poem also asserts the Scottish literary tradition; it is written as an
epistle addressed to a fellow Scottish poet and composed in a stanza form
used by Allan Ramsay in his own verse epistles. Moreover, although the
poem as a letter is a written event, it promotes oral poetry, conjuring up a
picture of a community experience, an oral tradition alien to the likes of
Pope, Steele, and Beattie:

> On Fasteneen we had a rockin,
> To ca' the crack and weave our stockin;
> And there was muckle fun and jokin,
> > You need na doubt;
> At length we had a hearty yokin,
> > At sang about.
>
> > > *(ll. 7–12)*

Unlike the literary epistles of Pope, for example, the aim of Burns's epistle is
to lead to further oral communication. Burns invites Lapraik to meet him at
Mauchline where they could "hae a swap o' *rhymin-ware*, / Wi' ane anither"
(l. 108). Robert Crawford has argued that Burns's juxtaposition of the high
and low in Burns's work constitutes a critique of the dominant literary culture of England. According to Crawford, Burns "frequently presents himself
in a guise both self-deprecating and confidently assured, constantly implying
that the manifestly little may stand confidently beside the mighty" (*Devolving*, p. 89). Crawford argues that "the effect of this technique is to upset established categories, raising questions about the way in which we casually as-

sign cultural value" (p. 89). In the "Epistle to John Lapraik," rather than promote one tradition above the other, however, Burns draws attention to the
possibility of the coexistence of the Scottish and English traditions within his
poem and within Britain. He sets a place for himself on the literary market
by expanding the possibilities of British literature.

Kenneth Simpson, Murray Pittock, and Robert Crawford have analyzed
Burns's disruption of contemporary ideas of the relationship of Scotland to
England.[9] In *The Protean Scot: The Crisis of Identity in Eighteenth-Century Scottish Literature*, Simpson suggests that Burns reflects the contradictory nature
of all Scottish writers, mingling elements of Scottish and English traditions
in a process of self-ironization. In *Poetry and Jacobite Politics in Eighteenth-
Century Britain and Ireland*, Pittock reads Burns's work as troubling the "in-
cremental history" that was promoted by the English imperial center. Crawford regards the poet's straddling of English and Scottish traditions as evidence of Burns's basic "Britishness" (*Devolving*, pp. 88–89). Both Crawford
and Pittock situate Burns's critique of the British national community within
an ideology of Scottish nationalism. Crawford comments, "There is a British
aspect to Burns's work, but it is potentially explosive Britishness, because the
poet is often hovering near the touch-paper of Scottish republican nationalism" (p. 109). Pittock asserts that Burns's merging of Jacobite and Jacobin
politics depends on his interpreting "the idea of Scottish history as a struggle
for liberty" (*Poetry and Jacobite Politics*, p. 219).[10] It is important, however, to
pay attention to Burns's articulations of the discontinuities in the Scottish nation, too. In fact, although he questions British hegemonic values in his poetry, his position on the margin of the dominant hegemony gave him insight
into the acts of invention and silencing that are necessary in the creation of
any nation, not just Britain. Accordingly, his poetry questions the "nationality" Boswell asserted for the mediating and "liberal-minded Scotsman."

His critique of the imagining of both nations can be seen in "The Vision."
The poem begins with a poet-narrator, who, after having finished threshing,
sits contemplating the time he has wasted "stringing blethers up in rhyme /
For fools to sing" (ll. 23–24) and raises his palm to swear "That I, henceforth,
would be *rhyme-proof* / Till my last breath—" (ll. 35–36), but the oath is
checked on his lips by the appearance of a supernatural being, a woman at-
tired in green with a crown of holly boughs. The narrator deduces correctly
that she is "some SCOTTISH MUSE . . . come to stop those reckless vows" (ll.
51–54) that he made against poetry. The woman, Coila, presents a set of contradictory values similar to those in the "Epistle to Lapraik." She praises the
bellelettristes Fullarton, Dempster, and Beattie. But she also asserts the importance of what she calls the "lower Order" of muses who cater to "the hum-

bler ranks of Human-kind" (ll. 175–76). She is herself one of those muses "bounded to a district space" (l. 193) who "guide and guard" the development of *"rustic"* bards. Her particular district is Kyle, and her special charge is the narrator himself. She watched him as a child, "fir'd" by the "simple, art-less lays" (l. 209) of past poets and inspired by Nature. She sees him, like the young Wordsworth later in *The Prelude*, experiencing Nature in its sublime and benevolent forms:

> I saw thee seek the sounding shore,
> Delighted with the dashing roar;
> Or when the *North* his fleecy store
>   Drove thro' the sky,
> I saw grim Nature's visage hoar,
>   Struck thy young eye.
>
> Or when the deep-green-mantl'd Earth,
> Warm-cherish'd ev'ry floweret's birth,
> And joy and music pouring forth,
>   In ev'ry grove,
> I saw thee eye the gen'ral mirth
>   With boundless love.
>
> *(ll. 211–22)*

Instead of recounting great deeds, the narrator is destined to observe and re-late the seasonal changes with which rural communities mark the year. Coila reassures him of his importance and counsels him not to bemoan his lot: "trust the UNIVERSAL PLAN / Will all protect" (ll. 269–70). The poem shows Burns accepting his status as "bounded to a district space" (l. 193). However, he also makes the local a place of power from which he can critique the dominant tradition.

For although Coila acknowledges a British poetic hierarchy, she also sub-verts the idea of a united Britain as she offers the narrator a kaleidoscope of geographical and historical images that inspire a feeling of Scottish patriotism in him:

> My heart did glowing transport feel,
> To see a Race heroic wheel,
> And brandish round the deep-dy'd steel
>   In sturdy blows;
> While back-recoiling seem'd to reel
>   Their Suthron foes.
>
> *(ll. 97–102)*

Such an image of Scottish patriotism is at odds with the hegemony of *belles lettres* that Coila asserts in her praise of poetry.

In addition, the poem's revelation of the ambiguity inherent in British national identity can be seen to apply to the construction of the Scottish nation too. "The Vision" suggests the tension between local and national affiliations and between high and low class members of the nation. The scenes revealed to the narrator by Coila are local scenes around the rivers Doon, Irwine, and Aire. Moreover, the "Race" that wheels heroically is identified as the Wallaces, a family that traced its roots to southwest Scotland. Burns's interest clearly lies in the relationship between the local and the national. A similar tension is found in the portrayal of both privileged and laboring classes within the poem. Coila informs the narrator that different spirits are responsible for the different classes of citizens in the nation:

> Know, the great *Genius* of this land,
> Has many a light, aerial band,
> Who, all beneath his high command,
>   Harmoniously,
> As *Arts* or *Arms* they understand,
>   Their labors ply.
>
> *(ll. 145–51)*

These beings share "Scotia's race" among them. Some attend to the higher order of soldiers, patriots, and bards of the nation; others "To lower Orders are assigned" (l. 175), namely the "rustic" bards, laborers, and artisans. Although Burns tries to indicate the importance of both high and low pursuits, he nevertheless reveals a tension between the grand aspirations of the upper classes and the lesser concerns of the laboring classes in creating national identity; agricultural lore may be important, but it does not earn its possessor the designation of "His COUNTRY'S SAVIOUR" (l. 103). Burns's "Vision" represents the nation as a negotiation between local areas and the general nation and between the nation's high-class and low-class members.

The scenes on Coila's mantle offer other comments about nation-formation. In particular, the nation is seen as coming into being by defining itself against an Other; the heroism of the Wallaces comes into relief only in struggle against "Their Suthron foes" (l. 102). But the poem also suggests the Other that exists within the supposedly united national Self, as it refers to the Pictish history of Scotland. An additional stanza in the Stair manuscript notes the "ancient, Pict-built Mansion" of Sundrum (Kinsley, 1: 83). The narrator remarks that "Coilus King of the Picts, from whom the district of Kyle is said to take its name, lies buried, as tradition says, near the family-seat of the Montgomeries of Coilsfield, where his burial place is still shown" (1: 84). Burns portrays a sense of the historical diversity within Scotland.

The poem ends with Coila's advice to the narrator to "Preserve *the dignity of Man*" and to trust that "the UNIVERSAL PLAN / Will all protect" (ll. 267, 269–270). Thomas Crawford, suggesting that this advice "sums up the aim of a national poet—indeed of any poet," argues that there "is . . . not the slightest conflict between Burns's nationalism and the interests of the broadest humanism. His is a patriotism compatible with internationalism, for it merges with 'the dignity of Man'" (*Burns*, p. 190). But although the conclusion sets out to reconcile the narrator (and the reader) to the workings of a "UNIVERSAL PLAN," the poem has already suggested some of the straining that accompanies knitting the nation together. Burns's "Vision" points to the leap of imaginative faith that is necessary in reconciling the differences within the nation.

Burns calls attention in "The Vision" to this very act of imagining the nation. He suggests that, faced with disparities within the nation, it is the poet who is to a great extent responsible for creating the nation, as he actively recalls the poetic creations of Scotland in two other poets' work. "The Vision" looks back for its title and its theme to Allan Ramsay's poem of the same name.[11] Ramsay's "Vision" is a dream poem in which the narrator contemplates the history of Scotland, specifically the thirteenth-century war that reestablished Scottish sovereignty, in relation to its present. In Ramsay's poem, the difficulties which Scotland faces are due to the fact that the Guardian, the male spirit of the nation, has left the land. The poem ends with a heavenly council promising that Scotland will be restored to its place of importance in Europe. Ramsay's "Vision" draws a parallel between the time of Wallace and the years after the 1707 Act of Union. The poet wants to construct a Scottish nation that is coherent both chronologically and diachronically; he presents a chronological narrative, but he suggests that this chronology consists of a series of similar situations that are replicated. This diachronic coherence is reinforced as Ramsay presents the poem as translated from medieval Latin into Scots. Burns's "The Vision" alludes as well to James Macpherson's infamous imagining of the Scottish nation in the *Poems of Ossian*. Burns divides his poem into two parts, using the word "Duan" to indicate each half. In a footnote, he calls attention to Macpherson's *Cath-loda*, indicating that the "Duan" is "a term of Ossian's for the different divisions of a digressive Poem" (*Works*, 1: 80). Writing in the 1780s, Burns could not have been unaware of the controversy surrounding the claims of Macpherson. By invoking Ossian, he nonetheless suggests the power of poetry, whether authentic or not, in constructing the nation.

Burns's "Vision" continues some of Ramsay's concerns but also examines more carefully the creation of the nation. Like Ramsay, Burns presents a noble image of the Scottish people: they are "a *Race*, / To ev'ry nobler virtue bred, / And polish'd grace" (ll. 88–90). He also indicates that these features of the nation are conveyed "in *Scottish Story*" (l. 87). And it is significant that the topography and history of Scotland appear on the mantle of "Scottish Muse." The "lights and shades" on the fabric mingle to create "A *well-known* land" (l. 72); the nation is directly connected to artistic representation. Indeed, Burns also hints at the tenuousness of the image of the nation at the end of the poem when he indicates that Coila and her national representation disappear "like a passing thought" (l. 275). Although Coila makes a loud enough entrance, as Burns does everything in his power to portray the creaking of the door and the snap of the lock as she comes in, he retreats from attempting to represent her reality at the end, instead emphasizing her insubstantiality. The question remains: has the entire construction of the nation been just a vision of the poet? Although, as Thomas Crawford suggests, in "The Vision" Burns is asserting "his right to be considered as part of a great and many-sided national movement" (*Burns*, p. 187), he is also showing the fissures that have to be sealed over by the poet—and the reader—through imagination.

"The Cotter's Saturday Night" also suggests how the nation is created through multiple acts of imagination. Burns paints the world of the cotter as a vital community, contrasting it with the graveyard scene of Gray's "Elegy Written in a Country Churchyard," which the poem invokes in its epigraph. The second stanza of Burns's poem echoes the cadences of the "Elegy," but it quickly turns not to a lonely graveyard, but to a cottage with a "wee-ingle blinkan bonilie" and to a loving family. Burns depicts an ideal household which, though poor, obeys both their human "Master's and . . . Mistress's command" (l. 46) and the "Creator's" universal plan, as outlined by the "priest-like Father" (l. 118). This passage offers a positive image of the Scottish laboring class. Moreover, Burns suggests how this class help to imagine the nation into being. In particular, the members of the cotter's family are shown to be inspired by the effect that earlier performances have in cementing the nation of Israel together. They respond to

> . . . how the *royal Bard* did groaning lye,
> Beneath the stroke of Heaven's avenging ire;
> Or *Job's* pathetic plaint, and wailing cry;
> Or rapt *Isiah's* wild, seraphic fire;
> Or other *Holy Seers* that tune the *sacred lyre*.
>
> (*ll. 122–26*)

The family members then turn their attention to their own Scottish nation through singing. For in addition to listening to Bible stories, they also participate in singing "the sweetest far of SCOTIA's holy lays" (l. 114): the songs of "*Dundee*," "*Martyrs*," "Or noble *Elgin*" (ll. 111–13), compared to which "*Italian trills*" (l. 115) are soul-less. The members of the family are put in tune with each other through "tun[ing] their hearts" in song (l. 110). Reciting Scottish songs fuses the cotter's family together as national subjects. Burns suggests that it is "From scenes like these [that] old SCOTIA's grandeur springs / That makes her lov'd at home, rever'd abroad" (ll. 163–64).

Other elements in the poem suggest a different kind of national imagining than the singing of traditional songs. The poem is "inscribed" for an individual of a different class than the cotter, Robert Aiken, Esquire, a friend of Burns, and it is designed to inspire readers of Aiken's class who will help to imagine the Scottish nation. At the end of the poem, Burns addresses the nation itself:

> O SCOTIA! my dear, my native soil!
> For whom my warmest wish to Heaven is sent!
> Long may thy hardy sons of *rustic toil*
> Be blest with health and peace and sweet content!
>
> *(ll. 172–75)*

Although he employs the "sons of *rustic toil*" as the objects of his national discourse, Burns intends by such an apostrophe to create his readers as subjects of that discourse who join him in the address to the nation. In Chapter 1, I examined the ambiguity involved in the narratives of Belhaven and Defoe as both attempted to unite Scottish and British citizens, respectively, in an immediate imagining of the nation. Belhaven conceived of that immediacy as primarily visual and aural, whereas Defoe tried to convey immediacy through the printed word. Burns represents both kinds of immediacy. The "double narrative movement" in the "Cotter's Saturday Night" suggests the several levels on which the nation must be imagined: both rustic, laboring citizens and more economically advantaged literary citizens must participate in conceiving the nation in both oral and written form.[12]

Burns also builds a double narrative of national imagining combining orality and literacy into "Halloween," again attempting to unify divergent groups through acts of imagination. The main narrative of the poem describes the activities of a group of rustic laboring characters on All Hallow's Eve as they attempt to discern their futures. Burns ties their activities into the imagining of the Scottish nation by invoking the memory of Bruce, "the great Deliverer of his country" (Kinsley, 1: 122):

> Amang the bonie, winding banks,
> Where *Doon* rins, wimplin, clear,
> Where BRUCE ance rul'd the martial ranks,
> An' shook his *Carrick* spear,
> Some merry, friendly, countra folks,
> Together did convene,
> To *burn* their nits, an' pou their stocks,
> An' haud their *Halloween*
>   Fu' blythe that night.
>
>   *(ll. 10–18)*

The characters serve to illustrate the history of Scotland, inasmuch as they are seen to practice the same folk customs that their ancestors have done for ages. When Jenny asks to participate in the ceremonies, Graunie describes the story of Rab McGraen, which she remembers "as well's yestreen" (l. 128). "Halloween" has been criticized for its failure to develop a standard narrative: "It revolves upon a single spot; and furthermore, it seems to narrow in smaller and smaller gyrations" (T. Crawford, *Burns*, p. 123). But the effect is important because it suggests the timeless past of Scottish history that is passed down through oral tradition.

The actions of these characters are mediated for the reader by the use of extensive footnotes. The poem begins with an anthropological note explaining what the reader is about to experience:

> The following POEM will, by many Readers, be well enough understood,
> but, for the sake of those who are unacquainted with the manner and
> traditions of the country where the scene is cast, Notes are added, to give
> some account of the principal Charms and Spells of that Night, so big
> with Prophecy to the Peasantry in the West of Scotland. The passion of
> prying into Futurity makes a striking part of the history of Human-
> nature, in it's rude state, in all ages and nations; and it may be some enter-
> tainment to a philosophic mind, if any such should honor the Author
> with a perusal, to see the remains of it, among the more unenlightened in
> our own. (Kinsley, 1: 122).

By including such elaborate explanations, Burns distances himself, and as-sumes the distance of his readers, from the community of "Western Scotland" that he is evoking. The rhetorical difference between narrative and footnotes, between the language of the peasants of the West of Scotland and the more "philosophic" reader suggests a fundamental split within the nation. Similarly, by presenting "the remains" of the peasants' superstitions, Burns also suggests the fragmentary nature of nation. The double narrative again suggests a Scotland which is contradictory.

Yet in this poem, as in "The Cotter's Saturday Night," Burns also works to suggest the relation between the contradictory members of the nation as all imagine their community into being. Burns gradually conflates the language of the peasants with that of the reader by shifting the footnotes from objective third-person description to second-person imperative. The first note begins, "The first ceremony of Halloween, is, pulling each a *Stock*, or plant of kail. They must go out, hand in hand, with eyes shut, and pull the first they meet with" (Kinsley, 1: 123). But the ninth footnote begins by addressing "Whoever would" try the spell, and continues with the directions:

> Steal out, all alone, to the *kiln*, and, darkling, throw into the *pot*, a clew of blue yarn: wind it in a new clew off the old one; and towards the latter end, something will hold the thread: demand, *wha haulds*? ie. who holds? and answer will be returned from the kiln-pot, by naming the christian and sirname of your future Spouse. (1: 125)

The remaining footnotes also use the second person, ordering the reader to "Take a candle" (1: 126), "sow a handful of hemp seed" (1: 127), "Take three dishes" (1: 130), and to conduct similar occult tasks. Burns's changing narrative position in the poem works to create a relationship between otherwise incommensurable sections of the Scottish nation.

Burns's sense of the contradictions inherent in Scotland, and in Britain, became stronger when he visited Edinburgh in 1787. Thanks to the encouragement of Thomas Blacklock, Burns moved to the capital to oversee a republication of his *Poems*. He found himself to be an object of fascination for the Edinburgh literati, valuable as representative of peasant rusticity, but also kept at arm's length because of his membership in that class. In a letter to Mr. William Greenfield dated December 16, 1786, he writes: "Never did Saul's armour sit so heavy on David when going to encounter Goliath, as does the encumbering role of public notice with which the friendship and patronage of some 'names dear to fame' have invested me . . . to be dragged forth, with all my imperfections on my head, to the full glare of learned and polite observation, is what, I am afraid, I shall have bitter reason to repent" (*Letters*, 1: 73–74). He expresses a similar fear to Mrs. Dunlop:

I assure you, Madam, I do not dissemble when I tell you I tremble for the consequences. The novelty of a poet in my obscure situation, without any of those advantages which are reckoned necessary for that character, at least at this time of day, has raised a partial tide of public notice, which has borne me to a height where I am absolutely feelingly certain my abilities are inadequate to support me; and too surely do I see that time when the same tide will leave me, and recede, perhaps, as far below the mark of truth. (*Letters*, 1: 85)

Burns's residence in the capital brought home to him the competition between different values and also the curious position he occupied, like Macpherson, as a negotiator between worlds. A letter to Dr. Moore indicates his apprehension about what he can have to offer: "in a language where Pope and Churchill have raised the laugh, and Shenstone and Gray drawn the tear; where Thomson and Beattie have painted the landskip, and Littleton and Collins described the heart; I am not vain enough to hope for distinguished Poetic fame" (*Letters*, 1: 88).

Burns makes his vision of the fractured imagined community—and the role of the writer within it—the theme of one of his most famous poems, "Tam o'Shanter." The poem was originally written as commentary for a picture of Alloway Kirk in Francis Grose's *Antiquities of Scotland* (1789 and 1791). A note in the Glenriddell manuscript indicates:

When Captain Grose was at Friars-Carse in Summer 1790 Collecting materials for his Scottish Antiquities he applied to Mr. Burns then living in the neighbourhood to write him an account of the Witches Meetings at Aloway Church near Ayr who complied with his request and wrote him the following Poem. (Kinsley, 1: 443)

In effect, Grose wanted Burns to supply him with a popular tale that would represent the Scottish nation as a Gothic, superstitious Other for English readers. Burns complies with the request to a certain extent, but "Tam o'Shanter" also comments on the process of imagining a community, either one's own or another, because it represents the Scottish nation not as a holistic cultural entity but as a split image. Both the familiar, comfortable world of the pub and the unsettling satanic community constitute a picture of Scotland. The world of the pub and market, which we encounter initially, for example, contains "lang Scots miles" of "mosses, waters, slaps and styles" (ll. 7–8). But the satanic community at the kirk is also Scottish, as the witches leap about to "hornpipes, jigs, strathspeys, and reels" (l. 117). Moreover, the devil plays the bagpipes: "He screw'd the pipes and gart them skirl" (l. 123). Rather than attempting to delineate the nation with one representation, Burns offers a picture of an imagined community ghosted by its *unheimlich* Other.[13] In doing so, he works against the attempt to write a cohesive national identity. His poem suggests to both British and Scottish readers the "dangers of the fixity and fetishism of identities" (Bhabha, *Location*, p. 9).

For what is crucial in "Tam o'Shanter" is not Tam's fixity in one identifiable place, but his ability to cross over from one location to another. The poem draws attention to the importance of crossing boundaries with the repetition of the image of the "key-stane." Tam saddles his mare for his supernatural journey at midnight: "That hour, o' night's black arch the key-stane" (l. 69). His return from the domain of the witches is marked by his crossing over "the key-stane of the brig" (l. 206). Keystones of time and space serve as boundaries that must be traversed. The loss of the mare's tail signals the alteration that constitutes such a crossing over: "But ere the key-stane she could make, / The fient a tail she had to shake" (l. 209–10). But identity finds another, more fluid, location in the recitation of the tale itself. The narrator finishes with a caution to the reader to "Remember Tam o'Shanter's mare" (l. 224). Membership in this imagined community is constituted by remembering the process of crossing boundaries and the losses and the gains that occur through such a process. Bhabha suggests that such celebrations of the in-between, such relocations of "the home and the world" are characteristic of "extra-territorial and cross-cultural initiations" (Bhabha, *Location*, p. 9). Burns was well adept at such initiations. "Tam o' Shanter" seems in many ways the culmination of such initiations, crossing as it does between Scottish dialect and English *belles lettres* as well as between the literary and the visual, the Gothic and grotesque, and the sentimental and satirical. In "Tam o' Shanter," Burns celebrates the ambiguities of national identity that he expressed in earlier poems.[14]

Burns's turn to music suggests an alternative to the national fracturing that figured so prominently in his writing. He contributed both to James Johnson's *Scots Musical Museum* (1787–1803) and George Thomson's *A Select Collection of Scottish Tunes* (1793–99). Music became a way of upsetting conventional notions regarding the distinction between popular and elite culture; the relationship between the individual poet and the nation; and the relationship between language and the nation. Notably, Burns chose to publish his contributions to both collections anonymously. His new vision of the nation imagines it, with all its disjunctures, as a web of anonymous activity, uniting author and the readers alike. In the song collections, national identity emerges through the denial of the individual. The collections offer a nonhierarchical imagining of the nation through active participation in its song culture. Burns also sought to remove the idea of the individual author from this reimagination of the nation by refusing to accept money for his contributions. In his letter of September 16, 1792, he wrote to George Thomson: "As to any remuneration, you may think my Songs either *above*, or *below* price; for they shall absolutely be one or the other.—In the honest enthusiasm with which I embark in your undertaking, to talk of money, wages, fee, hire, &c. would be downright Sodomy of Soul!" (*Letters*, 2: 149). Although the consumption of the image of the nation was still situated in the marketplace, its production in the hands of an individual author was removed from economic considerations. Furthermore, by turning to collecting songs, Burns suggests that it is music and lyrics, not printed language, that is most appropriate to convey national identity. In particular, this move attempts to legitimize a medium of national culture, music, in which the Scots had a strong tradition instead of accepting one, poetry, that was largely controlled by English standards.[15]

I have been suggesting the way in which Burns critiques but also participates in the imagining of the nation and the cultural power which allowed for its construction. But even though Burns foregrounded ambiguity in his poetic aesthetic, attempting to question the political and cultural order, he himself became an instrument of a larger marketing strategy for all of Scotland. In *Poetry as an Occupation and an Art in Britain, 1760–1830*, Peter Murphy examines Burns's attempts to claim his share of the literary market. According to Murphy, "all of Burns' strategies had to negotiate the tricky border between local and general, between coarse Robert Burns and the airy Poetic Plowman. The inevitable flaw in all of his schemes for material advancement is his simultaneous dependence upon and inability to control the appearance of his coarser side" (p. 65).

But Murphy does not consider the wider implications of Burns's desires for economic success, in particular, the implications of Burns's literary success on the place of Scotland in the British cultural realm. Another way of reading this "simultaneous dependence upon and inability to control the appearance of his coarser side" is to see it as Burns's calling into question the basis of both British and Scottish national culture. It is also important to realize that Burns was "recreated" not just by "the literary world" (p. 92) in general, as Murphy suggests, but first and foremost by the Scottish literary world in particular. Furthermore, his re-creation was not just a question of presenting "an inoffensive Burns," who "would not indecently step outside of the circle of refinement" (p. 92); it was also a question of presenting an image of a Burns who would represent an approved Scotland in the cultural realm.

It was the literati of Edinburgh who were largely responsible for Burns's popularity in the British market. Burns was promoted as associated with the rustic, natural world. His poetry inspired a new poetic interest in the language of the common man and a nature from which many people felt increasingly alienated as the population of urban areas grew. Burns became a market commodity, useful in the promotion of the very national coherence which he was in fact questioning. In their concern to promote the literary interests of Scotland, the literati seized upon Burns as a more up-to-date and less suspect natural bard than Ossian; Burns was living proof of his own authenticity. In order to satisfy the criteria for authenticity, however, Burns had to be seen as untutored, unlearned, and unaffected by present-day cares—exactly the way he had been packaged by critics right from the beginning. The first review of Burns's work, in the October 1786 issue of *Edinburgh Magazine*, presents an imagined interview between Burns and a curious critic asking about his background, education, favorite authors, and qualifications for "instructing or entertaining." The reviewer writes an imagined response, putting the words into Burns's mouth in the following catechism: "I am a poor country man; I was bred up at the school of Kilmarnock; I understand no languages but my own. . . . I have not looked on mankind *through the spectacle of books*. . . . Homer and Ossian, for any thing that I have heard, could neither write nor read" (Low, pp. 63–64). The notion of literature providing a spectacle from which the author views the world is reversed in the review; the world looks at the author himself as the spectacle, and his work mirrors what the public wants to see. The review quotes Horace, calling Burns "*Rusticus abnormis sapiens, crassaque Minerva* [a peasant, a philosopher unschooled and of rough mother-wit]" (Low, p. 64). The desire to promote the Scots as innocuous peaceful peasants can be seen in the advice of people like Hugh Blair to Burns regarding leaving out poems like "Love and Liberty" from *Poems, Chiefly in the Scottish Dialect* (R. Crawford, *Devolving*, p. 101).

Henry Mackenzie's review of the *Poems* in the *Lounger* further contributed to Burns's literary success, emphasizing the image of the rural bard. Entitled, "Surprising effects of Original Genius, exemplified in the Poetical Productions of Robert Burns, an Ayrshire Ploughman," this review presented Burns as an unlettered rustic who captured in his poetry "the divinity of genius" that is best seen in "the darkness of distant and remote periods" (Low, p. 67). Burns is regarded as an example of "original man" because he portrayed the way life may have been in an earlier era in the country, closer to nature, away from the busy crowds of the city. For those within the "commerce" of the modern world, reading Burns's poetry could be a way of experiencing a life closer to nature. Mackenzie's concern to promote this vision of a pastoral, peaceful Scotland, but also to indicate his nation's progress, can be seen in his qualification that "Even in Scotland, the provincial dialect which Ramsay and [Burns] have used, is now read with a difficulty which greatly damps the pleasure of the reader" (Low, p. 69). The role of rustic bard written for him by the Scottish reviewers was one that Burns encouraged, however grudgingly, in the effort to ensure his success.

Burns's role as national poet promoting an image of Scotland as a rural paradise of literate peasants continued after his death with James Currie's official collection of poems, letters, and biographical sketch in *Works of Robert Burns* (1800), albeit with moral overtones that suggested that Burns succumbed to his own "sensibility of nerves" (1: 214).[16] Of all the Edinburgh literati, Francis Jeffrey, editor and cocreator of the Whig *Edinburgh Review*, alone seems to have been aware of the negative implications of the association of Burns as a national Scottish poet with the rural and lower classes.[17] Jeffrey's comments on Burns in his January 1809 review of Robert Cromek's *Reliques of Robert Burns* reflect his vision of Scotland's changing role in Great Britain. While promoting a positive image of the Scots, Jeffrey wants to move away from identifying Scotland purely as a rustic wilderness of naive, oatmeal-consuming peasants. Jeffrey claims to want to assess Burns, not for his uniqueness as a peasant ploughman, as other reviewers had done, but for his own merits: "So much indeed are we impressed with a sense of his merits; that we cannot help thinking it a derogation from them to consider him as a prodigy at all; and are convinced that he will never be rightly estimated as a poet, till that vulgar wonder be entirely repressed which was raised on his having been a ploughman" (Low, p. 178). Continuing in this leveling vein, Jeffrey uses Burns to promote the rest of the Scottish population, implying that the remarkable thing is not that Burns became famous, but that the rest of his community did not: "It is evident, from the whole details of his history, as well as from the letters of his brother, and the testimony of Mr. Murdoch and others to the character of his father, that the whole family, and many of their associates, who have never emerged from the native obscurity of their condition, possessed talents, and taste, and intelligence, which are little suspected to lurk in those humble retreats" (Low, p. 194). Burns's epistles, for example,

> all contribute to show, that not only good sense, and enlightened morality, but literature, and talents for speculation, are far more generally diffused in society than is generally imagined; and that the delights and the benefits of these generous and harmonizing pursuits, are by no means confined to those whom leisure and affluence have courted to their enjoyment. (Low, p. 194)

Jeffrey reasons that this sharing of sense, morality, and literature between the classes is "peculiar to Scotland, and may be properly referred to our excellent institutions for parochial education, and to the natural sobriety and prudence of our nation" (Low, pp. 194–95). He does not rule out the possibility of a similar situation's occurring among English peasants, but he does not pursue that track; his concern is with Scotland. Instead of focusing on Burns's poetry as the remarkable effusions of a peasant poet, then, and "admiring it much in the same way as if it had been written with his toes" (Low, p. 181), Jeffrey suggests that Burns is the natural culmination of the talents and self-sufficiency of the Scots.

Jeffrey's comments on the Scottish language are also pertinent to his vision of Scotland's role in Britain. He asserts Scots as a separate language, one that has its own origins, not a derivative of English. The language is indicative of Scotland's separate national identity: "We beg leave too, in passing, to observe, that this Scotch is not to be considered as a provincial dialect, the vehicle only of rustic vulgarity and rude local humour. It is the language of a whole country,—long an independent kingdom, and still separate in laws, character and manners. It is by no means peculiar to the vulgar; but is the common speech of the whole nation in early life,—and with many of its most exalted and accomplished individuals throughout their whole existence" (Low, p. 186). Furthermore, says Jeffrey, "the Scotch is, in reality, a highly poetical language; and . . . it is an ignorant, as well as an illiberal prejudice, which would seek to confound it with the barbarous dialects of Yorkshire or Devon" (Low, pp. 186–87). Burns took more pains with the Scots than with the English, says Jeffrey, and it was a deliberate artistic choice he made. What is interesting, however, is how Jeffrey, even while making sure to praise the Scots language, also registers an awareness of its inappropriateness for the cosmopolitan role Scotland is to play in Britain. In laying out a few abstracts of Burns's poetry to readers, Jeffrey says he "shall be guided more by a desire to exhibit what may be intelligible to all our readers, than by a feeling of what is in itself of the highest excellence" (Low, p. 187). More telling than this bashfulness about the Scots language is the fact that Jeffrey's piece is written in standard English. Jeffrey wants to claim a unique national identity for Scotland based on historical origins at the same time as he desires to escape the marginalization that history has meant for the Scots in Britain.

Here is the paradox of Jeffrey's piece: he wants to promote Scotland, not a Scotland that is associated, as is the Scottish language, with "remembered childhood and domestic affection" (Low, p. 186), but a Scotland that has a place in cosmopolitan Britain. Ultimately, he wants to present a Scottish writer who can direct the cultural systems. Hence, Jeffrey criticizes Burns for his lack of morality and his "ungentlemanly" behavior: Burns "is perpetually making a parade of his thoughtlessness, inflammability and imprudence, and talking with much complacency and exultation of the offence he has occasioned to the sober and correct part of mankind" (Low, p. 183). His "leading vice" is his contempt for "prudence, decency and regularity," and especially his belief in "*the dispensing power* of genius and social feeling, in all matters of morality and common sense" (Low, p. 182). What Jeffrey objects to in Burns, in other words, is his individuality and his refusal to serve as a model for the readers around him. Burns offers an image of the Scots as ex-centrics who defy the center. Jeffrey wants to present an image of the Scots as ex-centrics who *define* the center.

In his review of Burns, Jeffrey writes the script for the role of a Scottish writer who would promote the new image. In fact, he asserts himself as Burns's replacement as the cultural representative of Scotland. Jeffrey's comments about Burns can also be seen as Jeffrey's promotion of himself. In particular, Jeffrey comments at length on the advantages of coming from the geographical and cultural periphery. He destroys the myth of Burns as just an unlettered genius, suggesting rather that Burns's talent was due to the fact that he could read and write without the anxiety of influence that comes from "perusing the most celebrated writers, and conversing with the most intelligent judges":

> The head of such a person [who comes from the center of culture] is filled, of course, with all the splendid passages of antient and modern authors, and with the fine and fastidious remarks which have been made even on these passages. When he turns his eyes, therefore, on his own conceptions, they can scarcely fail to appear rude and contemptible. He is perpetually haunted and depressed by the ideal presence of those great masters and their exacting critics. (Low, p. 179)

What Jeffrey is implying is that the most perceptive observations come not from the center of activity, but from the periphery. Jeffrey's praise for Burns, suggesting that Burns profited from being raised away from the hue and cry of the established literary world, can also be seen as a promotion of himself as a writer of the *Edinburgh Review* writing from his own position removed from the center. However, Jeffrey also distinguishes himself from Burns. By chastising Burns, Jeffrey shows his own moral superiority to the poet. And by writing a review of Burns's work, Jeffrey assumes the position Burns refused: the arbiter of morality and taste. In essence, Jeffrey is preparing the way for a shift in the cultural hegemony. Jeffrey's new world order would see Scotland directing the taste of Great Britain.

Jeffrey concludes his review with "two general remarks—the one national, the other critical" (Low, p. 194). What we see, however, is that both general remarks are national. The first promotes Scotland, the second demotes England. First, Jeffrey suggests that readers cannot read Burns's poetry "without forming a higher idea of the intelligence, taste, and accomplishments of the peasantry" (Low, p. 194)—particularly the Scottish peasantry. Second, he urges readers to compare the naturalness of Burns's poetry with that of the "new school of poetry," the English Lake poets. He contrasts the authentic rustics of Burns's "The Cotter's Saturday Night" with the "hysterical schoolmasters and sententious leech-gatherers" of Wordsworth (Low, p. 195).

It is significant that Jeffrey ends his comments on Burns with pejorative comments about Wordsworth because that Lake poet created an opposite image of Burns, promoting him as a rural Scottish poet and thereby countering Jeffrey's cosmopolitan image of the role of Scotland in Britain. Wordsworth, in his own peripheral position in northern England might, like Burns, have resorted to an assertion of local difference. He might have remained in the situation of border poet. However, Wordsworth was determined to move away from this position. Whatever his political beliefs may have been before 1789, it is clear that Wordsworth's ideals for the British nation were much less radical after the publication of the *Lyrical Ballads* (1798). It became of particular importance to him to create a nation that, unlike France, was free of dangerous differences. This political change had a profound effect on Wordsworth's aesthetics, too, as he became concerned not just with writing poetry, but with attempting to shape his audience. Wordsworth himself said that "every author, as far as he is great and at the same time *original*, has had the task of *creating* the taste by which he is to be enjoyed" (*Prose Works*, 3: 30). Instead of remaining in the contact zone of the border, then, in which the boundaries of England and Scotland, Self and Other, could shift constantly and challenge the center, Wordsworth attempts to establish a center in his work in the figure of the poet. Unlike Burns, who pointed out the disjunctures in national identity, Wordsworth set out to make his readers into a homogeneous and peaceful nation. His aesthetic of universalizing the local as representative of general natural laws served to make him into a popular author and to assimilate his readers by compelling them to follow the moral lead of the poet. Wordsworth was inspired by Burns's representation of the common man and the Scottish countryside. Ultimately, however, Burns came to represent for Wordsworth a difference within Britain which constituted a threat both to his sense of the nation and to his sense of his poetic Self.

Wordsworth's negotiations with Burns are reflected in *Lyrical Ballads* in the way in which Wordsworth embraces Burns's ideas, but differentiates his

own aesthetic from that of Burns. Russell Noyes has traced the specific in-
fluences of Burns on Wordsworth, noting more generally that Wordsworth
considered the work of the Scottish poet (along with that of Cowper) important enough to learn by heart (p. 813). Mary Jacobus suggests that "Burns
must be the most important influence on Wordsworth's writing" (p. 90).
Certainly, for Wordsworth, Burns offered a model of how to speak a "natural
language" of men in "low and rustic life." Wordsworth echoes the sentiments
Burns expressed. In "Epistle to John Lapraik," Burns had declared conventional education a waste of time: "Give me one spark o' Nature's fire / That's
all the learning I desire" (ll. 73–74). Wordsworth writes in "The Tables
Turned":

> Books! 'tis a dull and endless strife:
> Come, hear the woodland linnet,
> How sweet his music! on my life,
> There's more of wisdom in it.
>   . . .
> Come forth into the light of things,
> Let Nature be your Teacher.
>
> *(ll. 9–16)*

   Instead of merely reiterating Burns's sentiments, however, Wordsworth effects a refashioning of Burns's ideas of the common man. In his *Commonplace
Book*, Burns comments that he writes down his thoughts and poems because
"it may be some entertainment to a curious observer of human nature to see
how a ploughman thinks and feels under the pressure of Love, Ambition,
Anxiety, Grief" (*Works*, 3: 968). Burns suggests that "like cares and passions . . . however diversified by the modes and manners of life, operate
pretty much alike . . . in all Species" (3: 968). According to Burns, then,
everyone has the same capacity to feel. Wordsworth's interpretation of feeling
is invested in a different kind of politics, however. In the 1800 preface to the
Lyrical Ballads, he begins by asserting, unlike Burns, that in "Low and rustic
life," "the passions of the heart find a *better* soil in which they can attain maturity, are less under restraint, and speak a plainer and more emphatic language" (*Prose Works*, 1: 124, my italics). In rural conditions, he continues, "our
elementary natures exist in a state of greater simplicity, and consequently may
be more accurately contemplated and more forcibly communicated," because
passions "are incorporated with the beautiful and permanent forms of nature" (*Prose Works*, 1: 124). Wordsworth considers a ploughman to feel a
keener sense of the "Love, Ambition, Anxiety, Grief" than Burns's egalitarian

notions of sentiment would allow. But Wordsworth's glorification of the common man becomes inverted by his assertion that it takes a poet to appreciate this deep feeling. Where Burns offers an unexpurgated version of the sentiments of the common man, Wordsworth maintains that the language of the common man, even if it expresses the essential passions of the heart more than any other kind of language, must be filtered through the consciousness of the poet: "All good poetry is the spontaneous overflow of powerful feelings; but though this be true, Poems to which any value can be attached, were never produced on any variety of subjects but by a man who being possessed of more than usual organic sensibility had also thought long and deeply" (*Prose Works*, 1: 126). Emotion must be initially experienced by a poet and then "recollected in tranquillity" (*Prose Works*, 1: 148) so that ordinary things can be presented to the mind in an unusual way. Although Wordsworth asserts directly that the poet is a man speaking to other men, the argument of the preface suggests the contrary. The Wordsworthian poet acts as a creative medium, affecting and effecting the transmission of the image to the reader. Burns was seen to be offering an immediate picture of the land and people he described. Wordsworth in his poetry and criticism stresses mediation, emphasizing the importance of return, of revision, and of re-creation. Although his poetic manifesto gestures toward an equality between poet, reader, and common man, breaking out of the bounds of Augustan verse, in fact, it reinstitutes a poetics of power aligned with knowledge. Wordsworth's readers, like Fielding's, are assimilated by being guided by the author through their common experience of reading.

Wordsworth's refashioning of Burns and of Scottish material in the process of establishing his career after the *Lyrical Ballads* emphasizes his concern about difference within Britain, a concern that must have increased with the establishment of Napoléon as emperor and with France's conquests. Scotland and Burns symbolize a difference within Britain, which Wordsworth both acknowledges and attempts to deny by incorporating it into a universal scheme. His first tour of Scotland occurred in 1803, a year after he returned to France during the Peace of Amiens. Inspired, it would seem, by a desire to discover for himself the far regions of Britain, the nation he had now embraced wholeheartedly, Wordsworth makes his survey of Scotland serve as an antidote to the political mayhem of Europe.[18] The poems inspired by Wordsworth's first Scottish tour were published in *Poems, in Two Volumes* in 1807, a work divided into a number of sections. The arrangement of poems in the two volumes seems somewhat arbitrary, but there is a recurrent theme: the importance of the local objects is emphasized when seen in the context of national and historical events. The local is seen as natural and ahistorical and therefore preferable, and nature triumphs over history in the course of the two volumes. Wordsworth's tour of the country north of the Tweed allows him to observe difference, but also to absorb it into philosophical reflections on the relation between humanity and nature.

Volume 1 consists of four parts: an untitled group of poems concerned with nature, but ending abruptly with the stern "Ode to Duty"; "Poems, Composed During a Tour, Chiefly on Foot"; and a section of sonnets, including "Miscellaneous Sonnets" and "Sonnets Dedicated to Liberty." It ends with concerns about the European wars and the threat of political difference—but the threat is expressed chiefly in terms of the psychological impact on the individual. The poem "There is a bondage which is worse to bear" suggests the dissolution of personal integrity that can result from national conflict:

> There is a bondage which is worse to bear
> Than his who breathes, by roof, and floor, and wall,
> Pent in, a Tyrant's solitary Thrall:
> 'Tis his who walks about in the open air,
> One of a Nation who, henceforth, must wear
> Their fetters in their Souls. For who could be,
> Who, even the best, in such condition, free
> From self-reproach, reproach which he must share
> With Human Nature?
>
> *(ll. 1–9)*

"November, 1806," the last sonnet of the series dedicated to liberty, also translates political struggles into a struggle in human nature. It leaves the reader with the suggestion, "That in ourselves our safety must be sought" (l. 6).

Volume 2 provides the answer to these disturbing international and national affairs. The tour of Scotland and the changing of Scottish material into poetry of sensibility present a welcome way of finding the "safety" "in ourselves," concentrating on the beauty of nature and humans in a natural world and in the British nation; significantly, "Poems Written During a Tour in Scotland" is followed by "Moods of My Own Mind." Together they echo the themes of liberty and nature from the first volume, although now transferred into the mind of the poet. The final section, "The Blind Highland Boy, with Other Poems," provides an incorporation of the Scottish tour and the sensibility of "Moods" into the general theme of the benevolence of nature.

In order to highlight the theme of national unification, the "Poems Written During a Tour in Scotland" must integrate Scotland into England by erasing the specific history of Scotland and by universalizing Scottish scenery into general nature. The subject of Scottish history has been raised in a peculiar way in the "Sonnets Dedicated to Liberty" section in the twenty-fourth poem, "October, 1803," about the battle at Killiecrankie. This poem describes the conflict between the Williamite troops and the Highland Jacobites in 1689 as one between "Veterans practis'd in War's game" (l. 1) and "Shepherds and Herdsmen" (l. 4). Ironically, in the poem, Wordsworth wishes for a leader like the Jacobite Dundee, for then "Like conquest would the Men of England see" (l. 13) over their foes. Wordsworth's desire for a commander like Dundee co-opts the Scottish past of conflict with England into a unified present, an important gesture given the fear of possible French invasion through Scotland.

The first of the "Poems Written During a Tour in Scotland," "Rob Roy's Grave," further erases the Scottish past. Wordsworth himself says he will eschew giving the details of the story because "the History of Rob Roy is sufficiently known" (*Poems, in Two Volumes*, p. 179). An active participant in history, Rob Roy, is reduced to a marker on a "Traveller's" journey, part of the geography of the "Highlands of Scotland." In fact, Rob becomes a marker for Wordsworth's poetic journey, too. Wordsworth describes Rob Roy's aspirations to return to a "moral creed" without statutes or laws:

> Said generous Rob, "What need of Books?
> "Burn all the Statutes and their shelves:
> "They stir us up against our Kind;
>   "And worse, against Ourselves.
>
> *(ll. 21–24)*

Rob Roy's desire to return to nature's law echoes Rob Burns's desire to move away from books. And Wordsworth shows Rob Roy's aspirations to be failures also. According to Wordsworth, Rob Roy's problem in carrying out his plan was that he was out of step with the new economic system. He "came an age too late" (l. 64), and the "rents and Factors" and "rights of chace" (l. 69) then predominated. But Wordsworth uses Rob Roy, as he does Burns, for his own purpose. Instead of Rob Roy's teaching the world a lesson in morals, the task is taken up by Wordsworth, who teaches not through destroying books in favor of live examples, but through selecting his words and putting them in books. Wordsworth's shift to the subject matter of Scotland has wider implications, too. He draws a comparison between Robin Hood, who is "The English Ballad-singer's joy" (l. 2) and Rob Roy, in a sense negating the difference between the Scottish and English past. Both heroes are appropriate grist for the lyrical balladeer's mill. In fact, in line 109, Wordsworth refers to Rob Roy as "Robin." Furthermore, in writing about the Scottish hero, Wordsworth lays his own claim to that cultural tradition, proving himself "A Poet worthy of Rob Roy" (l. 15). In the rest of the sequence on Scotland, we see other examples of Wordsworth honing his poetic skills by absorbing and re-creating Scottish material.

In "Glen-Almain, or the Narrow Glen," written about the mythical burial site of another Scottish figure, the poet Ossian, Wordsworth places himself in a position to supplant Ossian. The speaker in the poem praises Ossian for his portrayal of stormy battles and notes that it would be more appropriate if the poet's final resting place were less tranquil. Wordsworth comments that Ossian is the poet of "every thing unreconciled" (l. 12) and invites the reader to compare his own sense of tranquillity with the turbulence of his predecessor. Although Ossian, the "last of all his race" (l. 31) is buried in a place "remote from men" (l. 1), the English poet emerges as the possessor of the sensibility to distinguish something "deeper" than silence (l. 26).

For Wordsworth, Scotland offers an alien landscape which has to be interpreted by the Traveler, who is given "spiritual right" to travel there, like the speaker in "Stepping Westward" (l. 15). This mediation, in which the poet generalizes the local into scenes of universal nature is seen in "The Solitary Reaper," inspired by a line in the manuscript version of *Tours to the British Mountains* (finally published in 1824) by Thomas Wilkinson, another English tourist. Wordsworth introduces a distancing into his poem directly by indicating not only his own presence in the scene, but that of the reader, to whom he addresses his introductory imperative: "Behold her, single in the field / Yon solitary Highland Lass" (ll. 1–2). The poem emphasizes that she is "solitary" and "single in the field," unlike the workers Burns often describes who work in pairs or groups. Although Wordsworth asks, "Will no one tell me what she sings?" (l. 17), not understanding the girl because she is singing in Gaelic, he proceeds to speculate on what her song might be about. It is not the specific meaning of the song that interests him, but the potentiality of finding meaning in it. He imagines that she is singing either of "old, unhappy far-off things / And battles long ago" (ll. 19–20) or of "familiar matter of today"— "natural sorrow, loss, or pain, / That has been, and may be again!" (ll. 23–24). In Wordsworth's representation, the reader experiences the thrill of the tourist, alienated from the landscape of work like the travelers in the "shady haunts" of Arabia described in the poem. Wordsworth further distances the scene through metaphor, comparing his singer to birds in anomalous situations: a nightingale in the sands of Arabia and a cuckoo off the farthest Hebrides. Her habitat, like her speech, is strange enough that it can be altered in the imagination of the poet. In "The Solitary Reaper," then, Wordsworth transcends the specific location of Scotland, rendering the scene strange, so that the reader's experience of it demands mediation, or translation, by the poet.[19]

There are similar occurrences of translation in "The Matron of Jedburgh and her Husband" and "To A Highland Girl." In the former, it is the poet who is able to perceive the spirit in the Matron, but only because he is outside the scene. In the latter, the girl's "Benignity and home-bred sense" (l. 24) is visible only in contrast to the "maidenly shamefacedness" (l. 29) which the speaker expects. He notes his desire to "have / Some claim upon thee, if I could, / Though but of common neighbourhood" (ll. 54–56). In the course of the poem, he stakes his claim as he forms the girl into a representation of an unchanging memory for him, which he bears away as "recompence." The girl herself becomes superfluous in this transaction, as the poet returns to his own reflection in tranquillity. "Yarrow Unvisited," the final poem in the Scottish sequence, completes the erasure of Scotland into nature, but this time it is not actual nature, but nature as a construct imagined by the poet. He rejects the actual scene of the famous Braes in favor of his own imagination:

> "Be Yarrow Stream unseen, unknown!
> "It must, or we shall rue it:
> "We have a vision of our own;
> "Ah! why should we undo it?
>
> *(ll. 49–52)*

Furthermore, while Wordsworth supplants the actual Scottish landscape with a scene from his imagination, he also supplants Scottish literature with his own poem. "Yarrow Unvisited" begins with a quotation from the "Ballad of Hamilton," and the speaker in the poem employs dialect phrases from the ballad: "*frae* Selkirk Town" and "Winsome marrow," for example. These literary borrowings serve to incorporate Scotland into the poem.

The journey through Scotland is ultimately designed to foster the growth of the poet's mind, to make him not only a "Poet worthy of Rob Roy," but also worthy to write of all the matter of Scotland and to integrate it poetically, and thus politically, within England. Moreover, Wordsworth's poems on Scotland are designed to instruct readers to use the poet as mediator. "Departure from the Vale of Grasmere, August, 1803," written retrospectively sometime after 1811, represents this kind of poetic colonization of Scotland. Wordsworth presents Scotland as a Miltonic chaos, a tract "of darkness and of cold" (l. 10). The English poet can travel into this chaos, extracting "luxuries . . . from bleakest moors" (l. 26) all the while, but only because he begins and ends his journey from the safe moral position of the "Elysian plains" of Grasmere. Accordingly, the reader uses the poet as guide through this unfamiliar territory.

Yet such an achievement of extracting the matter of Scotland is possible for Wordsworth only if he imagines the lack of an actual Scottish writer to perform the task of writing Scotland: specifically, if he imagines the death of Robert Burns.[20] The "Poems Written During a Tour in Scotland" are haunted by the trace of Burns, so much so that Burns is made present by his absence. Burns appears in the first volume, when Wordsworth refers to him glowingly in "Resolution and Independence" as "Him who walked in glory and in joy / Following his plough along the mountainside" (ll. 45–46). But Wordsworth neglects to give his Scottish counterpart a name. The "Poems Written During a Tour in Scotland" lead up to the grave of the Scottish poet before the final imaginative leap to Yarrow, but even at the scene of confrontation, Burns is omitted. Instead, the poem written at the grave is for his sons: "Address to the Sons of Burns after Visiting their Father's Grave (August 14, 1803)."

According to John Rudy, Burns's grave offered a place where Wordsworth could "meditate upon the connection between individual suffering and cosmic process" (p. 641). Jeffrey Robinson suggests further that Wordsworth's tour of Scotland presented an opportunity for Wordsworth to grapple with the legacy of his poetic father in order to assert his own creative ego. For Robinson, the Scottish poems are a battlefield on which Wordsworth proves his value by silencing Burns. In Robinson's analysis, Burns appears as the father whom Wordsworth must kill off before he can achieve poetic maturity. But Burns represents more than this. He also represents the difference of Scotland which Wordsworth seeks both to deny and to absorb. Burns's political threat is signaled by his association with Napoléon. "Address to the Sons of Burns after Visiting their Father's Grave (August 14, 1803)" calls attention to the date on which Wordsworth's visit took place, which is, significantly, the day after Napoléon's birthday. The Scottish poet is associated with a similar kind of disruption that Napoléon represented. By turning Burns's graveside into the scene of Burns's moral testing and subsequent failure, Wordsworth seeks to eliminate the challenge that Burns represents. "Address to the Sons of Burns" advocates an imaginative killing of the father, as Wordsworth urges the sons to be different from their father. He warns the sons that there are those who will use Burns's name to "make / a snare for [them]" (ll. 17–18). The last phrase of the poem, however—"be admonish'd by his Grave, / And think, and fear!" (ll. 23–24)—suggests Wordsworth's awareness of the continuation of the threat of the "Father's name" (l. 17).

Notably, Wordsworth leaves out "At the Grave of Burns" from this edition. The exposure of his own "wishes and . . . fear" (l. 11) which the "Spirit fierce" (l. 1) of Burns calls forth constituted too unsettling a portrayal, one that Wordsworth would avoid until 1842.[21] Wordsworth's concern in the "Poems Written During a Tour in Scotland" is after all to translate difference, historical and geographical, into common terms through the mediation of the poet, so that with the appearance of "The Blind Highland Boy," in the next section, the reader can feel that the material of Scotland has been successfully transformed into a representation of universal maternal affection. In that poem, Scotland is both deliciously foreign—"In land where many a mountain towers, / Far higher than these hills of ours!" (ll. 13–14)—and comfortably assimilable into a "Tale told by the [presumably English] fireside" (p. 221).

It is crucial to understand Wordsworth's concern about his relationship to Burns and about the relationship of Scotland within Britain in wider terms, however, as connected with his anxiety about the power of Scottish writers in the British cultural realm. At the same time that Wordsworth was assimilating Scotland figuratively in his poetry, Scottish writers were exerting control over the British literary market. While not scotophobic as such, Wordsworth was concerned about marketing his work and was all too conscious of the threat to the sales of his poetry coming from the Scottish front. Wordsworth's concerns about the literary marketplace were particularly relevant in this era, when, as Leslie Chard notes, due to "the increasing cost of goods, the mechanization of the printing industry, and an enormous increase in the size and an equivalent change in the taste of the reading public," "competition for authors and readers" in the book trade increased enormously (pp. 139, 150). The Scots had already made their mark on the market for literature in the area of book publishing and selling and had a reputation as a kind of literary mafia. As Patricia Srebrnik notes, "London had long been filling with Scottish publishers" like Andrew Millar, William Strahan, and John Murray, who "changed his name from McMurray in an attempt to deflect anti-Scottish prejudice" (p. 10).[22] Others, although they were based in Scotland, made their presence most strongly felt in London: "Blackwoods, Chamberses, Blacks, Constables, Collinses, and many other firms based in Edinburgh or Glasgow maintained London offices" (Srebrnik, p. 11). John Feather comments on the effect of these Scottish-based booksellers: "In the first two decades of the nineteenth century, four Scottish houses . . . represented the first serious and sustained challenge to London's domination of British publishing" (*History*, p. 122). In addition, Scots had been among the most adamant supporters of limited copyright. They had much to gain from a shorter copyright period. According to Trevor Ross, the decision in favor of limited copyright that resulted from the Donaldson / Beckett trial of 1774 was "a source of much resentment for Wordsworth, who, throughout his career, petitioned for the reinstitution of perpetual copyright" (p. 17).[23] Donaldson was, of course, a Scot.

In addition to the threat Scottish booksellers posed to Wordsworth's poetic career, there was also the matter of Scottish writers, in particular Scott and Byron. In a letter to Samuel Rogers, dated May 5, 1814, for example, Wordsworth compares the popularity of Scott and Byron with his own relative obscurity, lamenting, "for [with] Mr. Scott and your friend Lord B. flourishing at the rate they do, how can an honest Poet hope to thrive?" (*Letters: The Middle Years*, 3: 148). The phrase "honest Poet" is an echo of his letter to Catherine Clarkson written on New Year's Day 1814, in which he comments on Jeffrey's review of *The Excursion* and urges Clarkson to procure positive reviews of the poem in "the Philanthropist or any well circulated Periodical Publication to which you may have easy access." He admonishes her: "you see as the evil spirits are rouzed it becomes the good ones to stir, or what is to become of the poor Poet and his Labours?" (*Letters: The Middle Years*, 3: 182–83). He suggests that his enterprise, unlike Byron's or Scott's, is real poetry. Although Scott was a friend of his, Wordsworth could not entirely conceal his contempt for the style of writing of the Author of Waverley. Wordsworth again expresses a pejorative view of Scottish writing in his letter to R. P. Gillies of February 14, 1815. Here Wordsworth directs his comments to the inadequacies of Scottish authors, remarking, "what a hobbling pace the Scottish Pegasus seems to have adopted in these days" (*Letters: The Middle Years*, 3: 197). He decries the "insupportable slovenliness and neglect of syntax and *grammar*, by which James Hogg's writings are disfigured," and he comments that such errors are "excusable in him from his education, but Walter Scott knows, and ought to do, better" (*Letters: The Middle Years*, 3: 196). He notes of the writing of James Hogg and Walter Scott: "They neither of them write a language which has any pretension to be called English" (*Letters: The Middle Years*, 2: 196–97). In such comments, Wordsworth conflates his economic anxieties with national prejudices.

Wordsworth continued to be aware of Scottish influence in book publishing and writing, but it was a particular critical piece of Jeffrey's that occupied Wordsworth in the year in which he wrote his own review of Burns, the *Letter to a Friend of Robert Burns*. Jeffrey had included a review of *The Excursion* in the November 1814 *Edinburgh Review*, which began with the memorable statement, "This will never do." *The Excursion*, of course, did not do. Or at least, it did not do as well as Wordsworth had hoped. Defending his long (and expensive) work, Wordsworth called Jeffrey a "Coxcomb" and an "Aristarch" and declared he was glad to have had such a negative review, because now Jeffrey "will have the mortification of seeing a book enjoy a high reputation, to which he has not contributed" (*Letters:The Middle Years*, 3: 179–80). Nevertheless, Wordsworth's letters indicate that to a large degree he blamed Jeffrey's infamous review for *The Excursion*'s poor sales. Wordsworth's reactions to Burns can be seen as a reflection of his continuing animosity toward Jeffrey and the cultural shifts that were being implemented by North Britons.

Wordsworth makes the assimilation of Scotland part of his deliberate aesthetic program as his career progresses. In *Poems, 1815*, he shows a desire to fashion an English aesthetic, one that either excludes or subsumes Scotland and Scottish writing. *Poems, 1815*, demonstrates Wordsworth's growing concern to shape a nation of readers, as in the "Essay, Supplementary to the Preface" in that work he acknowledges how the interpretation of literature may be manipulated to advance ideological interests. He notes, "So strange indeed are the obliquities of admiration, that they whose opinions are much influenced by authority will often be tempted to think that there are no fixed principles in human nature for this art to rest upon" (*Prose Works*, 3:71). Getting one's work of literature accepted, then, becomes a strategic play for power: "Genius is the introduction of a new element into the intellectual universe: or, if that be not allowed, it is the application of powers to objects on which they had not before been exercised, or the employment of them in such a manner as to produce effects hitherto unknown. What is all this but an advance, or a conquest, made by the soul of the poet?" (*Prose Works*, 3: 82). Again, we see the language of government, and in this case of empire, employed to discuss literature: "Is it to be supposed that the reader can make progress of this kind, like an Indian prince or general—stretched on his palanquin, and borne by his slaves? No; he is invigorated and inspirited by his leader, in order that he may exert himself. . . . Therefore to create taste is to call forth and bestow power, of which knowledge is the effect." (*Prose Works*, 3: 82).

Wordsworth suggests a parallel between literary activity and empire building and sets out to provide a route map through English literature, to build the foundation of national taste. He is determined to redraw incorrect maps of the past and, in particular, to incorporate Scotland, as we see in his remark in the letter to R. P. Gillies regarding the "Essay": "You will find a few hits at certain celebrated names of Scotland, I do not mean persons now living" (*Letters:The Middle Years*, 2: 196). He wants to identify authentic national poets and to comment on those works that have demonstrated poetic genius in the past—the correct boundaries of the nation—and to expose those works that owed their popularity to a manipulation of the reading public—the false boundaries of genius. His "Essay" attempts to show the discrepancy between critical praise for literary works and their actual value. In addition, in the "Essay," he seems to want to set the Scots in their place. A major source of Wordsworth's anti-Scottish sentiments is James Macpherson, as the *Poems of Ossian* come in for particularly pointed invective. Macpherson's work is depicted as a bastard of literature: "The Phantom [Ossian] was begotten by the snug embrace of an impudent Highlander upon a cloud of tradition—it travelled southward, where it was greeted with acclamation, and the thin Consistence took its course through Europe" (*Prose Works*, 3: 77). According to Wordsworth, even if Macpherson's derivation of his poems was authentic, his imagery would be spurious because his art is too far removed from life. Wordsworth notes that, whereas in nature, "everything is distinct, yet nothing defined into absolute independent singleness," in Macpherson's work "it is exactly the reverse; every thing (that is not stolen) is in this manner defined, insulated, dislocated, deadened,—yet nothing distinct. It will always be so when words are substituted for things" (*Prose Works*, 3: 77). Wordsworth's denunciation of Macpherson echoes Defoe's comments on the insubstantiality of Belhaven's conjurings. To finish his expulsion of Macpherson from the canon, Wordsworth announces that the poems of Ossian "have been wholly uninfluential upon the literature of the Country. No succeeding writer appears to have caught from them a ray of inspiration" (*Prose Works*, 3: 78). He concludes, "This incapacity to amalgamate with the literature of the Island, is, in my estimation, a decisive proof that the book [*Poems of Ossian*] is essentially unnatural" (*Prose Works*, 3: 78). Again, Wordsworth's evaluations establish the dominance of England when he suggests, "Contrast, in this respect, the effect of Macpherson's publications with the Reliques of Percy, so unassuming, so modest in their pretensions!" (*Prose Works*, 3: 78). In *Poems, 1815*, Wordsworth also rearranged the Scottish pieces, adding one extra poem on Scotland, "Yarrow Visited," but eliminating the poems' specific Scottishness by mixing them into categories like "Poems Founded on the Affections" and "Poems of the Imagination." Exclusion and amalgamation seem to be the two possibilities for Scottish literature in Wordsworth's new English canon.

A year later, in his *Letter to a Friend of Robert Burns* (1816), Wordsworth comes back to the haunting presence of Burns, performing just such an amalgamation and exclusion of the Scottish poet that he had mapped out in the "Essay." Wordsworth composed the *Letter* after James Gray sent him a copy of Alexander Peterkin's 1815 *Review of the Life of Burns*. Peterkin included a preface with evidence "in refutation of some foul charges against the moral qualities of BURNS, and his poetry, which have of late been propagated" (ix). Gilbert Burns was interested in publishing a new account of his brother's life and applied to Wordsworth for advice. In his *Letter*, Wordsworth suggests that Gilbert could remedy the slur on his brother's reputation in Currie's *Works* by publishing the poems before the sketch and by writing a condensed version of Burns's biography himself. Gilbert and James Gray had hoped for a strong statement from Wordsworth. They were sorely disappointed, for instead of offering a vindication of Burns, Wordsworth seems to confirm his crimes. Wordsworth's reaction to Burns in his *Letter* can in fact be seen as a statement of the English poet's aesthetic of promoting the universal over the local. Wordsworth's protests are aimed not at Currie's biographical sketch of Burns, but at the fact that Currie would publish such intimate details; Currie was in his own words an "entire stranger" to Burns. Wordsworth performs an equally destructive postmortem on Burns as did Currie, one disguised as being interested in the poet's aesthetic sensibility, but one that ultimately condemns him. Behind Wordsworth's own comments on Burns we can also sense his reaction to Jeffrey's exercise of power over the literary market. Using the figure of Burns, Wordsworth attempts to reassert control of the marketplace by marginalizing Scotland. Such an assertion only thinly disguises the underlying anxieties.

Wordsworth praises Burns for his ability to convey his closeness to his subject matter: "Neither the subjects of his poems, nor his manner of handling them, allow us long to forget their author. On the basis of his human character he has reared a poetic one, which with more or less distinctness presents itself to view in almost every part of his earlier, and, in my estimation, most valuable verses" (*Prose Works*, 3: 123). He also writes that Burns "avail[s] himself of his own character and situation in society, to construct out of them a poetic self,—introduced as a dramatic personage—for the purposes of inspiriting his incidents, diversifying his pictures, recommending his opinions, and giving point to his sentiments" (*Prose Works*, 3: 125). This praise quickly turns into an analysis of Burns's problem, however. Essentially, suggests Wordsworth, Burns did not distinguish carefully enough between art and life. This made it too easy for him to give way to the "impulses of nature, both with reference to himself and in describing the condition of others" (*Prose Works*, 3: 124). Wordsworth's final analysis of Burns is that there is much merit in his poems, but that their usefulness depends on their interpretation by the reader: Burns can "put the reader into possession of [intelligent] sympathy," qualifying him for "exercising a salutary influence over the minds of those who are thus deplorably enslaved" (*Prose Works*, 3: 124). In other words, the real work of Burns's poems goes on outside the poem in the mind of the reader.

In the *Letter to a Friend of Robert Burns*, Burns's failings are traced to the fact that he was too responsive to the "impulses of nature," lacking reason and tranquil reflection to buffer him. Although professing disagreement with Currie, Wordsworth essentially concurs with the assessment of Burns's weakness that Currie offered. And by emphasizing the frailties of Burns, Wordsworth also establishes himself as an authority and a better poet. Burns was too enmeshed in the matter of Scotland to be universal and objective; in contrast, Wordsworth cultivates his own image as a poet who speaks from the "general heart" of men. The *Letter* suggests a view of Burns as a poet whose chief claim to genius lay in his ability to respond to "impulses of nature," but who was ultimately undone by an inability to distinguish between those impulses in life and art. Taken further, Wordsworth's interpretation of Burns implies that anyone who identifies himself as a Scot is incapable of making judgments based on true taste and imagination. This is opposite to Jeffrey's claim that it is precisely a Scot, a person on the periphery, who is most capable of objective thinking because he has not been corrupted by the tired culture of the metropolis.

Wordsworth shifts, in what he describes as a transition "too natural to require an apology" (*Prose Works*, 3: 128), to an ad hominem attack on Jeffrey. The excuse for this attack is Jeffrey's assessment of Burns. Wordsworth quotes Jeffrey's comment that Burns's vices "have communicated to a great part of his productions a character of immorality at once contemptible and hateful" (*Prose Works*, 3: 126). According to Wordsworth, Jeffrey's problem, it seems, like Burns's, centers on an inability to separate art and nature, or in Jeffrey's case, the poem from the poet. Behind the disagreement with Jeffrey's view of Burns, however, we can see the real issues. What Wordsworth particularly reacts against is Jeffrey's power to influence the reading population, his audacity in "framing a summary of the contents of volumes that are scattered over every quarter of the globe, and extant in almost every cottage of Scotland" (*Prose Works*, 3: 127). Jeffrey is a "persevering Aristarch" who uses every "original work of genius" which comes before him to "re-proclaim to the world the narrow range of his own comprehension" (*Prose Works*, 3: 127). Yet although he noted Burns's ungentlemanliness, Jeffrey was on the whole favorably disposed to Burns's poetry. Wordsworth, then, is responding not so much to Jeffrey's view of Burns, but to Jeffrey's view of Wordsworth, and, most recently, of *The Excursion*.

What is particularly interesting in Wordsworth's comments about Jeffrey is the analogy Wordsworth draws between reviewing literature and shaping the state. Employing the language of government and of law, Wordsworth objects that Jeffrey was "self-elected into the office of a public judge of the literature and life of his contemporaries" (*Prose Works*, 3: 127) and compares him to two

men who controlled the political destiny of France: Napoléon (the "intoxi-
cated despot") and Robespierre. Although Wordsworth admits that comparing "these redoubtable enemies of mankind with the anonymous conductor
of a perishable publication" may seem absurd, he nevertheless affirms that
"the moving spirit is the same in them all" and that they operate in the same
way: "by professions of reverence for truth, and concern for duty—carried to
the giddiest heights of ostentation, while practice seems to have no other re-
liance than on the omnipotence of falsehood" (*Prose Works*, 3: 128). In this hy-
perbolic comparison, however, we sense that the deep concern Wordsworth
had in how the fate of the nation is tied in with the fate of its literature. Burns
provided an effective subject through which to explore that connection.

Wordsworth's final view of Burns, and, arguably, of Scotland, is found in
two poems not published until 1842 and later included in *Memorials of a Tour
of Scotland, 1803*, in 1845: "At the Grave of Burns, 1803, Seven Years after his
Death," which was composed on the spot, and "Thoughts Suggested the Day
Following, on the Banks of Nith, near the Poet's Residence," which was partially composed at the time but completed later. Both work to translate
Burns out of the actual circumstances of his life into "the general heart of
men" ("Thoughts," l. 47). "At the Grave of Burns" presents an ambivalent relationship between the dead Scottish poet and the English poet who comes
to pay him tribute. The "Spirit fierce and bold" (l. 1) of Burns oppresses the
beholder of his grave, arousing mixed feelings of both "wishes" and "fear."
Wordsworth seeks to take possession of the body and spirit of Burns. He
draws attention to the similarity between himself and Burns: "Neighbours we
were, and loving friends / We might have been" (ll. 41–42). But he also establishes the difference between them; they might have been "True friends
though diversely inclined" (l. 43). Wordsworth suggests his debt to Burns:

> I mourned with thousands, but as one
> More deeply grieved, for He was gone
> Whose light I hailed when first it shone
>   And showed my youth
> How Verse may build a princely throne
>   On humble truth.

> *(ll. 31–36)*

But what is interesting here is how Wordsworth both praises Burns as his literary predecessor and also sets out the major criterion that elevates his poetic
aesthetic over that of Burns: according to Wordsworth, a poet must have the
capacity to feel "more deeply" than the common man. Though he and Burns

might have been "True friends" joined "heart with heart and mind with mind" (l. 44), it is ultimately the English poet who extracts the moral message from the scene. As he leaves the grave, he half-creates and half-perceives a universal spirit in place of the actual Spirit of Burns:

> Sighing I turned away; but ere
> Night fell I heard, or seemed to hear,
> Music that sorrow comes not near,
>   A ritual hymn,
> Chanted in love that casts out fear
>   By Seraphim.
>
> *(ll. 79–84)*

"Thoughts Suggested the Day Following" completes the translation of Burns into a Wordsworthian universal image. Wordsworth leaves the scene of the grave and literally takes the place of Burns, walking along the same pathways as the poet while reading with "his Book in hand" (l. 27). Burns becomes common property:

> What need of fields in some far clime
> Where Heroes, Sages, Bards sublime,
> And all that fetched the flowing rhyme
>   From genuine springs,
> Shall dwell together till old Time
>   Folds up his wings?
>
> *(ll. 49–54)*

Although he suggests that he is at the "command" of "each sweet Lay" of Burns, in fact it is Wordsworth who has the power here, the power to generalize Burns out of the specific location of Scotland into a universal reference point:

> But why to Him confine the prayer,
> When kindred thoughts and yearnings bear
> On the frail heart the purest share
>   With all that live?—
> The best of what we do and are,
>   Just God, forgive?
>
> *(ll. 61–66)*

Looking back in 1842 on his discovery of Burns, Wordsworth suggests that, along with Cowper and Percy, Burns helped save him from the evils of Continental aesthetics. Burns's writing, along with Percy's *Reliques of Ancient English Poetry* (which I will examine further in Chapter 5), "powerfully counteracted the mischievous influence of Darwin's dazzling manner, the extravagance of the earlier dramas of Schiller, and that of other German writers upon my taste and nature [sic] tendencies" (Low, p. 163). Wordsworth indicates a concern to protect British writers of the future from foreign contamination, adding, "may these few words serve as a warning to youthful Poets who are in danger of being carried away by the inundation of foreign literature, from which our own is at present suffering so much, both in style and points of far greater moment" (Low, p. 163). Like Edward Young, Thomas Gray, and William Collins, Wordsworth was interested in finding an original poetry to save literature in England from falling into foreign debt. Burns represented an answer to this dilemma, although only after his presence had been thoroughly subjected to Wordsworth's process of mediation. Through Wordsworth's mediation, Burns and Scotland become, like the Lake District which Wordsworth presented to British readers in his *Guide to the Lakes*, "a sort of national property, in which every man has a right and interest who has an eye to perceive and a heart to enjoy" (*Prose Works*, 2: 225). In his representation of Burns and of Scotland throughout his long career, Wordsworth creates his idea of the homogeneous nation, united under the guidance of the poet.

This chapter has concentrated on the debate on the role of Scotland in the British cultural realm in the beginning of the nineteenth century. Burns himself attempted to redefine both British and Scottish cultural identity, but he was refashioned by Scottish literati who were eager to promote their own image of a unique Scottish culture within a unified Britain. Consequently, Wordsworth capitalized on their image of Burns as an inspired peasant in order to fix the place of Burns and of Scotland during a time when Scottish writers, publishers, and reviewers were controlling the literary market.[24] As will be seen in the concluding chapter, the comparison of Burns and Wordsworth by nineteenth-century critics came to play an important part in the construction of the canon of English literature.

CHAPTER 5

Citing the Nation: Thomas Percy's and Walter Scott's Minstrel Ballads

This chapter explores Walter Scott's reconfiguration of the relationship between Scotland and England within British literature a century after the Union. Within the large corpus of Scott's work, I have chosen to focus on Scott's first substantial published project addressing the subject of Scotland within Britain, *The Minstrelsy of the Scottish Border* (1801–3), and on the 1830 republication of that work with two new introductory essays. I want to examine Scott's perspective in the two versions of the *Minstrelsy* as a negotiation both with his two Scottish predecessors examined in earlier chapters, Macpherson and Burns, and with the English antiquarian Thomas Percy. In promoting his particular view of Scotland within Britain in the 1801–3 *Minstrelsy*, Scott seeks to avoid the taint of Macpherson's inauthenticity and Burns's rustic associations. Scott presents the work first and foremost as a response to Percy's *Reliques of Ancient English Poetry*, featuring the matter of Scotland to counter Percy's English nationalism. More than this, Scott's 1801–3 *Minstrelsy* suggests a different version of British history than that found in Percy. Rather than just see the Borders as a site of barbarity that survived longer because it was on the periphery of more civilized society, this first edition of the *Minstrelsy* presents the Borders as constituting an important alternative to Percy's homogeneous vision of history.

This perspective is still visible in the 1830 republication of the *Minstrelsy*, but with important qualifications, most notably suggested in the two additional essays, "Introductory Remarks on Popular Poetry" and "Essay on the Imitation of Ancient Ballads." Whereas the earlier edition of the *Minstrelsy* suggested an alternative history of Britain, the 1830 edition offers an alternative history of British literature. Scott still emphasizes the distinct origins of Scotland within Britain and Scotland's contribution to British literature, but he also questions the authority of both literary origins and literary originality. In the 1830 *Minstrelsy*, he establishes himself obliquely as the literary heir of Macpherson and Burns.

Scott was influenced by Macpherson both indirectly, through Percy, and directly, through his own reading of the poems of Ossian. Macpherson's popularity had been an important factor in Thomas Percy's decision to publish his ballads. Percy commented that "hardly one reader in ten Believes the specimens already produced to be genuine," and speculated "how much greater attention would be due to an editor, who rescues the original itself from oblivion, and fixes it's meaning by an accurate version" (Johnston, p. 77). According to Arthur Johnston, Shenstone used the example of Macpherson to persuade Percy to alter the Folio texts to suit the taste of the reading public (p. 79). Whereas Percy could make such comments as a relative outsider, however, Scott saw himself as a literary descendent of Macpherson, responsible for recuperating the scholarly reputation of Scottish writers, which his predecessor had called into disrepute. In particular, Scott felt himself under a burden to ensure the authenticity of his *Minstrelsy* project in the light of the suspicion with which his fellow countryman was viewed. In a letter to R. Cleator in 1802 he suggests, "I have been very desirous as far as possible to ascertain the authenticity of the old poems which I have given to the world, as literary forgeries have been but too often and too justly imputed to the Scottish antiquaries" (*Letters*, 1: 141).[1]

Scott had written a paper on Ossian during his student days, but it is his review of interpretations of Ossian published in the *Edinburgh Review* in July 1805 that indicates most clearly the relationship he sought to negotiate with the legacy of Macpherson. The review examines the *Report of the Committee of the Highland Society* regarding Ossian together with Malcolm Laing's damning edition of Macpherson's poems.[2] Scott used the *Report* to encourage closure of the debate: "The celebrated controversy seems now to be finally at issue. Both parties have arrayed their arguments, and marshalled their proofs, so that it can hardly be expected that much will hereafter be added to the strength of either side" (p. 429). He states the case clearly: "We believe no well-informed person will now pretend that Ossian is to be quoted as historical authority, or that a collection of Gaelic poems does any where exist, of which Macpherson's version can be regarded as a faithful, or even a loose translation; always excepting those which he himself was pleased to produce in a state entirely unauthenticated" (p. 429). Nevertheless, Scott, like the Highland Commission, emphasizes the existence of a body of authentic work from which Macpherson drew: "There existed before the times of Macpherson, a sort of general basis of tradition, on which the poems, whether collected or composed by himself, appear to have been founded" (p. 429). Scott ends the review, which is extensive, by pointing in two opposite directions. On one hand, he promotes the establishment of "historical authority." In particular, he recommends publication of translations of the Gaelic poetry that the Highland society had discovered alongside the originals, in a manner similar to that found in Charlotte Brooke's *Reliques of Irish Poetry* (1789). On the other hand, he suggests the importance that even an inauthentic work can have on the literary canon, as he praises Macpherson's contribution not only to English letters but to European literature: "Our national vanity may be equally flattered by the fact, that a remote, and almost barbarous corner of Scotland, produced, in the 18th century, a bard, capable not only of making an enthusiastic impression on every mind susceptible of poetical beauty, but of giving a new tone to poetry throughout Europe" (p. 463). Scott's comments directly contradict those of Wordsworth in his "Essay, Supplementary to the Preface" suggesting that the works of Macpherson "have been wholly uninfluential upon the literature of the Country" (*Prose Works* 3: 78). In Scott's interpretation of the legacy of Macpherson, Scotland is valuable as the site of both authentic ancient bards and modern literary innovators. Nevertheless, by adopting the persona of the objective reviewer commenting on the transgressions of Macpherson, Scott, like Francis Jeffrey, also carves out a role for Scottish writers as astute and honest critics. Scott is anxious to redeem Macpherson as far as he can. In an 1806 letter to Anna Seward he goes so far as to claim that Macpherson's renditions of Ossianic poetry are authentic Gaelic poems because Macpherson originally spoke Gaelic. He continues, "We know from constant experience, that most highlanders after they have become compleat masters of English, continue to *think* in their own language" (*Letters*, 1: 323).[3] But he also dissociates himself from Macpherson genealogically by identifying him as a Highlander and professionally by passing judgment on him.

Scott inscribes for himself a similar ambivalent relationship with Burns as he does with Macpherson. He presents himself as very much a supporter of Burns, subscribing to the monument for the earlier poet on Calton Hill and writing in his journal: "Long life to thy fame and peace to thy soul, Rob Burns! When I want to express a sentiment which I feel strongly, I find the phrase in Shakespeare—or thee" (Low, p. 260). Yet in his anonymous review of Cromek's *Reliques of Robert Burns* for the *Quarterly Review* in February 1809, Scott also critiques Burns as he did Macpherson. Scott accepts Currie's model, outlined in the previous chapter, that Burns was a "child of impulse and feeling" who "was unfortunately divested by the violence of those passions which finally wrecked him" (p. 25).[4] Scott praises Burns's feelings of sensibility, which "were so native to the soul of this extraordinary man, and burst from him so involuntarily, that they not only obtained full credence as the genuine feelings of his own heart, but melted into unthought of sympathy all who witnessed them" (p. 28). Scott concurs with Currie in linking the undisciplined nature of Burns's sensibility to his political positions, suggesting that Burns's impulsiveness explains his Jacobitism and subsequent republicanism. Viewing Burns's politics as a manifestation of weakness helps Scott to excuse him; like Currie, however, he also suggests that politics were the ultimate cause of Burns's death, as after losing his hope for promotion in the Excise "his tendency to dissipation hurried him precipitately into those excesses which shortened his life" (p. 29).

Scott differs from Currie, however, in foregrounding the feminine aspects of Burns's sensibility. Much of Scott's review of Cromek's *Reliques* is concerned with feminizing Burns or at least connecting him with domestic discourse. Scott comments that "it was within female circles that his powers of expression displayed their utmost fascination" (p. 28). He sees Burns as wasting his time writing songs: "We cannot but deeply regret that so much of his time and talents was frittered away in compiling and composing for musical collections" (p. 32). In Scott's view, such collections are associated with domestic discourse. Burns took on, says Scott, "the monotonous task of writing love verses on heaving bosoms and sparkling eyes, and twisting them into such rhythmical forms, as might suit the capricious evolutions of Scotch reels, ports, and strathspeys" (p. 32). Scott had written to Currie on October 18, 1800, asking for any unpublished Border ballads that Burns had in his collection. In the letter, he associates Burns not with the masculine Riding Ballads, which he promoted chiefly in the *Minstrelsy*, but with "Scottish Ballads of merit upon romantic and popular subjects" (*Letters*, 12: 104). This involvement with domestic discourse, like the involvement with politics, is also a kind of dissipation, inasmuch as it renders him incapable of turning his attention to more important, masculine projects. In his review Scott notes that "this constant waste of his fancy and power of verse in small and insignificant compositions, must necessarily have had no little effect in deterring him from undertaking any grave or important task" (p. 32). Writing love verses "diverted the poet from his grand plan of dramatic composition" (p. 32).

In particular, according to Scott, writing love songs prevented Burns from accomplishing a larger project, a drama combining tragedy and comedy concerning Robert the Bruce's adventures "while wandering in danger and disguise after having been defeated by the English" (p. 33). Such a project would have allowed Burns to exercise once more "the masculine and lofty tone of martial spirit which glows in the poem of Bannockburn" (p. 33) and would have served as a more "substantial monument to his own fame and to the honour of his country" (p. 33). But although he condemns Burns for not accomplishing this project, Scott also implies that Burns would have been incapable of succeeding at it anyway; he would "undoubtedly have wanted that tinge of chivalrous feeling which the manners of the age, no less than the disposition of the monarch, imperiously demanded" (p. 33). According to Scott, Burns possessed sufficient resources to convey "the energy of a hero" (p. 33) but lacked the class standing to have portrayed an aristocrat appropriately. Similarly, he lacked the ability to write in English, which is the only way Scott believes Burns could have succeeded in having his dramatic composition produced on the stage. "No man ever had more command of this ancient Doric dialect than Burns" (p. 35), writes Scott. However, his expression in English was "confined and embarrassed" (p. 35).

As a Scottish writer beginning his career just after the turn of the century, Scott was able to capitalize on Macpherson's and Burns's popularization of the matter of Scotland, but he was also careful to establish the difference between him and his predecessors. Both of his Scottish predecessors offered images of Scotland which Scott found quite limiting. In Scott's view, Macpherson conveyed the impressive spirit of chivalry of the Scots in a language designed for the entire British nation, but he compromised the culture he ostensibly represented by ignoring standards of scholarly accuracy. Burns offered the authenticity which Macpherson lacked, but was unable to translate that authenticity to an English public. Moreover, his authenticity lacked the "chivalrous feeling" and, often, the masculine energy which Scott wanted to associate with the Scottish nation. In contrast, the *Reliques* of Percy offered Scott a model of a national identity that combined masculine chivalry with authenticity, as it presented adventurous Riding Ballads alongside antiquarian notes.

Scott's description of his first encounter with the *Reliques* conveys his excitement at finding this perfect combination of attributes. The passage appears in the autobiographical fragment which he first wrote in 1808, then revised in 1826, and which is included in the first volume of Lockhart's *Life of Sir Walter Scott*:

> I then first became acquainted with Bishop Percy's Reliques of Ancient
> Poetry. As I had been from infancy drawn to legendary lore of this na-
> ture, and only reluctantly withdrew my attention, from the scarcity of
> materials and the rudeness of those which I possessed, it may be imag-
> ined, but cannot be described, with what delight I saw pieces of the same
> kind which had amused my childhood, and still continued in secret the

Delilahs of my imagination, considered as the subject of sober research, grave commentary, and apt illustration, by an editor who shewed his poetical genius was capable of emulating the best qualities of what his pious labour preserved. (1: 38)

The gendering of the process is significant in this passage. The legends are associated for Scott with childhood, but they now represent a debilitating feminization such as that which prevented Burns from promoting his own fame and that of his country. They are the "Delilahs" existing to threaten Scott's Samsonian imagination. In Percy, however, the feminine effect of the legends is legitimized by "sober research, grave commentary, and apt illustration." As well as providing a happier ending to the story of Samson and Delilah, Scott also rewrites the story of the Garden of Paradise in this episode:

I remember well the spot where I read these volumes for the first time. It was beneath a huge platanas-tree, in the ruins of what had been intended for an old fashioned arbour in the *garden* I have mentioned. The summer day sped onward so fast, that notwithstanding the sharp appetite of thirteen, I forgot the hour of dinner, was sought for with anxiety, and was still found entranced in my intellectual banquet. To read and to remember was in this instance the same thing, and henceforth I overwhelmed my schoolfellows, and all who would hearken to me with tragical recitations from the ballads of Bishop Percy. (1: 38–39)

The site of the discovery becomes enshrined as myth in Scott's mind, with the Gothic arbor and the plantain tree occupying the place of Eden and the Tree of Knowledge. In this case, however, Scott's tasting of his "intellectual banquet" and sharing it with others results not in punishment but rather in enlightenment. Scott purchased a copy of Percy as soon as he could and attested "nor do I believe I ever read a book half so frequently, or with half the enthusiasm" (1: 39). Robert Anderson also indicated Scott's indebtedness to Percy, as he wrote to Percy introducing the young Scottish advocate. He forwarded to Percy two of Scott's ballads, "The Eve of St. John" and "Glenfinlas," "in testimony," he wrote, "of his high respect for your character and of his gratitude to the Editor of 'The Reliques,' *upon which he formed his taste for ballad thinking and expression.*"[5] Scott himself referred to the episode under the plantain tree at the start of his correspondence with Percy: "The very grass sod seat to which (when a boy of twelve years old) I retreated from my playfellows, to devour the works of the ancient minstrels, is still fresh and dear to my memory" (*Letters*, 1: 108).

It is worth examining Scott's regard for Percy more closely, however, to determine why Scott chose a model south of the Tweed on which to base the articulation of his own nation's identity. Part of Percy's appeal for Scott lay not only in the masculine national image which he conveyed, but also in the important role he gave the minstrels as the "genuine successors of the ancient Bards" (1: 346). In their original role in mainland Europe, suggests Percy, minstrels were historians, prophets, and religious leaders highly esteemed by rulers. By the medieval era, as a result of demographic and social changes, they had lost some of the original power accorded to them, but, according to Percy, they still enjoyed great honor. The minstrels' arts of poetry and harping "rendered them extremely popular and acceptable in this and all the neighboring countries; where no high scene of festivity was esteemed complete, that was not set off with the exercise of their talents; and where, so long as the spirit of chivalry subsisted, they were protected and caressed, because their songs tended to do honour to the ruling passion of the times, and to encourage and foment a martial spirit" (1: 345–46). Susan Stewart notes the appeal of the minstrel's "natural" position in a feudal world in comparison to that of the eighteenth-century author, who was "caught between the decline of patronage and the rise of commercial publishing" (p. 113). Percy's dedication to Elizabeth, Countess of Northumberland, makes a point of trying to reestablish the "bonds" of feudal loyalty:

> By such bonds, Madam, as I am now introducing to your presence, was the infancy of genius nurtured and advanced, by such were the minds of unlettered warriors softened and enlarged, by such was the memory of illustrious actions preserved and propagated, by such were the heroic deeds of the Earls of Northumberland sung at festivals in the hall of Alnwick; and those songs, which the bounty of your ancestors rewarded, now return to your Ladyship by a kind of hereditary right; and, I flatter myself, will find such reception as is usually shown to poets and historians, by those whose consciousness of merit makes it their interest to be long remembered. (1: 2)

Percy's reference to "poets and historians" echoes the minstrels' combination of these two roles, as he represents himself as a minstrel offering the *Reliques* as the "hereditary right" of the family of Northumberland. Percy, then, provided Scott with an image of the minstrel in an organic community, which Scott then imagined himself re-creating by subjecting first "all who would hearken to me" to his oral renditions of Percy's ballads, then later readers to his own published versions of ballads. Where Percy represented himself as minstrel to the Northumberland family, Scott uses the publication of the *Minstrelsy* to re-create the honored position of bard to the clan, as he writes to the Duke of Buccleuch: "Your Grace I hope will pardon me if I say that such a work has in some degree a legitimate claim to your protection for besides your being the Chieftain of an ancient & illustrious Border Clan, there are several poems in which the exploits of your Ancestors are particularly commemorated in a strain of poetry which would do honor to a more polished age" (*Letters*, 12: 100). When Scott comments in his autobiographical fragment that Percy proved that his "poetical genius was capable of emulating the best qualities of what his pious labour preserved," he refers not just to Percy's composition of ballad stanzas, but also to the possibilities Percy raises for translating the close communion between minstrel, aristocratic chief, and audience to the relationship between modern author, patron, and reader.

But whereas Scott identified strongly from a very young age with his Scottish heritage, Percy's *Reliques*, despite containing a number of Scottish ballads, are decidedly Anglo-Saxon. Percy goes to great pains to distinguish the Gothic pedigree of his minstrels from that of the Celtic bards. He makes a point of indicating the Teutonic predisposition for poetry, remarking that although bards were found in the communities of "almost all the first inhabitants of Europe, whether of Celtic or Gothic race," they were admired "by none more than by our own Teutonic ancestors, particularly by all the Danish tribes" (1: 346). The honors paid to bards were continued when "our Anglo-Saxon ancestors" moved to Britain, although when the Saxons converted to Christianity and began to have the use of letters, there was a separation of the roles of poet and minstrel: "Poetry was cultivated by men of letters indiscriminately, and many of the most popular rhymes were composed amidst the leisure and retirement of monasteries. But the Minstrels continued a distinct order of men for many ages after the Norman Conquest, and got their livelihood by singing verses to the harp at the houses of the great" (1: 347). While the skalds were greatly honored in Europe, the Anglo-Saxon minstrels, who were more entertainers than instructors, nevertheless enjoyed "no small portion of public favour" (1: 350). The historical examples that Percy provides prove the existence and importance of minstrels in Anglo-Saxon Britain. In a note to the main essay, Percy uses etymology to show that the instrument native to Anglo-Saxon minstrels was the harp: "That the harp (*cithera*) was the common musical instrument of the Anglo-Saxons, might be inferred from the very word itself, which is not derived from the British, or any other Celtic language, but of genuine Gothic original, and current among every branch of that people" (1: 390).

Percy seeks to present an English identity that is essentially homogeneous.

Accordingly, he points out the common ancestry of all the Anglo-Saxons, whether Jutes, Angles, or Saxons; those who settled in Britain were "only different tribes of the same common Teutonic stock, and spoke only different dialects of the same Gothic language" (1: 349). But it is not just the Angles, Saxons, and Jutes who constitute the Teutonic influence responsible for promoting minstrelsy in Britain. Percy suggests that the Normans, too, are of Teutonic origin and "had been a late colony from Norway and Denmark, where the Scalds had arrived to the highest pitch of credit" (1: 353). In fact, Percy suggests that even if the Anglo-Saxon culture had not valued minstrels, the conquest of 1066 would have ensured the promotion of minstrels: "The Norman Conquest was rather likely to favour the establishment of the minstrel profession in this kingdom, than to suppress it" (1: 354). As good Teutons, the Normans honored their own minstrels. In suggesting that England's minstrels derived their Teutonic ancestry from both the Anglo-Saxon and Norman invasions, Percy rewrites English history. Instead of presenting the English as, in Defoe's terms, "Heterogeneous Thing[s]," whose blood is mixed from a series of invasions, Percy imagines them as the progeny of layerings of Teutonic cultures.

Just as Percy presents the minstrels as of Teutonic origin, so he is eager to claim Gothic roots for the tales of chivalry that they related. Rejecting the hypothesis that the chivalric tales originated with the Moors who invaded Spain, then were conveyed to Britain by the bards of Armorica, Percy sets out to prove in his essay "On the Ancient Metrical Romances, &c," published as an appendix to volume 3, "That our old romances of chivalry may be derived in a lineal descent from the ancient historical songs of the Gothic Bards and Scalds" (3: 341). Although he concurs that chivalry "as a distinct military order" arose as a characteristic of feudal society, he nevertheless argues that the notion of chivalry "as in embriyo" can be found in "the customs, manners, and opinions of every branch" of the Gothic people (3: 341).

Significantly absent from Percy's essay in the *Reliques* is any substantial reference to the heterogeneous nature of Britain. Although he gives passing mention to Edward I's alleged massacre of the Welsh bards, he also writes in such a way as to suggest that the "original inhabitants" of Britain, those who existed at the time of the Norman Conquest, were of Anglo-Saxon derivation (1: 355). The essays elide differences within Britain, although the preface to the *Reliques* does acknowledge the non-Anglo-Saxon presence in Britain, noting that "select ballads in the old Scottish dialect, most of them of first-rate merit, are also interspersed among those of our ancient English minstrels" (1: 9). Ironically, this difference within Britain seems to be responsible for the production of ballads, inasmuch as border clashes inspire poetry. Percy comments that most of the English minstrels are represented as being from North England: "There is scarce an old historical song or ballad wherein a minstrel or harper appears, but he is characterized by way of eminence to have been 'of the North countreye:' and, indeed, the prevalence of the Northern dialect in such compositions shews that this representation is real" (1: 378). Similarly, he comments, the finest Scottish ballads are found in the south of Scotland near the border with England. He concludes, "The martial spirit constantly kept up and exercised near the frontier of the two kingdoms, as it furnished continual subjects for their songs, so it inspired the inhabitants of the adjacent counties on both sides with the powers of poetry" (1: 379). Although Percy does not elaborate on the ethnic derivations of the Scottish Borderers, he does emphasize their national difference. The paradox of the *Reliques* is that it both erases and depends on differences within Britain. In his essays, Percy wants to prove that pure Teutonic ancestry is responsible for the prodigious poetry of the minstrels. The preface and the body of the *Reliques*, however, suggest that the poetry arises from cultural and national conflict.

Scott identified his ambitions with Percy's. In a letter to Percy dated October 6, 1800, Scott offers his services for the fourth volume of the *Reliques*, which was being proposed under the supervision of Percy's nephew. He suggests that the *Minstrelsy* "humbly follow the plan of the R. of Anct. Poetry" (*Letters*, 12: 168) in providing notes and introductions for each ballad, and he writes to Percy, "That you are pleased to approve of my intended work, will prove to me an additional stimulus in the execution" (*Letters*, 1: 108). But Scott is also anxious to establish his difference from Percy. In his letter of January 11, 1801, Scott explains his hopes for the *Minstrelsy*, specifically setting out his interest in Scottish material: "An early partiality to the tales of my country, and an intimate acquaintance with its wildest recesses, acquired partly in the course of country sports, and partly in pursuit of antiquarian knowledge, will, I hope, enable me at least to preserve some of the most valuable traditions of the south of Scotland, both historical and romantic" (*Letters*, 1: 108–9). Scott was interested in providing a positive image of Scotland in the *Minstrelsy* to counteract Percy's single-minded attention to the Anglo-Saxon origins of the minstrels. In addition, Scott builds on Percy's hint about the creative potential of the Borders, constructing a much more elaborate place for the Borders in British history.

Scott offered, if not an epic of Scotland, then at least a series of sketches that would suggest epic possibilities. He devoted himself to the area of "Border Clans." Instead of including a wide range of ballads, both historic and literary, from a number of different geographical areas, Scott concentrated on

ballads from the area he knew best.[6] Although he included some of the same
ballads found in Percy's collection, he selected the Scottish variations, even
when they were not as ancient. In a letter to Percy he comments, "I have
published (that is, printed) in the Minstrelsy of the Scottish Border, the Scottish account of the Battle of Otterbourne; a ballad evidently much more
modern than that published in the Reliques on the same subject" (*Letters*, 1:
109). In the notes to the "Battle of Otterbourne," Scott says that his account
is essentially different from that published in the *Reliques of English Poetry* and
points out Percy's promotion of English poetry: "The author, with a natural
partiality, leans to the side of his countrymen" (1: 279). He also notes that his
work is living history. Where Percy's *Reliques* are taken from manuscript editions of ballads, Scott indicates that his versions have the added element of
being part of an oral tradition. The "Battle of Otterbourne" was also published by David Herd in 1774, says Scott, but he chooses to correct his version from copies of "the recitation of old persons residing at the head of Et-
trick Forest" (1: 281). Scott takes pains to emphasize the heterogeneous history of Britain by including a Scottish and oral perspective.[7]

The Borders are a natural site for exploring this heterogeneous history.
Like Percy, Scott emphasizes the wars that have taken place on the Borders.
The Borders embody geographically the clash of different cultures in Britain:
"From the remote period, when the Roman province was contracted by the
ramparts of Severus, until the union of the Kingdoms, the Borders of Scotland formed the stage, upon which were presented the most memorable conflicts of two gallant nations" (1: 55). The Borderers are unique in the nation
of Britain, set apart from other peoples by their wildness. Scott constructs a
different kind of history of Britain than that found in Percy. In the *Reliques*,
Percy had argued that the Borders represent an arrested stage of social development: whereas, he writes, London "must have been ever the scene of novelty and refinement, the northern countries, as being most distant, would preserve their ancient manners longest, and, of course, the old poetry, in which
those manners are peculiarly described" (1: 379). Furthermore, although he
draws on anecdotes to demonstrate to his readers the importance of the minstrels to medieval society, he was in general not interested in portraying the
society of the time. Scott, on the other hand, wants to show the cultural differences that existed in Britain. He states his intent to present to the reader
such incidents of Border life "as may introduce to the reader the character of
the Marchmen, more briefly and better than a formal essay upon their manners" (1: 111), and he then moves into a sharper focus, discussing "more
minutely, some of their peculiar customs and modes of life" (1: 111). He portrays Border life as a unique culture with values that are not so much precur-

sors to a more civilized philosophy as they are functional in their own right.[8] The Borderers' morality, for example, "was of a singular kind. The rapine, by which they subsisted, they accounted lawful and honourable" (1: 111). Encouraging a cultural relativism in his readers, he notes, "This strange, precarious, and adventurous mode of life, led by the Borderers, was not without its pleasures, and seems, in all probability, hardly so disagreeable to us, as the monotony of regulated society must have been to those who had been long accustomed to a state of rapine" (1: 116). The Border way of life exists as an indication of heterogeneity in Britain, a heterogeneity to which the ballads bear witness.

Paradoxically, this heterogeneity also encourages a unique version of union between Scottish and English inhabitants. For one thing, Scott suggests that the Scottish border clans are in fact ethnically identical to their southern neighbors. Saxon families who fled from "the exterminating sword of the Conqueror" made up the "most powerful Border chiefs" (1: 56). These chiefs then were exiled and "upon their ruins was founded the formidable house of Douglas" (1: 57). Like Macpherson in his *History of Great Britain*, Scott writes Scotland and England together ethnically. However, he displaces the difference that exists *between* the nations to the difference *within* Britain that the border represents, emphasizing the way that the Borderers on both sides of the Tweed differ from the other citizens of the two nations. The Borderers are, he suggests, "a kind of outcasts, against whom the united powers of England and Scotland were often employed" (1: 116).

Moreover, Scott notes that there were "habits of intimacy betwixt the Borderers of both kingdoms, notwithstanding their mutual hostility and reciprocal depredations" (1: 118). Instead of being arranged politically or legally, this union was an organic part of Border life: "A natural intercourse took place between the English and Scottish Marchers, at Border meetings, and during the short intervals of peace. They met frequently at parties of the chase and football; and it required many strict regulations, on both sides, to prevent them from forming intermarriages, and from cultivating too close a degree of intimacy" (1: 118–19). Even the custom of blackmail "introduced a connection betwixt the countries," developing alliances of protection or antagonism across borders (1: 119). "Hence, a union rose betwixt the parties, founded upon mutual interest, which counteracted, in many instances, the effects of national prejudice. The similarity of their manners may be inferred from that of their language" (1: 119). They were often moderate toward each other in open war. Not only do the Borders represent an alternative culture to that found in the rest of Britain, they also represent an alternative politics, an ideal mixture of unity with diversity.

Scott's attitude in the *Minstrelsy* anticipates the ambiguity found in much of his later work, as he both regrets the passing of the old ways of life and normalizes their passing. The actual Union destroys the potential of the Border's alternative political site, as the Borderers are either subsumed within the rest of Britain or eliminated. Scott describes this spatially as the end of the periphery: "The accession of James to the English crown converted the extremity [the Borders] into the centre of his kingdom" (1: 108). The east marches were civilized, while in the western and middle marches where outlaws still existed, measures such as execution and exile were pursued until "the Border marauders were, in the course of years, either reclaimed or exterminated" (1: 110). It took almost a century, but finally "their manners were altogether assimilated to those of their countrymen" (1: 110). Scott himself suggests that he has undertaken the project only because the uniqueness of his nation is disappearing: "the peculiar features" of the manners and character of Scotland "are daily melting and dissolving into those of her sister and ally" (1: 175). He finishes the introduction by quoting a poem that symbolizes such a melting, *Albania* (1742). The poem, written before the '45 uprising, takes as its subject the independent history of Scotland, a "state unconquer'd by the fire of war" (1: 175–76). But, ironically, the poem is also written in standard English, suggesting the cultural conquest which Scotland had undergone even then. Penny Fielding suggests that Scott's project "is to frame and delineate the Scottishness of his subject, as that Scottishness becomes conversely absorbed into a greater British identity" (p. 51). Despite all its equivocation, however, it is important to recognize to what extent the *Minstrelsy* is a direct negotiation with the homogeneous model of Britain which Percy put forward in his historical collection of English poetry. Although it participates in uniting Scotland to the rest of Britain, the *Minstrelsy* sets out to make Scottish ballads important not as the poetry of Britain's periphery, but as a central aspect of British heritage.

Scott went on to write his own poetic compositions, combinations of history and romance set in Scotland. Peter Murphy calls Scott's poems "vacations from consequence" (p. 240), but in fact they have important consequences for the construction of Britain, which was at the time involved in the Napoleonic Wars.[9] Scott's first ballad imitation, *The Lay of the Last Minstrel*, extends the project of his *Minstrelsy* by drawing attention to the Scottish culture within Britain. In the preface to the *Lay of the Last Minstrel*, Scott explains the purpose of the poem: "to illustrate the customs and manners which anciently prevailed on the Borders of England and Scotland," which, because they were in danger of being erased, were particularly conducive to "poetical ornament" (*Poetical Works*, 6: 37). He elaborates on this in the introduction to

The Lady of the Lake: "The ancient manners, the habits and customs of the aboriginal race by whom the Highlands of Scotland were inhabited, had always appeared to me peculiarly adapted to poetry. The change in their manners, too, had taken place almost within my own time. . . . I had always thought the old Scottish Gael highly adapted for poetical composition" (8: 274). Poetical composition, for Scott, is built on representing tensions, a process he continued when he moved to the historical novel.

Scott's novels present a complicated view of the divisions between Scottish and English identity, showing the existence of difference within an ostensible picture of national unity.[10] A reviewer in the *British Critic* of August 1814 commented that *Waverley* depicts "a period to which no Briton can look back without the strongest emotions . . . the last fatal year when the blood of our countrymen was spilt on its own shores, when Briton met Briton on his native land" (Hayden, p. 68). The review praises the novel because it can help the British people detect the "first symptoms" of the recurrence of such civil strife. But it is equally true to say that as the novels appeared, each featuring a different time period of British division and subsequent assimilation, they suggested a continual need to confirm the contemporary state of affairs. Like Defoe's nation, Scott's Britain seems to depend on the constant reiteration of the process of union.

Under the anonymous mask of "The Author of Waverley," Scott was able to continue his process of writing the nation together while increasing his personal estate until 1826. In that year, his machinations behind the scenes in the printing and publishing worlds caused his financial downfall. Ballantyne and Company's failure was due to a decision by Hurst (of the London book publishers Hurst, Robinson and Company) to speculate in hops. Hurst, Robinson and Company was the London agent of Archibald Constable, who was the source of financial stability for Ballantyne and Company, and therefore for Scott. After the domino effect of his financial ruin, Scott was left owing £120,899 (*Journal*, p. xxiv). Instead of declaring bankruptcy, however, he chose to write his way out of debt. Trustees were appointed, and the profits of his work for the rest of his life were put under the surveillance of the trustees. In order to help pay off his debts, Scott set to work on a republication of all of his previous novels in a *Magnum Opus* edition. In fact, the edition inaugurated an important change in the business of publishing. Jane Millgate observes that the forty-eight-volume collected edition between 1829 and 1833 "marked a crucial stage not only in the development of the texts of those particular novels but in the general history of publishing" (p. vii). The idea of republishing the works had been suggested earlier by Constable, but his idea then was to produce an expensive edition. When the bankruptcy occurred, Constable renewed his suggestion, and Robert Cadell also urged publishing the complete works in a cheaper edition for a mass market. Among the republished works was a new edition of the *Minstrelsy*, published in 1830.

Graham Sutherland argues that the economic collapse caused fundamental changes in Scott (p. 306). In a similar vein, Caroline McCracken-Flesher contends that Scott's perspective on Scottish-English relations changed after his financial collapse. McCracken-Flesher notes that before the collapse, "Scott composed pieces that appeared to foreground Scottish difference, but that sold well in England, and that thus inscribed their author as successful within both England's economic narrative and Scotland's national one," but that in 1826, "events conspired to reveal to him that he stood not as transcendent Scot, but as grotesque Other" (p. 75). McCracken-Flesher concentrates on how the *Letters of Malachai Malagrowther* serve to strike back at the cultural and economic hegemony which Scott had earlier promoted. I want to fit the 1830 republication of the *Minstrelsy* within the contexts that Sutherland and McCracken-Flesher discuss, arguing that it constitutes a more critical evaluation of the British nation and of the literature which had historically served to imagine that nation than found in Scott's earlier work. The financial downfall and the preparation of the new edition affected Scott's own perception and presentation of his work and his perception of the relationship between Scotland and England. The 1830 edition includes more notes than the earlier edition, but, more important, it features two essays derived from material that Scott had published between the time of the two editions. Now "Introductory Remarks on Popular Poetry" precede the "Introduction," reiterating observations Scott had made in previous journalistic pieces such as "On Ellis's Specimens of the Early English Poets" and "On Ellis's Specimens of Early English Metrical Romances and Ritson's Ancient English Metrical Romances" (published in 1804 and 1806, respectively, in the *Edinburgh Review*). Scott also added an "Essay on the Imitation of Ancient Ballads" in the 1830 edition of the *Minstrelsy*. The inclusion of both these essays alters the *Minstelsy*'s effect, creating a more problematic relationship between history, literature, the market and the construction of the British nation.

The 1830 edition, like the previous edition, emphasizes the importance of Scotland and the Borders as heterogeneous elements in the history of Britain. But where the introduction of the 1801–3 edition discussed the shared ancestry of the Scottish and English Border clans, the leaders of both having derived from Saxon lords, "Remarks on Popular Poetry" concentrates on the Celtic essence of Scotland. Now Scott includes in his ballad collection the theory that the Picts were of Celtic origin:

It is now generally admitted that the Scots and Picts, however differing otherwise, were each by descent a Celtic race; that they advanced in a course of victory somewhat farther than the present frontier between England and Scotland, and about the end of the eleventh century sub-dued and rendered tributary the Britons of Strathcluyd, who were also a Celtic race like themselves. Excepting, therefore, the provinces of Ber-wickshire and the Lothians, which were chiefly inhabited by an Anglo-Saxon population, the whole of Scotland was peopled by different tribes of the same aboriginal race. (1: 15–16)

Just as Percy saw the various Angles, Saxons, and Jutes as uniformly Teutonic, Scott now presents the peoples of Scotland (apart from the Anglo-Saxon Bor-der lords) as a homogeneous Celtic race. And where Percy claimed that the Teutonic peoples were particularly musically inclined, Scott sees musicality as a Celtic characteristic. The Celts were, he asserts, "a race passionately addicted to music, as appears from the kindred Celtic nations of Irish, Welsh and Scot-tish, preserving each to this day a style and character of music peculiar to their own country, though all three bear marks of general resemblance to each other" (1: 16). Although all of these nations have impressive musical his-tories, "That of Scotland, in particular, is early noticed and extolled by an-cient authors" (1: 16). This skill also went hand in hand with talents for the literary arts, in particular for "a species of poetry, adapted to the habits of the country, celebrating the victories of triumphant clans, pouring forth lamen-tations over fallen heroes, and recording such marvellous adventures as were calculated to amuse individual families around their household fires, or the whole tribe when regaling in the hall of the chief" (1: 16).

Scott suggests how this Celtic essence was changed by the gradual en-croachment of English into Scotland: "While the music continued to be Celtic in its general measure, the language of Scotland, most commonly spo-ken, began to be that of their neighbours the English" (1: 16). The English language was introduced into Scotland by Saxons who attended the court of Malcolm Canmore, by prisoners of war taken in Border raids, and by the hegemonic influence of Berwickshire and the Lothians, whose inhabitants were of Saxon derivation. Moreover, says Scott, this introduction happened because English was more "refined," had been "long since reduced to writ-ing," and it was "capable of expressing the wants, wishes and sentiments of the speakers" better than "the jargon of various tribes of Irish and British ori-gin, limited and contracted in every varying dialect, and differing, at the same time, from each other" (1: 17). He is anxious to assure his readers, however, that Scottish people "retained their Celtic music, and many of their Celtic

customs, together with the Celtic dynasty" (1: 17), even though they shifted
to expressing the music and the customs using the English language. It was
Celtic verse that was used to celebrate the "genealogy of the monarch" (1:
17), and Celtic elements would continue in the Lowland popular culture for
a quite a while. The 1830 edition of the *Minstrelsy* suggests more strongly
than the earlier edition that the uniqueness of Scottish culture continued
even when it began to be assimilated to England.

More important, however, at the same time that it offers an account of the
cultural distinction of Scotland within the nation of Britain—however, one
that draws attention to the authentic Celtic spirit that exists in Scottish culture even in the present—the 1830 edition also problematizes issues of authenticity, particularly literary authenticity, which had proved so important in
forging the nation. To begin with, the "Essay on the Imitation of Ancient Ballads" suggests how dependent literature is on the material conditions of the
marketplace, calling into question the purity of any kind of cultural spirit.
Scott describes the effects of changes in the media on culture and its practi-
tioners, using the example of the minstrels: "The invention of printing necessarily occasioned the downfall of the Order of Minstrels, already reduced
to contempt by their own bad habits, by the disrepute attached to their profession, and by the laws calculated to repress their licence" (4: 1). A century
before Walter Benjamin, Scott was drawing attention to the effect of the age
of mechanical reproduction on the work of art.[11] Scott's minstrels, like Percy's,
were highly trained professionals who composed their own works, or sometimes sang those composed by others. Printing, it seems, while it allowed a
greater number of people access to poetry, also lowered standards. When the
metrical romances were "in the hands of every one," the occupation of the
minstrel was rendered unnecessary. Scott's account unsettles the image of literature and culture as a transcendent practice, suggesting rather that literature
is intricately connected with material conditions and market demand.

More than this, Scott also puts into question standard literary history by
describing an alternative history based not on originality, but on imitation.
The deterioration of the original metrical romances, he claims, precipitated
the birth of a new genre of poetry, the imitation. This genre did not directly
reflect the culture and society of the time, but attempted instead to re-create
works of the past in the present. In the "Essay on the Imitation of Ancient
Ballads," Scott attempts to establish an authentic pedigree for these inauthentic poems, or, in his terms, "the fair trade of manufacturing modern an-
tiques" (4: 13). He accomplishes this first by identifying illegitimate forms of
imitations: the deliberate forgeries (although Macpherson is notably absent in
this discussion). Then he devotes his attention to defining two categories of

authentic imitations. On one hand, there are those authors who merely adopt unquestioningly the standards of the past: those who "have attempted to imitate the language, the manners, and the sentiments of the ancient poems which were their prototypes" (4: 14). On the other hand, there are those who imagine an ideal standard for ancient ballads based on the standards of the present: "those, on the contrary, who, without endeavouring to do so, have struck out a particular path for themselves, which cannot with strict propriety be termed either ancient or modern" (4: 14). He assures his readers that this new genre also had its own standards; it "is capable of being subjected to peculiar rules of criticism, and of exhibiting excellences of its own" (4: 9). But, as he makes clear, one of these standards is the erasure of originality. Neither of the two authentic kinds of imitation is altogether original. The imitation, then, serves as a peculiar kind of intervention in the market system. In the genealogy of the genre which Scott establishes, the imitation of the metrical romance is a response to the deterioration of literature which resulted from the advent of printing. Scott presents the romance imitation as a recalcitrant practice in the face of changing demands on the market. If the market favors novelty and accessibility, the ballad imitation would appear to defy both those desires.

Scott goes on to trace the history of the new genre of poetry, and in so doing, he creates an alternative history of British literature and British writers. While Scots like Robert Anderson were busy collecting the lives and works of the greatest writers in Britain, Scott writes the story of those writers who imitated other writers' work. Percy plays the role of the father of the genre, says Scott. He was "remarkable for his power of restoring the ancient ballad, by throwing in touches of poetry, so adapted to its tone and tenor, as to assimilate with its original structure, and impress every one who considered the subject as being coeval with the rest of the piece" (4: 14). In establishing his literary history of imitation, Scott includes other writers normally praised for their originality: "Southey, Wordsworth, and other distinguished names of the present century, have, in repeated instances, dignified this branch of literature" (4: 16). A special place is also reserved for Coleridge. Notably, however, Scott's brief alternative sketch of the history of British literature also allows more room for Scottish writers, who, although they may be given short shrift in conventional literary histories, occupy an important place in the history of imitations: John Leyden, James Hogg, and Allan Cunningham "have all three honoured their country, by arriving at distinction from a humble origin, and there is none of them under whose hand the ancient Scottish harp has not sounded a bold and distinguished tone" (4: 16). Scott even includes Anne Bannerman, despite her mystical effusions. More than just supplying quantity, however, the Scots also supply quality. The greatest honors of the genre go to a Scot, one who had been particularly influential on Scott earlier: "The poet, perhaps, most capable, by verses, lines, even single words, to relieve and heighten the character of ancient poetry, was the Scottish bard Robert Burns" (4: 15). Scott does not praise "the avowed lyrical poems of [Burns's] own composition," but rather "the manner in which he recomposed and repaired the old songs and fragments, for the collection of Johnson and others" (4: 15). Burns's powers of originality are commended only insofar as he subdues them for the good of the nation in perpetuity: "his genius contributed that part which was to give life and immortality to the whole" (4: 15). Scott's rewriting of the literary canon according to imitation disrupts the Enlightenment narrative of literature as a reflection of the society that produced it, operative at least since Thomas Blackwell's *An Enquiry into the Life and Writings of Homer* in 1735. The authors whom Scott canonizes are praised for their translucence: they avoid being marked in historical time. This is a radical break for an author who built his career out of writing novels that take as their theme the historical progress of societies.

Scott leads up to a discussion of his own contribution to the development of the genre. Jane Millgate observes that Scott often substitutes autobiographical details for analysis, beginning with the *Lay of the Last Minstrel*: "The subjection of his own poetry to the kind of editorial treatment normally reserved for ancient texts serves to modify the authorial role itself, to detach Walter Scott, Esq, in some degree from the troubling figure of the poetic creator" (p. 18). According to Millgate, this editorializing impulse is "not a purely retrospective activity"; rather it is "intrinsic to the working of the creative impulse itself" (p. 18). What seems clear as genealogy gives way to autobiography in the 1830 *Minstrelsy*, however, is Scott's concern to indicate his own recalcitrance against the forces of literary history and the market, as he argues that none of his poetic endeavors have any claim to originality and that he failed at each opportunity to anticipate market demand.

Scott presents his work as dependent in each case upon a previous writer's example. His first excursion into the literary field, the translation of "Lenore," was inspired by Laetitia Aikin, later Mrs. Barbauld's, recitation of William Taylor's translation of the ballad. Scott was not present at the recitation, but his friends' enthusiasm for the ballad convinced him to try to obtain a copy and produce his own translation. Even then, his rendition was not completely his own work. Because "my object was much more to make a good translation of the poem for those whom I wished to please, than to acquire any poetical fame for myself" (4: 39), he says, he retained two lines of Taylor's translations.

The originality of Scott's imitated ballads is next brought into question. Scott suggests that with "Glenfinlas" he was influenced by Macpherson. "Glenfinlas" was "supposed to be a translation from the Gaelic," but, Scott says, "A versification of an Ossianic fragment came nearer to the idea I had formed of my task" (4: 44). "The Eve of St. John," although not influenced by any other writer (Scott says the incidents were "entirely imaginary" [4: 45]), is also a qualified form of literature, being written as part of a bargain with Mr. Scott of Harden, to prevent him from allowing the dilapidation of Smailholm Tower. The ballads' literariness is further questioned by Scott's indication of Matthew Lewis's criticism of them on technical grounds: "I was quite unaccustomed to the mechanical part of poetry, and used rhymes which were merely permissable, as readily as those which were legitimate" (4: 49). With the *Minstrelsy*, Scott again acknowledges his debt to another writer, noting "my attempt to imitate the plan and style of Bishop Percy, observing only more strict fidelity concerning my originals" (4: 52). This effort, however, unlike the previous attempts, was "favourably received by the public, and there was a demand within a short space for a second edition" (4: 52). Furthermore, in the appendixes Scott includes, in addition to letters from Lewis criticizing his poetry, Byron's accusation that Scott had plagiarized from Coleridge:

> But for [Coleridge], *The Lay of the Last Minstrel* would never have been thought of. The line,
> "Jesu Maria shield thee well!"
> is word for word from Coleridge. (4: 53)

Although Scott defends himself from "parodying Mr. Coleridge" (4: 58), his inclusion of Byron's remark emphasizes the lack of originality that Scott had been pointing out in the rest of the essay.

Scott ends the "Essay on Imitations" at the point of his success, directing the reader to another of his works for more details of the rest of his career: "My progress in the literary career in which I might now be considered as seriously engaged, the reader will find briefly traced in an Introduction prefixed to the *Lay of the Last Minstrel*" (4: 52). In the *Minstrelsy*, however, he is more concerned with the failures than the successes. In the background of Scott's story of his career are his clashes with the literary market. In the case of "Lenore" and the "Wild Huntsman," for example, he writes, "I distributed so many copies among my friends as, according to the booksellers, materially to interfere with the sale; and the number of translations which appeared in England about the same time . . . were sufficient to exclude a provincial

writer from competition" (4: 40). The whole venture to publish the ballads in
Lewis's *Tales of Wonder* is also presented as a market failure: "Thus, owing to
the failure of the vehicle I had chosen my efforts to present myself before the
public as an original writer proved as vain as those by which I had previously
endeavored to distinguish myself as a translator" (4: 51). This apparent failure
to understand the market amounts to a refusal to comply with it, however.
He notes that this failure turned him away from caring about market pressures: "I found pleasure in the literary labour in which I had, almost by acci-
dent, become engaged, and laboured, less in the hope of pleasing others,
though certainly without despair of doing so, than in the pursuit of a new
and agreeable amusement to myself" (4: 41–42).

In the "Essay on Imitations," Scott presents the genre of imitation as a recalcitrant response to the material conditions of the market. He attempts to
establish an alternative aesthetic and an alternative literary history based on
imitation, not authenticity, or, perhaps more accurately, on authentic imitation. Similarly, Scott offers his own career as a recalcitrant response to the literary market, as he presents himself as depending on other writers, even engaging at times in forms of plagiarism, or failing to read market conditions.
Such recalcitrance is embodied in the publication history of the *Minstrelsy*.
The notable thing about that work, Scott says, is its publication by an unknown quantity on the literary market. Ballantyne was "editor of a provincial newspaper" at that time, and when the book came out "the imprint,
Kelso, was read with wonder by amateurs of typography, who had never
heard of such a place, and were astonished at the example of handsome printing which so obscure a town produced" (4: 51–52). In *Legitimate Histories*,
Fiona Robertson suggests that with the "autobiographical voice introduced in
the Magnum Opus edition" Scott "creates an authorial persona whose pro-
nouncements about origins and authority have been more difficult to refute
than those of Peter Pattieson or Dr. Jonas Dryasdust" (p. 18). In the editorial
apparatus of the republication of the *Minstrelsy*, the authorial persona calls
into question the "origins and authority" of literature itself and, by extension,
of literature's role in forming a national culture.

In his autobiographical fragment and his letter to Percy, Scott had mythol-
ogized his first exposure to Percy as a fortunate feast of forbidden knowledge. His reference to Percy in the 1830 republication of the *Minstrelsy* has
less Edenic overtones. Scott notes that "the tree is still in my recollections, beneath which I lay and first entered upon the enchanting perusal of Percy's
Reliques of Ancient Poetry" (4: 35). But now he adds that the actual tree "has
long perished in the general blight which affected the whole race of Orien-
tal plantanus to which it belonged" (4: 35). In the original 1801–3 *Minstrelsy*,

Scott had been concerned to rewrite Percy's history of the imagined community of Britain. While Percy's text remains an important influence in the
1830 *Minstrelsy*, in that edition, Scott fashions himself as negotiating with the
entire history of British literature and standards of originality. Refusing the
role of transcendent genius, Scott presents himself not as an author of literary
texts, but as a "pedlar" with his wares: "Thus I was set up for a poet, like a
pedlar who has got two ballads to begin the world upon, and I hastened to
make the round of all my acquaintances, showing my precious wares, and re-
questing criticism" (4: 46). In the 1830 *Minstrelsy*, Scott "recollects" not just
Percy, but also Macpherson and Burns. Scott corrects Macpherson's violations
of scholarship by presenting antiquarian notes with authentic ballads, but he
also vindicates the practice in which Macpherson can be said to have been
engaged of writing imitations of ancient literature. Like Macpherson, Scott
shows himself to be "a bard, capable not only of making an enthusiastic impression on every mind susceptible of poetical beauty, but of giving a new
tone to poetry throughout Europe." And he presents himself in his alternative
genealogy of British literature as a descendent of Burns, "The poet, perhaps,
most capable, by verses, lines, even single words, to relieve and heighten the
character of ancient poetry." Whereas in the 1801–3 *Minstrelsy* Scott moved
the Borders, and himself as a Border writer, from the periphery to the center
of British literature, in the 1830 edition he questions the authenticity of that
center. The 1830 edition, then, represents Scott's movement away from the
model of literature and history found in Percy's *Reliques* toward a renewed
acceptance of the literary ancestors of his own nation.

In *The Achievement of Literary Authority: Gender, History, and the Waverley
Novels*, Ina Ferris examines the way Scott endowed the historical novel with
a sense of legitimacy, establishing himself in the role of patriarch. Ferris also
notes, however, the shift in public opinion and literary standards that resulted
in Scott's exclusion from the literary canon. According to Ferris, Scott was a
victim of the same literary structures he had helped to create. It is worth investigating Scott's fall from literary grace further for its connection to the ongoing struggle to represent Britain in the cultural realm. Scott was able to
satisfy both Scottish and English audiences and, in the words of Harriet Mar-
tineau, to "soften national prejudices" (Hayden, p. 340). But his very popularity and subsequent financial downfall, highlighting as it did the relationship between the market and the nation which he portrayed in the 1830 *Minstrelsy*, made the inclusion of his work into the confines of the canon of
English literature impossible.

In an essay for the *London and Westminster Review* in 1838, Thomas Carlyle
uses Scott, and particularly the *Minstrelsy of the Scottish Border*, in his own en-

terprise of defining "great" English literature. Scott, says Carlyle, represents
not a great writer, but one who was engaged "largely in trade" (Hayden, p.
356). Whereas a great writer delivers an important message to an eagerly
awaiting public, Scott does no such thing, according to Carlyle: "In this nineteenth century, our highest literary man, who immeasurably beyond all others commanded the world's ear, had, as it were, no message whatever to de-
liver to the world; wished not the world to elevate itself, to amend itself, to do
this or to do that, except simply pay him for the books he kept writing"
(Hayden, p. 357). The *Minstrelsy* epitomizes the best and the worst about
Scott, according to Carlyle. The popularity of the ballads is understandable,
he suggests, because "there was the indisputable impress of worth, of genuine
human force, in them" (Hayden, p. 358). Contrasted with the effusions of the
Della Cruscans, Scott's work gave the public a more positive image of "vig-
orous whole-life" (Hayden, p. 358), which was especially important in the beginning of the nineteenth century, "an age fallen into spiritual languor, des-
titute of belief, yet terrified at Scepticism; reduced to live a stinted half-life,
under strange new circumstances" (Hayden, p. 358). But the problem was
that the *Minstrelsy* encouraged a passivity in its readership. The stories were
enjoyable and easily digested; there was "no call for effort on the reader's part;
what excellence they had, exhibited itself at a glance" (Hayden, p. 358).
Scott's writing supplied his British readership with instant and superficial
gratification, a service which Carlyle likens to the efforts of a body-worker:
"What the Turkish bathkeeper is said to aim at with his frictions, and sham-
pooings, and fomentings, more or less effectually, that the patient in total
idleness may have the delights of activity,—was here to a considerable extent
realized" (Hayden, p. 358–59).

Carlyle's essay indicates how closely Scott's literary fortune was linked to
the downfall of his actual fortune, for Scott's financial failure drew undeni-
able attention to the material relationship between writing and money. Carlyle concludes with his reflections on the higher aspirations of literature: "Literature *has* other aims than that of harmlessly amusing indolent languid men:
or if Literature have them not, Literature is a very poor affair" (Hayden, p.
366). Moreover, Scott's literary ambitions are directly connected to his class
ambitions. Carlyle presents him as a suburbanite who aspires to aristocratic
heights: "Walter Scott, one of the gifted of the world, must kill himself that
he may be a country gentleman, the founder of a race of Scottish lairds"
(Hayden, p. 363). But Scott is not a country gentleman, Carlyle implies; he is
middle-class. In particular, Carlyle associates Scott with interior decorating:
Scott writes daily "with the ardour of a steam-engine, that he might make
15,000 & a-year, and buy upholstery with it" (Hayden, p. 363).

With its connection to consumer commodities and the marketplace, a connection which, as we have seen, Scott himself foregrounds in his "Essay on the Imitation of Ancient Ballads," Scott's work does not serve as an example of the transcendent values which Carlyle seeks to promote. Carlyle excluded Scott's work from the category of great literature, but he devotes much attention to his predecessor, Burns. In the concluding chapter I examine how Carlyle, and subsequently Matthew Arnold, used Burns, not Scott, to position Scotland and Scottish writers within the canon of English literature.

Runes of Empire: Scotland and the Margins of English Literature

The previous chapters have examined how the conflicted articulations of national identity by Scots and English writers combined to create a British identity, but one that was intrinsically unstable, demanding constant renegotiation. This renegotiation took different shapes at different historical junctures, and I have attempted to acknowledge the relationship between those specific historical circumstances and the project of writing the nation. I want to conclude with a consideration of how the conflicted identity of Britain as represented through these various literary efforts affected and was affected by the institutionalization of English literature in the nineteenth century.

At that time, in addition to operating within the already complex parameters of the literary marketplace, the articulation of the British nation became associated with the highly political activity of creating a canon of English literature. An important part of nineteenth-century canon formation, I suggest, involved the incorporation of the Celtic periphery into the English hegemonic center, and Scotland served as an ideal periphery for this purpose. First, although it was outside the hegemonic center, Scotland was, unlike Ireland or Wales, similar enough religiously, culturally, and linguistically to England to be incorporated. Second, the work of incorporation had already been partially accomplished during the past hundred years in the work of writers like those examined in the previous chapters. In keeping with the design of this book to foreground the dialogism of the British nation by juxtaposing Scottish and English writers' perspectives, I will explore this negotiation of English dominance and Scottish supplementation as it is represented in the work of Thomas Carlyle, a Scottish critic whom we have already encountered in Chapter 5, and Matthew Arnold, an English critic who had enormous influence over the institutionalization of English literature in the later nineteenth century.

As Robert Crawford and Franklin Court suggest, the institutionalization of English literature actually had its origins in the Scottish university system. Crawford credits the Scots with the invention of English literature, observing that the literati of mid-eighteenth-century Scotland, concerned to improve their knowledge and pronunciation of English, devoted a great deal of attention to studying English rhetoric and *belles lettres* (*Devolving*, p. 15). Court concentrates his observations on Adam Smith and Hugh Blair, both of whom included the study of English literature in their course curricula at Glasgow and Edinburgh (Court, chapter 1). Crawford quotes Smith's comments on learning proper English describe the operative hegemony at the time:

> Our words must not only be English and agreeable to the custom of the country but likewise to the custom of some particular part of the nation. . . . It is the custom of the people that forms what we call pro-pri[e]ty, and the custom of the better sort from whence the rules of purity of stile are to be drawn. As those of the higher rank generally frequent the court, the standard of our language is therefore chiefly to be met with there. (*Devolving*, p. 29)

Smith advocated the study of English literature as a means of achieving access to the English culture to which he so clearly aspired. Blair, however, used the study of English to promote a more nebulous philosophy of taste. According to Blair, possession of such taste would enable individuals to identify universally great works and thereby improve their prospects. Both of their methodologies can be seen as encouraging Scottish participation in the cultural affairs of the nation.

Ironically, this institution of English literature, established originally by Scots to ensure increased Scottish participation in an English-centered British hegemony, was employed south of the border in the nineteenth century to reinforce that hegemony. According to Terry Eagleton, the study of English literature in nineteenth-century England was designed to instill a sense of common universal purpose into all classes as a way of overcoming material inequities (*Literary Theory*, p. 25). Court concurs with Eagleton's assertion: "The idea of an all-encompassing national identity, which in time would assume its own mythic proportions, in the early years of the century they designated as an opportunity for the reconciliation of all classes" (pp. 40–41). Court links the study of literature directly to the desire to promote industrial development and the growth of the British empire, noting the structure whereby this was accomplished:

> The "institution" of literature . . . gradually evolved into a recognizably hegemonic phenomenon that by the end of the nineteenth century combined, in its capacity as a cultural and political determining force, not only the controlling ideologies but also, as Louis Althusser suggests, the formal state apparatuses which made possible the transmission through time of those ideologies. (p. 4)

We can see the groundwork laid for the linking of literature with national progress in the writing of Thomas Carlyle, who was concerned with establishing a Britain that would be a leading power in the world. Although he was himself a Scot, Carlyle liked to emphasize his Teutonic origins; accordingly, his ideological agenda rests on the denial of Scottish difference. Notably, he focuses his attentions on a fellow Scot, not Walter Scott, who, as we have seen, he expels from the canon of "great" literature, but Robert Burns, who serves his ideological purposes more clearly. Following Wordsworth's lead, Carlyle incorporates Burns into the canon of English literature as a marginalized figure.

In his *Essay on Burns*, published originally as a review of Lockhart's *Life of Robert Burns* in the *Edinburgh Review* in 1828, Carlyle confirms Burns's importance in the world of letters. Burns is one of few individuals who "deserve" to be subject to "the great end of Biography" ("Burns," p. 261). Carlyle is effusive in his praise of Burns: "Strictly speaking, perhaps no British man has so deeply affected the thoughts and feelings of so many men, as this solitary and altogether private individual, with means apparently the humblest" (p. 287). Like Wordsworth, Carlyle notes that Burns helped give English literature the infusion of "originality" it needed. Just before Burns appeared on the scene, writes Carlyle, English literature was suffering from "a certain attenuated cosmopolitanism" (p. 287): "Our Grays and Glovers seemed to write almost as if *in vacuo*," not really for "Englishmen" but for "certain Generalizations which philosophy termed men" (p. 288). Carlyle admires Burns for providing a model of how to avoid foreign affectation by being both "natural" and "national": specifically, he says, Burns was responsible for a "remarkable increase of nationality" in Scottish literature.

We can see here how much Carlyle is concerned with furthering an all-encompassing "British" nationalism. Even while noting that Burns has done wonders for Scottish literature, he also recruits Burns into representing the "British" nation, expressing the opinion that Burns is not only a "true British poet," but also "one of the most considerable British men of the eighteenth century" (pp. 4–5). Furthermore, Burns's songs "are already part of the mother-tongue, not of Scotland only, but of Britain, and of the millions that in all ends of the earth speak a British language" (p. 26). However, in this process of ap-propriating Burns for the republic of English letters, Carlyle also marginalizes him. He presents Burns as battling hard against many handicaps, but ulti-mately succumbing. He lists the poet's weaknesses, suggesting that Burns was underprivileged because he was not exposed to truly elevating (English) lit-erature; all Burns had for standards of beauty were the rhymes of Fergusson and Ramsay. What is interesting here is how Burns's weaknesses are described as his lack of maturity, according to standards of coherence. His genius "could never show itself complete"; it "wanted all things for completeness: culture, leisure, true effort, nay, even length of life" (p. 266). Burns made it only part-way up the poetic scale, because, according to Carlyle, he never really grew up; even at thirty-seven, he was "still, as it were, in youth," lacking moral man-hood (p. 30). Ultimately, Carlyle suggests that Burns is most important not for the sake of his poetry but for the sake of his struggles in life.

In *On Heroes, Hero-Worship, and the Heroic in History*, Carlyle indicates his awareness of the larger cultural project which literature can serve: defining a nation. Originally delivered in 1840 as a series of six lectures, *On Heroes* pre-sents Carlyle's concerns about mass rule. Carlyle idealizes a society based on loyalty, faith, and the reverence of heroes who embody the best values of so-ciety. Hero-worship is the method he invents for achieving social cohesion, because hero-worship guarantees consensus despite diversity. According to Carlyle, the kind of hero who is able to achieve that consensus in the present society is the "*Man of Letters*" (p. 133). Carlyle sees writing at the present time as a form of government: "Literature is our Parliament. . . . Printing, which comes necessarily out of Writing . . . is equivalent to Democracy" (p. 141). But Carlyle also wants to control the impact of the democracy. Hence, he selects his literary representatives carefully: Shakespeare, and, with some qualification, Burns.

Carlyle effuses that Shakespeare "is the grandest thing we [English] have yet done" for "our honour among foreign nations" and is "an ornament to our English Household" (p. 96). Drawing an analogy between literature and commerce, Carlyle examines Shakespeare's potential "as a real, marketable, tangibly-useful possession" for uniting England in the nineteenth century (p. 96). Shakespeare as hero-poet can become the equivalent of a monarch, yet better than one, for his reputation is immortal: "Here is an English King, whom no time or chance, Parliament or combination of Parliaments, can de-throne!" "King Shakspeare" will serve as "the noblest, gentlest, yet strongest of rallying-signs" (p. 97). Englishmen will be united by revering Shakespeare because when they revere him they acknowledge sharing the same moral values. Carlyle speculates on whether it would be better to part with England's rule over India or with Shakespeare, and he decides that Shakespeare is less expendable. As he reasons, "Indian Empire or no Indian Empire; we cannot do without Shakspeare! Indian Empire will go, at any rate, some day; but this Shakspeare does not go, he lasts forever with us" (p. 96). He continues, suggesting the universal bond that Shakespeare provides: "From Paramatta, from New York, wheresoever, under what sort of Parish-Constable soever, English men and women are, they will say to one another: 'Yes, this Shakspeare is ours; we produced him, we speak and think by him; we are of one blood and kind with him'" (p. 97). Carlyle recognizes that cultural hegemony is actually the means to a bigger empire than any particular piece of land. By controlling Shakespeare (and the criticism which validates him), England can control the means of cultural production: "before long, this Island of ours, will hold but a small fraction of the English: in America, in New Holland, east and west to the very Antipodes, there will be a Saxondom covering great spaces of the Globe" (p. 96). Carlyle makes Shakespeare, once master of the theatrical Globe, into master of the world globe, a master who will "keep all these together into virtually one Nation, so that they do not fall-out and fight, but live at peace, in brotherlike intercourse, helping one another" (p. 96).

But Carlyle suggests there is yet another "true poet" who will help keep English-speaking people united: Robert Burns. In *On Heroes*, Carlyle elaborates on what he had written in his *Essay*, praising Burns's "sincerity" as his best quality. His "noble rough genuineness; homely, rustic, honest; true simplicity of strength" helped to counteract the skepticism that Carlyle saw as characteristic of the eighteenth century (p. 163). Carlyle notes, "The largest soul of all the British lands came among us in the shape of a hard-handed Scottish Peasant" (p. 162). However, Carlyle also repeats Burns's difficulties. Burns, Carlyle says, was "uninstructed, poor, born only to hard manual toil; and writing . . . in a rustic special dialect known only to a small province of the country he lived in" (p. 162). These faults proved too much to overcome. Although Carlyle at first praises Burns for his "originality," he ultimately relegates him to a minor status, to being a child in comparison to the more mature English poets. It is significant, then, that he refers to Burns as "a King in exile" ("Burns," p. 7), suggesting that Burns, too, can also help fashion the "one Nation." Whereas Shakespeare is a king over all the English-speaking world, Burns is an example of a hero-poet found on the margins of English literary history who can be useful in rallying the marginalized people. Carlyle indicates Burns's appeal to the different social and regional groups in the

British Isles and in the English-speaking empire. He is read by all classes, from duchesses to waiters and ostlers (*Heroes*, p. 163). Burns, like Shakespeare, is a universal poet, but Burns's role is more specific; he is to be a unifying point for the disenfranchised groups within the larger framework: the lower classes and the non-English. Carlyle notes:

> He has gained a certain recognition, and is continuing to do so over all quarters of our wide Saxon world: wheresoever a Saxon dialect is spoken, it begins to be understood, by personal inspection of this and the other, that one of the most considerable Saxon men of the Eighteenth century was an Ayrshire Peasant named Robert Burns. ("Burns," 162)

Burns represents for Carlyle both the desire for inclusion and the actual marginalization of peripheries. Burns was indeed a "King in exile," a necessary figure whose existence as an outlaw ultimately ensures the power of the de facto ruling power.

Carlyle's writing prefigures the ethnographic and imperial concerns which influenced the direction of English literary study in the later nineteenth century. Court points out that "dogmatic political and racial overtones" came increasingly to characterize English literary study:

> English studies in the academy would gradually incorporate into its pedagogical focus a uniform vision of an Anglo-Saxon empire deemed superior in the wide spectrum of western civilization in large measure because of the Teutonic basis of its racial heritage. The responsibilities of English professors were to analyze the highly signifying language patterns that most vividly recalled the past greatness of the race and to isolate and preserve for posterity the works of those visionary authors who best captured the Saxon essence, the political and spiritual essence of the nation. (p. 73)

Perhaps the most important commentator on this subject is Matthew Arnold, who, as a literary critic and a school inspector, had an immense impact both on the controlling ideologies and on the state apparatuses. In *The Social Mission of English Criticism, 1848–1932*, Chris Baldick comments on Arnold's importance in the institutionalization of English, noting how he attempted to address the disillusion and discontent in the public sphere by "introduc[ing] into English critical writing a new sense of self-consciousness, a new sensitivity to the wider social and cultural duties befitting its special guardianship" while at the same time claiming criticism's "disinterestedness," its purity from practical matters (p. 19). Arnold was concerned, especially after the 1860s, with ethnography, in particular with promoting Teutonic superiority. In *On the Study of Celtic Literature*, for example, he recommends the subordination of the "Celtic spirit" to the Saxon "genius." Arnold's writing relies on the containment of Scotland as a model for the assimilation of class and ethnic difference both in the British Isles and in the wider British empire. According to Arnold, the incorporation of Scotland can be seen as an indication of the success of British imperial culture.

Like Carlyle, Arnold pays particular attention to Robert Burns as a representative of the margins. Arnold, too, subordinates Burns by privileging the quality of "completeness." In his *Study of Poetry*, Arnold evaluates touchstones for their "completeness" of thought and content. Arnold seeks to reevaluate English literature chronologically, beginning with Chaucer, to show how certain works for which there has been critical agreement have been mistakenly valued. Chaucer, Dryden, and Pope, he determines, have been overrated due to "historic estimate"—they appeared at particularly important spots of time. Burns has been overrated because of "personal estimate." Critics were so impressed by his achievement in overcoming the detrimental effects of his background that they gave too much value to his poems. Arnold sets out to devalue these poets' "currency," and judging by the amount of space he devotes to Burns, he is particularly anxious to dispel the high estimation of the Scottish poet. His methodology is to attack what had been most praised by Burns's critics: his originality. Arnold proceeds through a number of Burns's works praised by critics, in an effort to show how each in its turn fails to represent the "real" Robert Burns.

First of all, Arnold dismisses the English poetry which Burns writes for not reflecting "the real Burns." Arnold draws on Burns's own complaint about his lack of facility with the English language to dispute the originality of his poems in that tongue: "I have not the command of [English] that I have of my native tongue. In fact, I think my ideas are more barren in English than in Scotch" (9: 182).[1] Arnold says that although "we English turn naturally, in Burns, to the poems in our own language," this is not where the "real" Burns is found (9: 182). It would appear, however, that the real Burns is not to be found in the "Scotch" poems, either. "There is something in [the Scotch poems] . . . which makes us feel that we have not the man speaking to us with his real voice; something, therefore, poetically unsound" (9: 182), pronounces Arnold. He does not accept anything Burns says as registering sincerity, utilizing instead adjectives like "shrewd" and "arch" to describe Burns's style. He maintains that Burns is most himself when he utilizes irony or pathos, suggesting, in essence, that Burns is most himself when he is not himself, when he is acting a part. Here, Arnold's criticisms contradict those of

Carlyle and other critics who praised Burns for writing so naturally about his native environs.

In fact, it is not Burns's voice that Arnold dismisses as being nonpoetic, but his nationality. Much of Burns's Scots poetry deals with "Scotch drink, Scotch religion, and Scotch manners," he says, which is familiar to the Scots, but not to the English, and it seems that accessibility to an English audience is an important criterion of "greatness" to Arnold: "This world of Scotch drink, Scotch religion, and Scotch manners is against a poet" (9: 184). Arnold says that Burns is at a disadvantage because he is portraying "a harsh, a sordid, a repulsive world," and he is doing this without even the seriousness found in bacchanalian poetry. Arnold's final analysis of Burns's poetry, then, effectively discounts all of Burns's work. Arnold objects that when Burns writes in English he cannot write in a truly poetic manner, and when he writes in his native Scots he lacks serious poetic matter. For Arnold, there is only one kind of acceptable originality, that which is most truly English. By using the figure of Burns, Arnold, like Carlyle before him, succeeds in reasserting the dominance of England over the Celtic provinces in aesthetic concerns. Arnold twists the view of Burns as a natural or "original" poet that made him so popular, suggesting that a poet like Burns can never be considered "original" because he is on the periphery of the cultural community of readers who set standards of taste. In essence, Arnold makes "originality" equal Englishness. Burns's eventual placement on the cultural margin, then, becomes useful for defining the boundaries of the center.

Arnold's *On the Study of Celtic Literature* (1867) proposes a more general model for the assimilation of Celtic into English culture. In this project, Arnold's more immediate target is Ireland. But Scotland serves as an example of a successfully integrated Celtic nation, one whose importance lies in its supplemental position. Arnold draws on stereotyping and mythology to identify the ancestral strains of the modern British people, the Celtic and the Saxon geniuses, reversing many of Macpherson's assertions in the process. According to Arnold, the typical Saxon is steady and honest, although inclining to dullness. The Celt is passionate and impractical, always reacting against "*the despotism of fact*," a characteristic that explains why he accomplishes so little of practical worth, according to Arnold (3: 344). The Celt is "undisciplinable, anarchical, and turbulent by nature" (3: 347), although he can devote himself to a leader wholeheartedly. Arnold contrasts this dogged devotion of the Celt with the Saxon temperament, which is "disciplinable and steadily obedient within certain limits, but retaining an inalienable part of freedom and self-dependence" (3: 347). This difference in self-reliance leads Arnold to conclude that the Saxon is the more mature of the two. Arnold also relegates the Celts to the realm of nature, not civilization. They have "a peculiarly near and intimate feeling of nature and the life of nature" (3: 347). This association with nature also leads Arnold to speculate on the parallels between the Celtic and the feminine: "The sensibility of the Celtic nature, its nervous exaltations, have something of the feminine in them." The Celt is "peculiarly disposed to feel the spell of the feminine idiosyncrasy . . . he is not far from its secret" (3: 347).

Arnold's purpose in delineating the Celt and Saxon characters is to show how the two can be conjoined for the ultimate benefit of Britain. He observes that the Celtic and Saxon nations already share a point of origin, but that the intermixture that occurs as a result of encounter is more important. The science of philology, he says, has already proved the common origin of the Celt and the German in the Indo-European language. But, says Arnold, the affinity between races still "in their mother's womb" counts for little (3: 336). It is only when "the embryo has grown and solidifies into a distinct nature," when races have developed "marked, national, ineffaceable qualities to oppose or to communicate" (3: 336), that similarities between them mean the most. Arnold suggests that the amalgamation of nations is a "natural" law. He clinches his argument when he notes that "Science,—true science,—recognises in the bottom of her soul a law of ultimate fusion, of conciliation" (3: 330). The totalizing effect of Arnold's project to unite the British Isles is evident:

> The fusion of all the inhabitants of these islands into one homogeneous, English-speaking whole, the breaking down of barriers between us, the swallowing up of separate provincial nationalities, is a consummation to which the natural course of things irresistibly tends; it is a necessity of what is called modern civilization, and modern civilization is a real, legitimate force. (3: 296–97)

The "consummation" Arnold describes here, however, is actually a unilateral action: the consuming or "swallowing up" of the Celtic provinces by England and the eradication of any languages other than English. Although Arnold claims in *On the Study of Celtic Literature* that he wants to provide both the Celts and the English with information about each other so that they can better know each other, the power of this knowledge lies on only one side: that of the English. In the final part of the essay, Arnold encourages the establishment of a chair of Celtic at Oxford, which would oversee instruction in the Celtic languages and literatures. Arnold recommends reducing Celtic languages to products that would be consumed within the English university system.

It is important to Arnold's argument that he shows that the natural course of things will lead to the fusion of Celt and Saxon. But in a sense he suggests that this fusion has already occurred; its manifestation is the "English genius": "I say that there is a Celtic element in this English nature, as well as a Germanic element, and that this element manifests itself in our spirit and literature" (3: 341). By the end of the essay, it is clear that even the teaching of Celtic would demonstrate how the Celt has already been absorbed into English culture: "in the spiritual frame of us English ourselves," says Arnold, "a Celtic fibre, little as we may have ever thought of tracing it, lives and works" (3: 384). Arnold suggests that England's geographical proximity to the Celtic nations has occasioned this cultural crossover. Except for "early, frequent, and various contact" with the Celtic race, Arnold suggests, "Germanic English would not have produced a Shakespeare" (3: 376). His proof for this cultural fusion is found in English literature, as he directly identifies Celtic magic in "Shakespeare's touch in his daffodil, Wordsworth's in his cuckoo, Keats's in his Autumn." He adds, "The main current of English Literature cannot be disconnected from the lively Celtic wit in which it has one of its sources" (3: 376). For Arnold, then, English literature is a manifestation of a cultural fusion that has already taken place as well as a model for future fusion.

The position of Scotland in this cultural delineation proves especially vital in Arnold's argument, as he uses the literature of that nation to articulate the supplemental position he prescribes for Celtic culture. Macpherson's Ossian is particularly important in promoting a Scottish culture that is unique, but that has already been defeated. The epigraph of *On the Study of Celtic Literature* is taken from Macpherson's "Cathloda." It suggests the essential ineptitude of the Celts: "They went forth to war, but they always fell" (3: 291). The line is repeated within the essay. Arnold suggests that Ossian "carried in the last century this [Celtic] vein of piercing regret and passion like a flood of lava through Europe." He seeks to present the Ossianic poetry as pure "Celtic spirit":

> Make the part of what is forced, modern, tawdry, spurious, in [*Fingal*] as large as you please; strip Scotland, if you like of every feather of borrowed plumes which on the strength of Macpherson's *Ossian* she may have stolen from that *vetus et major Scotia*, the true home of the Ossianic poetry, Ireland . . . there will still be left in the book a residue with the very soul of the Celtic genius in it, and which has the proud distinction of having brought this soul of the Celtic genius into contact with the genius of the nations of modern Europe, and enriched all our poetry by it. (3: 371)

Ossian is here credited with "having brought this soul of the Celtic genius" into common currency. Arnold points out that the only poetry which has the "proud distinction of performing this task" comes from an inauthentic tradition, as the real tradition is Irish. Furthermore, he implies it is only when the residue of the spirit is isolated that the Celtic spirit can have an effect on "the nations of modern Europe." The Celtic spirit, then, is something which is created onlythrough falseness, distillation, and intermixture. It is of necessity already partially assimilated. Scotland serves as a Celtic nation which, like the disembodied "Celtic spirit," is always already incorporated into Britain. In this process, Scotland itself vanishes, reduced to a mere "residue," while the Celtic soul "enriches" or nourishes European, especially English poetry.

Paradoxically, however, Arnold's description of Macpherson's "residue" of Celtic spirit also suggests that the actual Irish tradition from which Ossian's poetry is derived remains, but that it is entirely inaccessible to the "nations of modern Europe." It cannot be translated by attempts like Ossian's. Although Arnold tries to deny the threat of Ireland by referring to it with the appellation "*major Scotia*," he cannot erase the haunting presence behind the name. *On the Study of Celtic Literature*, then, while seeking to fuse Celtic difference into the English "genius" also reveals the impossibility of this task. Behind Arnold's manifesto of 1867 lies a legacy of struggles and conflicts between England and the Celtic nations, of which, as we have seen, Macpherson's Ossian is only a recent embodiment.

In *Masks of Conquest: Literary Study and British Rule in India*, Gauri Viswanathan considers the connection between the "institutionalization of English in India and the exercise of colonial power, between the processes of curricular selection and the impulse to dominate and control" (p. 3). He argues, "The checkered history of English studies in India points to the inherent contradictions of the British sociocultural project that allowed it to fail in its own (heterogeneous) terms" (p. 168). In this study, I have examined the source of one of these inherent contradictions, drawing attention to the complex negotiations involved in literature as it developed within Britain itself, the cracks in the "masks of conquest" caused by the tensions between England and Scotland. The efforts of Belhaven, Defoe, Smollett, Fielding, Macpherson, Johnson, Burns, Wordsworth, Percy, and Scott in the cultural realm to represent the nation reveal nothing so much as the incommensurabilities that exist within Britain, incommensurabilities written and rewritten in literature at different times and in different configurations.

On September 11, 1997, Scottish voters resolved to renegotiate a Union that had been in existence for nearly three hundred years. (Welsh voters followed suit a week later, approving an assembly that would have more limited powers than the Parliament of Scotland.) The practical issues that the institution of a Scottish Parliament in the year 2000 raises are mind-boggling. What will happen to the number of Scottish MPs in Westminster? How will the population-based equation for determining spending in Scotland known as the "Barnett" formula be calculated now? How will the combination of "first past the post" and proportional representation operate? There are other more theoretical questions to be raised as well. The White Paper on *Scotland's Parliament* published by the Scottish Office concludes optimistically: "The Government believe that the establishment of a Scottish Parliament on the basis set out here will be good for Scotland, and good for the UK; responding to the wishes of the people of Scotland for a greater say in their affairs can only strengthen democracy in this country" (p. 36). But a Scottish Parliament can also offer the opportunity for a rethinking of the concepts of national identity and political representation, a rethinking that would have implications for both "the UK" and "democracy."

A Scottish Parliament may (and we should emphasize the conditional tense here, for the extent of the changes remains to be seen) serve to reorient the rest of Britain toward more regional identity and provide a environment more receptive to the concerns of previously underrepresented groups. Writing in another context, John Rajchman poses the question: "what would a democracy be which allows for the unpredictable movement of those unnamed 'others' within, without, or 'in-between' that would serve to transform the very idea of who comprises it, and therefore, of what it is and can do?"[2] In order to maximize the potential for such a rethinking, it is crucial to turn our attention to the many ways in which the nation has been created in the past and to the gaps that such acts of creation attempted to cover over. It is my hope that this book will be read not just as an account of an era of literary history, but also as an ongoing interrogation of how writing has served both to invent and to challenge the nation of Britain.

REFERENCE MATTER

Introduction: Acts of Union

1. Recent studies of nationalism relevant to this study include Breuilly (1993), Gellner (1983), Hobsbawm (1990), and A. Smith (1991). Ahmad (1992) offers a critique of current academic concerns with the nation.

2. A. Smith writes, "The formation of nations in the nineteenth and twentieth centuries has been profoundly influenced by the examples of England, France and Spain" (p. 59). Similarly, Anderson (1991) proposes that the nations in Europe developed particular characteristics that became "modular," capable of importation to other contexts (p. 4).

3. Nairn (1981) argues that Britain, as the first industrial nation, followed a unique path of evolution rather than invention. My study argues that it was in fact continually invented in response to historical events.

4. See also Lerner and Ringrose (1993) for a collection of essays that takes Anderson as a starting point, but also seeks out "strategies for countering the totalizing effects of the nationalist discourse" (p. 4).

5. He writes: "Nationalism denies the alleged inferiority of the colonized people; it also asserted that a backward nation could 'modernize' itself while retaining its cultural identity. It thus produced a discourse in which, even as it challenged the colonial claim to political domination, it also accepted the very intellectual premises of 'modernity' on which colonial domination was based" (p. 30).

6. In his more recent book, *The Nation and Its Fragments* (1993), Chatterjee continues his explorations for a method to circumvent the kind of monolingual discourse that has produced analyses of nationalism: "Against [a subject-centered reason] critics have been trying to resurrect the virtues of the fragmentary, the local, and the subjugated in order to unmask the will to power that lies at the very heart of modern rationality and to decenter its epistemological and moral subject" (p. xii). He suggests that "materials from colonial and postcolonial situations" (p. xii) can play an important part in this enterprise. I would add that materials from the colonizing situations can also shed light on the problem.

7. As is apparent from the current discussion of devolution, however, the

cultural realm will no longer bear the burden of holding the political nation together; another political formulation is necessary at this point.

8. Julia Kristeva's phrase "the strangeness within ourselves" (1993, p. 29) is
useful here, although I am not using the same model of national identity that
she does. Addressing the problem of nationalism in France, Kristeva reads the
formation of national identity as a psychosexual drama. Starting from a Freud-
ian perspective that links rejection of the Other with the child's differentiation
from its mother, she suggests that a nation's ego is formed by projecting difference within itself onto others.

9. For a discussion of Scottish literature before the Act of Union, see Lindsay
(1977), Watson (1984), and Kratzmann (1980).

10. For a history of events leading to the Union, see Ferguson (1964).

11. In his admirably detailed book *Britannia's Issue* (1993), Howard Weinbrot
examines the assimilation of "Scottish Celtic and Hebrew Jewish cultures" into
Britain (p. 1).

12. Murray Pittock's *Inventing and Resisting Britain* is a healthy alternative to
Colley's and Weinbrot's formulations of British unity.

13. Daiches (1964) notes, "Those poets who did not emigrate to England
and write in English in an English tradition either wrote in Scotland in English
for an English audience or turned to a regional vernacular poetry in a spirit of
sociological condescension, patriotic feeling, or antiquarian revival" (p. 21).

14. Crawford's recent edited collection of essays *The Scottish Invention of
English Literature* (1998) continues to explore this theme.

15. Situating her study around the figure of the bard, Trumpener (1997) argues that Irish, Welsh, and Scottish writers developed a sense of cultural nationalism in relation to English hegemony, which English writers then co-opted
and altered. She traces this dialogue from Britain's internal colonial situation
to its external empire, arguing that the construction of cultural nationalism became employed in both the establishment and contestation of Britain's imperial
identity.

16. Daiches (1964) comments on the attempt to erase scotticisms from the
language. He suggests that this streak of purism was particularly prominent after the 1745 rebellion, when Scottish writers tried to change the telltale signs
of being from North Britain. There were public lectures on proper pronunciation. (Richard Sheridan, a good Anglo-Irishman, delivered one such talk in Edinburgh.) Guides and grammars featuring proper English and listing examples
abounded, with titles like *The English Spelling-Book* (1798), *A New Grammar
with Exercises of Bad English; or, an Easy Guide to Speaking and Writing the English
Language Properly and Correctly*, and *The Only Sure Guide to English Tongue; or
New Pronouncing Dictionary* (1776).

17. McCrone (1992) suggests that Scotland illustrates the falseness of the as-

sumption "that the nation-state is equivalent to society" (p. 2). He explores how Scotland struggles to assert its own identity and to diverge from England, even though it has continued to be part of a centralized Britain.

18. Williams (1963), too, hints at this: "The idea of culture describes our common inquiry, but our conclusions are diverse, as our starting points were diverse. The word, culture, cannot automatically be pressed into service as any kind of social or personal directive" (p. 285).

19. Murphy (1993) suggests this by the fact that four out of the five writers he studies as models of professional writers in the late eighteenth century are Scottish. Murphy himself refuses to consider the implications of his work when he writes in the first sentence of his book: "In spite of the Scottish cast to the list of writers on the table of contents, this is not a book about Scottish writers" (p. 1).

20. Contemporary work on postcolonialism is too extensive to present comprehensively, but see especially Ashcroft et al. (1989), Jameson (1986), Parry (1987), Said (1994), and Spivak (1987).

Chapter 1: Writing the Nation in 1707

1. For previous interpretations of the Union, see R. H. Campbell (1964), Ferguson (1964) and (1977), Levack (1987), Phillipson and Mitchison (1970), Pryde (1950), Riley (1978), and Smout (1964) and (1969). See Whatley (1994) for an examination of the historiography of the Act of Union.

2. Quoted from Defoe's poem, "On the approaching UNION of the two Kingdoms":

> PEACE from the *North dawns* like the rising Day,
> And *jarring Nations* calmer laws obey:
> *Uniting Britain* from Contention free,
> Shall change her Feuds and Chains for Peace and Liberty.
> The envying Nations for Defence prepare,
> The vast Conjunction learns the World to fear.
>
> *(ll. 1–6) ("Review" 4, no. 1, p. 2)*

3. His first published book was actually a work on trade entitled *An Essay on Projects* (1697). Dijkstra (1987) notes that Defoe himself professed that "his major preoccupation, both in his writings and his personal life had always been 'trade', and its 'Method, Manner and Consequences'" (p. 4).

4. Colley (1992) notes, for example, that in 1700, England took one-half of Scottish exports (p. 12). See also Mason (1994) for an account of relations between the two countries at the time of the Union of Crowns.

5. In 1695 the Licensing Act expired when the House of Commons and the House of Lords failed to agree on the details of its renewal. Restrictions on

publication were lifted and there was a huge growth in the print industry. See
Plumb (1982), pp. 265–85. See also Feather (1980), p. 21.

6. Poems on the affairs of state had been circulated in manuscript form for
a considerable time. An anthology of such poems was published in 1689, before
the Licensing Act expired. George de F. Lord (1975) suggests that there subsequently arose a growing popularity for printed state poems, reflecting both "an
expanding society of authors" and "an expanded reading public" (p. xviii).
More people were able to read and be influenced by printed debate than ever
before. See also Backscheider (1986), p. 67, and Plumb (1982), pp. 268–73.

7. Pittock (1991) observes, "Within the context of the British state . . . in-
cremental history's essential premiss is the Revolution of 1688/89 and the constitutional developments which, flowing from it, established the state itself and
consolidated the British Empire" (p. 1).

8. As Feather (1980) notes, "Harley was . . . the first major politician ever
to be exposed to a more or less free press at a time of great political discord"
(p. 23).

9. See *Defoe's Review*, vol. 1, p. xviii, for publication details.

10. *Defoe's Review*, vol. 1, "Preface."

11. Ibid.

12. This new form of journalism was a clearly a success. Downie (1979) es-
timates that each *Review* sold five hundred copies, and a substantially greater
number of people would actually read it (p. 9). In fact, the *Review's* popularity
was cause for some consternation because it was read by lower-class members
(p. 6). Backscheider (1986) quotes Charles Leslie, a rival journalist, in his preface to *The Rehearsal*, on this phenomenon: "The greatest part of the *people* cannot read at all, but they will gather around one that can *read*, and listen to . . .
[a] *Review* (as I have seen them in the streets)" (p. 153).

13. In the same letter in which he set down his understanding of his mis-
sion, he had written to Harley of his intention to bring up the issue of the
Union in the *Review*: "I have been Considering About Treating of Union in the
Review and Unless your judgment and Orders Differ believe as I shall Man-
nage it, it Must be Usefull, but beg hints from you if you find it Otherwise"
(*Letters*, p. 128).

14. See Dickey (1995) and Armitage (1995).

15. See W. R. McLeod and V. B. McLeod (1979) for a comprehensive listing
of works concerned with the Union.

16. Pittock (1991) suggests that the idea of the ethnically pure nation corresponded originally with the project of Stewart restoration, and that although at
first it was a view of Scotland popular only among Jacobites, "the measures
leading to Union widened its appeal" (*Invention of Scotland*, p. 25).

17. Craig was also author of *De Unione Regnorum Britanniae Tractatus* (1605),

however, which advocated the union of the two nations into an imperial British monarchy. Craig dispenses with the assertion that Scotland had paid homage to kings in England before the Norman conquest, arguing that "fee" and "homage" did not come into English vocabulary before the conquest. Furthermore, he turns the claims of English historiographers on their heads. He points out that the unification of England was accomplished only through conquest of outsiders. England was not a united nation before the Romans, says Craig, nor could they remain united on their own. Once the Romans had left, the people were unable to fend off the attacks of the Scots and the Picts and had to call in Saxons to help them. In a sense, then, he suggests that the unification of England can be traced to the actions of the Scots. In contrast to England's history of conquest, Craig asserts Scotland's national independence.

18. The burning of his work in no way deterred him. In *The Superiority and Direct Dominion of the Imperial Crown of England Over the Crown and Kingdom of Scotland . . . Reasserted* (1705), Atwood further attacks the idea of Scottish independence: "In Alfred's Time, the Scots, (though many of them might line up and down within his Monarchy) were so far from having a distinct Government in this Island, that they were not so much as a distinct Nation within it" (p. 13).

19. According to Kidd (1993), Buchanan "constructed an ancient constitutional history of Scotland, relying on a theory of popular sovereignty in which the 'people' meant an assembly of the nobles and clan chiefs" (p. 20).

20. For biographical information on Belhaven, see the entry for "John Hamilton (1656–1708)" in *The Dictionary of National Biography*, 8: 1081–83.

21. Pittock (1991) comments on the way Belhaven appropriated biblical language to his cause (*Invention of Scotland*, pp. 35–36).

22. *The Lord Beilhaven's Speech in the Scotch Parliament, 2 November 1706* (Edinburgh, 1706), p. 3.

23. See Strong (1984).

24. *A Second Defense of the Scotish Vision* has been attributed to Belhaven. See Macaree (1978).

25. Others include the Earl of Cromartie, Lord Hamilton, and Andrew Fletcher of Saltoun.

26. Lennard Davis (1983) writes of the "profound changes . . . occurring in the general attitude toward language" during the eighteenth century because of the development of print culture, the result of which he identifies as "a kind of confusion of signification" (p. 141). According to Davis, "Print was becoming not only legitimate but the guarantor of immortality, fame, and public existence, taking on the capacity to embody within its representation the entire scope and shape of a human life in the form of biography and pseudobiography. At the same time, because of the enforcement of libel laws, printers and writers

had to become more and more circumspect in their references and representations. . . . To a certain extent narrative became so interpretable that it became difficult to know for sure if a reference to one thing might not be a disguised reference to something else" (p. 141).

27. The conflicts regarding the printing of the *History* further suggest the impossibility of the task. Backscheider (1989) notes that Defoe suffered "increasingly vicious personal attacks" during his time in Scotland, culminating in the prepublication attack on his *History* (*Life*, p. 259). In particular, Defoe was attacked for presenting an inaccurate account of the part the Reverend James Clark played in the Glasgow riot of November 7, 1706. Twenty years later, Defoe faced some of the same problems when he turned to a new narrative form of national imagining with *A Tour Thro' the Whole Island of Great Britain* (1724–26). See Schellenberg (1995) for an account of the problems in Defoe's *Tour*.

28. See Daiches (1964, pp. 13–30), and Ross and Scobie (1974) for commentary on these collections.

29. The National Library of Scotland contains the following editions of Belhaven's speech: *The Late Lord Belhaven's speeches . . . consider'd* (London, 1719 and 1733); *Belhaven's Three Speeches: as also, the Articles of Union, as ratified in Parliament Jan. 16, 1707: with the tenor of the Act for securing the Protestant religion, and Presbyterian Church government* (Edinburgh, 1725); Reay Sabourn, *The Scotch Prophecy: or, the Lord Belhaven's Remarkable Speech Before the Union, Examin'd and Compar'd with the Articles afterward Concluded, and now Subsisting. Wherein The Advantages accruing to Scotland by the Union, are discovered* (London, 1737); *Belhaven's Speeches in the Parliament, holder at Edinburgh November 1706* (Edinburgh, 1741); and editions for G. Alston (Edinburgh, 1779) and J. Bryce (Glasgow, 1784). Other editions, published in 1731 (London), 1751 (Edinburgh), 1766 (Edinburgh), and 1780 (n.p.) are cited in the British Library Catalogue and the National Union Catalog. The *Dictionary of National Biography* entry on John Hamilton, Lord Belhaven, notes that the speech is "the only specimen of Scotch parliamentary oratory which has found its way into English collections of rhetorical masterpieces" (8: 1082).

Chapter 2: Narrating the '45

1. See also Lenman (1980), chapter 7. It should be noted that only certain Highland clans rose against the house of Hanover. Recent scholarly attention to the Jacobite 1745 Rebellion has yielded fresh insight into its historical circumstances. The complexity of the new interpretations was made evident at the Eighteenth-Century Scottish Studies conference on Jacobitism held from July 29 to August 3, 1995, in Aberdeen.

2. Similarly, Hunter (1994) argues that "Practicing novelists took from a va-

riety of sources what they could . . . and much of what they took came from popular, not literary sources" (p. 135).

3. Michael McKeon (1987) argues that the novel gained its "modern, 'institutional' stability and coherence" because of its "unrivaled power both to formulate, and to explain, a set of problems that are central to early modern experience" (p. 20). In particular, McKeon proposes that the novel helped to mediate in two interrelated crises: that of epistemology ("how to tell the truth") and that of social relations ("how the external social order is related to the internal, moral state of its members") (p. 20).

4. I employ the Scottish spelling of the name here, which reflects the family's historical connection with the occupation of stewardship.

5. Upon hearing of Charles's landing, George II issued a proclamation offering £30,000 for the seizure of the man who would be king. Charles issued a counterproclamation, claiming that George was a fraud and attesting that George's proclamation was only a "scandalous and malicious Paper published in the Stile and Form of a Proclamation" (Proclamation, August 22, 1745).

6. The proclamation of December 23, 1743, declared that Charles was now Regent and noted that he promised "dissolution of the Union and abolition of the Malt Tax" (Jones [1954], pp. 225–26).

7. Cited in Fielding (1987).

8. Coley (Fielding [1987]) says that "with the exception of some published sermons and some editorializing in the newspapers, there was not a great deal yet in print, though much was about to be" (p. xxxv).

9. References to Locke's edition of the *True Patriot* are indicated in the text. All other references are to Coley's edition.

10. Locke (1964) divides the letters into three groups: those that are obviously imaginary; those that are meant to be of real correspondence; and those that are actual correspondence (pp. 21–23).

11. Forbes was a Scot.

12. See Prebble (1961), Hook and Ross (1995), and Speck (1981) for discussions of the aftermath of the '45.

13. Lennard Davis (1983) sees the marriage of Tom and Sophia at the end of the novel as an allegory of the unification of the nation: "Like George I and his line, Tom is welcomed to a union with England's rich fields; and with the destruction of the competing presumptions at Culloden, even the Tory guardian of these fields—Western, of the Country interest—is now persuaded and delighted" (p. 289).

14. Hudson (1990) points out that the characters in the novel "are repeatedly faced with the task of interpreting the words and actions of others: like us, they are 'readers,' and their habits of interpretation contribute to our sense of what forms of judgement we should adopt or avoid" (p. 17).

15. Cerny (1992) suggests, "He makes the reader learn on his own, not by telling him what he thinks is right, but by letting him discover sense and nonsense for himself" (p. 143).

16. For diverse critical interpretations of this scene, see Battestin (1967), Brown (1979), Carlton (1988), Cleary (1984, chapter 6), Lennard Davis (1983, chapter 11), Kearney (1973), and Schonhorn (1981). See also McCrea (1981, chapter 5).

17. In contrast to Basker's (1991) and Simpson's (1988) examinations of Smollett's ambiguities, Goldberg (1959) argues that, viewed in the context of the Scottish School of Common Sense, "Smollett is neither ambiguous nor contradictory" (p. 5).

18. *Poems, Plays, and The Briton*, pp. 23–26.

19. These lines from the poem are similar to lines found in *The Regicide*, which was written earlier, but which was published later than the poem. The phrase from *The Regicide* is as follows: "Weep, Caledonia, weep—thy peace is slain— / Thy father and thy king!" (p. 111).

20. The first incident in the confrontation took place as a result of Smollett's assertion that, despite Fielding's claims to the contrary, he had actually been paid to write the *True Patriot*. Smollett also attacked Fielding in the first edition of *Peregrine Pickle* (1751), though by the second edition he had removed the offending passages. In retaliation for this comment, Fielding attacked Smollett in the second number of the *Covent Garden Journal* (January 7, 1752). *A Faithful Narrative of the Base and Inhuman Arts That Were Lately Practised upon the Brain of Habbakuk Hilding, Justice, Dealer and Chapman, Who Now Lies at His House in Convent-Garden, in a Deplorable State of Lunacy: A Dreadful Monument of False Friendship and Delusion* was published a week after Fielding's description of the Grub Street battle. The author, most probably Smollett, attacks the legitimacy of Fielding's fiction, complaining that Fielding had taken the characters of Partridge and Jenny Jones from his own characters, Strap and Miss Williams.

21. See Armstrong (1987) for a complementary account of the novel form as a representation and agent of the change from the realm of politics to the realm of culture. Armstrong focuses on how "domestic fiction actively sought to disentangle the language of sexual relation from the language of politics and, in so doing, to introduce a new form of political power" (p. 3).

Chapter 3: Origin of the Specious

1. For a discussion on the changes in the Highlands, see Withers (1988).

2. David Hume's *Treatise of Human Nature* (1739–40), Frances Hutcheson's *System of Moral Philosophy* (1755), and Adam Ferguson's *Essay on the History of Civil Society* (1766), for example, addressed variously the best means by which

to cultivate "civic virtue." For commentary on the Scottish Enlightenment, see Dwyer (1987), Hont and Ignatieff (1984), and Rendall (1978).

3. See Introduction, pp. 8–11. See also Basker (1991).

4. See Sher (1985).

5. See Newman (1987) and Lucas (1990).

6. See Langford (1989, p. 327) for reflections on the virulence of anti-Scottish sentiment at the time.

7. Colley (1992) suggests that the "extremism" of anti-Scottish sentiment in Bute's era "was testimony to the fact that the barriers between England and Scotland were coming down" (p. 121).

8. My account of this debate differs in emphasis from that of Trumpener, who also regards it as crucial to the construction of the British nation. Trumpener (1997) reads Macpherson's project as more subversive than I do, suggesting that his promotion of orality indicates his involvement with a Scottish Enlightenment nationalist project invested in demonstrating how "although cultural forms originate in one specific historical epoch, they can survive into the next" (p. 74). In addition, Trumpener suggests that *Ossian* "drew readers into an unfamiliar, threatening, and alien cultural world, making it appear to them, for the first time, as sublime, heroic, and tragically doomed" (p. 76). Although Trumpener's readings are acute, I suggest here that the Ossianic poems' subversive nature is compromised by their promotion of British hegemonic values. Similarly, Trumpener reads Johnson's *Journey* as an attempt to establish "the primacy of a cosmopolitan and imperial vision of Enlightenment activity over what it sees as Scotland's nationalist Enlightenment, of the forces of linguistic normalization over those of vernacular revival, and of a London-centered, print-based model of literary history over a nationalist, bardic model based on oral tradition" (p. 70), whereas in this chapter I concentrate on Johnson's refutation of Macpherson's view of Britain, which I read differently than Trumpener does, and on the complications in Johnson's own imagining of the British nation.

9. See Gaskill (1991), Macqueen (1982), and Pittock (1991).

10. Stafford (1988) also comments on this passage (p. 56).

11. See Sher (1982).

12. Ironically, the Highlanders defended him strongly. As Smart says: "Long after Macpherson was dead, patriotic societies endeavored to foster their study: a copy of *Ossian* was presented to every parish school in the northern counties" (pp. 41–42).

13. See Conclusion (pp. 173–78).

14. See also *A Short History of the Opposition During the Last Session of Parliament* (1779), which examines the strife within the British government caused by the party system, a discord which Macpherson claims has fomented the American rebellion by exposing Britain's weakness. He announces: "The vehemence

of the present Opposition seems to have carried them to extremities, which supersede all former descriptions of party. . . . With a want of prudence, as well as of decency, they tie up the hands of their country in the hour of danger. They not only justify rebellion, against her authority, but indirectly promote a foreign war against her very existence. By magnifying the power of her opponents, they endeavor to depress her spirits; by exposing her real or pretended weakness, they wish to inspire her enemies with a confidence of success" (p. 40).

15. Although both *Fingal* and *Temora* were immediate successes, many people were suspicious about Macpherson's claims for the origins of the epics. Criticism of Macpherson's "discoveries" began less than three months after *Fingal* was published. In 1762, Ferdinando Warner, who was studying manuscripts in Dublin, brought forth a pamphlet denouncing the authenticity of Macpherson's work and revealing that the stories which Macpherson claimed for the Highland tradition were actually derived from Irish tales (*Remarks on the History of Fingal*). Even Macpherson's supporters changed their minds once more evidence came to light. William Shaw, who was preparing a Gaelic dictionary in which he hoped to include some of Macpherson's work, found stories of Finn and Cuchullain after doing six months' research in the Highlands in 1778, but nothing to verify his fellow countryman's translations. David Hume, too, eventually abandoned Macpherson's cause.

16. The committee reported that Ossianic poetry "was common, general, and in great abundance" and "that it was of a most impressive and striking sort, in a high degree eloquent, tender, and sublime" (Scott, *Report*, p. 151). Even in 1804, however, John Sinclair asserted that the publication of the Gaelic poems which Macpherson was working on when he died and which he bequeathed to John MacKenzie, "will satisfy every impartial reader, acquainted either with the Gaelic, or with the Latin language into which it is now translated, that the Gaelic is the only *possible original* . . . and that the Latin translation by Mr. Macfarlan, which is a plain literal version in the manner of Clarke's Homer, has as just a claim to boast of originality, as the English one published by Mr. Macpherson" (Sinclair, *Prospectus*, p. 12).

17. Fleeman (S. Johnson [1985]) discusses how Johnson altered and disseminated this letter.

18. See also Cannon (1994), pp. 215–47.

19. See also Lynch (1990).

20. Paradoxically, Johnson sees his own position as equivalent to that of a foreign invader, a Roman soldier. In his initial "Plan," he comments to his patron, the Earl of Chesterfield:

> When I survey the Plan which I have laid before you, I cannot, my Lord, but confess, that I am frighted at its extent, and, like the soldiers of Caesar, look on Britain as a new world, which it is almost

madness to invade. But I hope, that though I should not complete the conquest, I shall, at least, discover the coast, civilize part of the inhabitants, and make it easy for some other adventurer to proceed further, to reduce them wholly to subjection, and settle them under laws. (5: 21)

21. Vance (1984) suggests that Johnson regretted the fact that he was unable "to wander through a living museum of the past, where he could examine more of the domestic and cultural ceremonies and practices steeped deeply in antiquity" (p. 73). At the same time, however, Vance argues, Johnson wants to use the ruins in Scotland as a negative example from which to learn: "By understanding the *symbolic* properties of decayed churches and castles, England itself stood to gain much from Johnson's depiction of Scotland's ruins" (p. 80). Curley (1974) suggests that Johnson uses his Highland expedition to illustrate a moral: "namely, a traveler's disillusionment with foreign manners as his fancied preconceptions clash with sad realities abroad in a growing threnody of disappointments" (p. 186).

22. Interestingly, Johnson agrees with Macpherson that mountainous areas, in Britain's case Wales and the Highlands, "commonly contain the original, at least the oldest race of inhabitants, for they are not easily conquered" (Johnson, *Journey*, 9: 43). Like Macpherson, Johnson maintains that national character is "rather produced by situation than derived from ancestors" (9: 45). Johnson uses this logic to explain that the Highlanders are warlike because "a tract intersected by many ridges of mountains, naturally divides its inhabitants into petty nations" (9: 45) who war with one another. Similarly, they are thieves because they are poor, and, having the resources for neither "manufactures nor commerce" (9: 45), the only way they can get rich is by stealing. But Johnson takes issue with Macpherson's suggestion that the Highlanders developed a civilized chivalrous society when they were geographically isolated. He maintains that civilization occurs only through interaction: "Men are softened by intercourse mutually profitable, and instructed by comparing their own notions with those of others" (9: 43–44). As evidence for this, he notes that the Highlanders have remained savage for a much longer time than Lowland people, who practice agriculture and trade their goods with other societies.

23. For essays concerning Johnson and Jacobitism, see *The Age of Johnson: A Scholarly Journal*, vol. 7 (1997).

24. Rogers (1995) points out that Boswell constructed his narrative of the events of the '45 from accounts by Flora Macdonald, Malcolm Macleod, John Mackenzie, and possibly Dr. Murdoch Macleod, Raasay's brother (p. 158).

25. According to Turnbull (1987), Boswell was unable to find the strong sense of identity he craved through identification with Scotland, which he regarded as a country divided by faction and fragmented by uncertainty (p. 159).

26. Despite their differences, we should note the practical connections between Macpherson and Johnson in the project of writing the nation. Both authors, for example, were given pensions by Bute. Macpherson, as we have seen, had courted his fellow countryman and was so rewarded for his exertions. Johnson received his pension of three hundred pounds at the suggestion of Alexander Wedderburn in the same year in which Macpherson dedicated *Temora* to Bute. According to Walter Jackson Bate, Bute agreed to fund Johnson in an attempt to refute his critics' complaints of his patronage of Scots (see Bate [1977], p. 354). Johnson's financial security thus depended ironically on Bute's favor. Finally, both Macpherson and Johnson are buried in Westminster Abbey, where they lie together, a monument to the ambivalent negotiation of the British republic of letters.

27. Boswell and Johnson, under the guidance of Sir Allan M'Lean, view the ruins of Iona and are both moved by the presence of history. Boswell repeats Johnson's expostulation in his own account: "That man is little to be envied, whose patriotism would not gain force upon the plan of *Marathon*, or whose piety would not grow warmer among the ruins of *Iona*!" (5: 334). Boswell presents Johnson and himself as conjoined in patriotism and piety. Not only do Boswell and Johnson physically embrace (5: 334), but Boswell quotes directly from Johnson, suggesting the union of their minds in this matter.

Chapter 4: The Poetry of Nature and the Nature of Poetry

1. Agitation for burghal reform by merchants and burghers was reined in by the tight grip of Henry Dundas but nevertheless persisted. See Fry (1992).

2. James MacIntosh, in *Vindiciae Gallicae*, writes about the spirit of liberty of old Scotland corresponding with the new French constitution. See Meikle (1969), p. 57.

3. Fry (1992) suggests the agitation in Scotland "seemed to present uncomfortable parallels with that in France" (p. 12). Although it may be true, as Lenman (1981) argues, that the actual threat of opposition in Scotland was "in no way remarkable," the perception of the situation was different, both because of the higher percentage of lower class involvement and because of the persistence of the history of the "Auld Alliance," both of which had the effect of alarming the officials (p. 102).

4. For commentary on Wordsworth's escape from politics to poetry, see Chandler (1984), Levinson (1986), and Liu (1989). D. Simpson (1993) attempts to restore a sense of Wordsworth's radicalism (pp. 152–59).

5. Manning (1990) suggests the conceptual similarities between this kind of provincialism and Calvinist doctrine.

6. For discussion of heteroglossia in Burns's poetry, see Morris (1987) and McGuirk (1991).

7. In *Keats's Life of Allegory*, Levinson presents Keats as involved in a similar project of questioning political relations by foregrounding the construction involved in his poetry.

8. Blair and Home, of course, are Scottish, and Goldsmith is Irish. Their appropriation of the *belles lettres* tradition gives weight to R. Crawford's (1992) argument that the establishment of British, as opposed to distinctly English, literature occurred in the geographical peripheries.

9. Burns's representations of the nation are in fact contradictory. For example, he often adopts a British perspective. He wrote that he had always been a fervent supporter of the Hanoverian cause and the "sacred KEYSTONE OF OUR ROYAL ARCH CONSTITUTION" (*Letters*, 2: 529). He also joined the Dumfries Volunteers during the war against France and requested (and obtained) a military funeral. See McIntyre (1995), p. 398.

10. For a further reading of Burns's Scottish nationalism, see Noble's "Burns and Scottish Nationalism" (1994).

11. See T. Crawford et al., *Longer Scottish Poems*, 2: 31–43.

12. See Bhabha (1993), p. 145.

13. The *unheimlich*, says Freud, is "the name for everything that ought to have remained . . . secret and hidden but has come to light" (quoted in Bhabha [1993], p. 10). R. Crawford (1997, pp. 15–20) also provides an interesting perspective on "Tam o'Shanter."

14. The national fractures represented in *Poems, Chiefly in the Scottish Dialect* and "Tam o'Shanter" are further reflected in Burns's representation of his own poetic self as fundamentally unstable. In poems such as "A Bard's Epitaph," for example, he defies the concept of consistent individual and national identity. In his other poems and his letters, he writes himself similar multiple identities: he is Rab the Rhymer, Rob Mossgiel, Sylvander, his Bardship. Most tellingly, he plays with the concepts of naming and death in "Elegy on the Death of Robert Ruisseaux." The translation of his own name into French makes it approximate that of the "father of the French Revolution," Jean-Jacques Rousseau. Appearing at the same time as the controversy about the rights of individual citizens, Burns's portrayal of the unstable subjectivity of the writer within that nation suggests the instability of the nation itself. Burns embodies the contradictions of cultural values in Britain in his image of his poetic self, suggesting that the only way of writing an authentic national identity within a tradition of English literature is to adopt multiple positions, multiple names. See also K. Simpson (1988), chapter 7, and R. Crawford (1992), pp. 88–110, for commentary on Burns's multiple personae, and Roe (1997) for a fascinating discussion of Burns and the notion of authenticity.

15. See also D. Johnson (1972).

16. Elsewhere I have argued that Currie emphasized Burns's hypochondria-

sis in order to distract readers' attention from his political views, which might
have threatened the advancement of Scots in Britain after the French Revolution. I further suggest that Currie uses Burns's body as an image of Scottish national culture, which is, in Currie's words, "embalmed" as a monument "to the
expiring genius of an ancient and once independent nation" (1: 30). See Leith
Davis (1997).

17. On the importance of the review in the Romantic era, see Butler
(1993) and Klancher (1987).

18. Wordsworth's desire to use Scotland as an alternative vision to the political scene of Europe can be seen in his next visit to Scotland in 1814, this time
with his wife. Wordsworth notes in a letter to Samuel Rogers that instead of
going to London for the festivities celebrating Napoléon's defeat at Leipzig and
subsequent exile in Elba, he will go to Scotland, where "I hope to fall in occa-
sionally, with a Ptarmigan, a Roe, or an Eagle; and the living bird I certainly
should prefer to its Image on the Panel of a dishonoured Emperor's Coach"
(*Letters: The Middle Years*, 2: 148). He turns from politics to the natural world,
which he wants Scotland to represent.

19. See also Buzard (1995) on translation.

20. Liu (1989) argues that for Wordsworth the Self emerges out of a relationship with history and nature. According to Liu, the Wordsworthian imagination is constituted from the denial of history. Liu concentrates on
Wordsworth's reactions to events in France. I argue that Wordsworth's poetic
and political self was also fashioned in relation to the British internal Other:
Scotland. Wordsworth's interest in Burns reflects his desire to deny the threat to
the national Self.

21. See note in *William Wordsworth: The Poems*, ed. Hayden, 1: 998. The
Scottish poems were dissolved into other subject areas in the 1820 edition of
Wordsworth's poems, but "Memorials of a Tour in Scotland, 1803" and "Memorials of a Tour in Scotland, 1814" appeared as discrete sections in the 1827, 1832,
1836–37, 1845, and 1849–50 editions.

22. Srebrnik explains the proliferation of Scottish booksellers as a function
of the Scottish educational system, which was better for the average citizen
than that of England. "For a publisher, more than most businessmen, could
profit from just such a [liberal] education, whereas many an Englishman of a
class to enjoy the same education would have regarded himself as superior to
the work of retail bookselling or, even worse, job printing—two occupations
inextricably bound up, in the nineteenth century, with the business of publishing" (p. 13).

23. See also Eilenberg (1989).

24. Although Wordsworth's various writings may have been paramount in
determining the British reading public's attitude toward Burns and Scotland, it

is important to realize that several Scottish writers, including John Wilson and James Hogg, took issue with his interpretation of their fellow countryman. Wordsworth's *Letter to a Friend of Robert Burns*, in fact, provoked a vehement debate in the journals of the day, journals that were primarily run by Scots. Low (1995) writes that John Wilson is "a key figure in the process of deterioration in Scottish literary culture which in the Victorian period was to lead to domination by 'Kailyard' novelists and poetasters . . . Wilson sentimentalized Burns for a new age as thoroughly as Mackenzie had done in 1786. He made much of nationality, and minimized any implications in Burns's writings which might disturb conservative imaginations" (p. 39). Carol McGuirk (1994) also comments on Wilson's effect on Burns's image in the Victorian age, noting how in 1844 at a reception to "honour the surviving legitimate sons of Burns upon the return (after years of service in India) of Lieutenant-Colonel James Glencairn Burns" (p. 36) Wilson provided "what might be called the Tory line on Burns" (p. 37). See also Nash (1997) for a discussion of Burns and the Kailyard school.

Chapter 5: Citing the Nation

1. Any discomfort was eased by the approval of J. Ritson. Scott notes, "I was particularly desirous to give [Ritson] every information in my power concerning the authenticity of my Border Ballads & I believe I succeeded perfectly in removing every doubt from his mind" (*Letters*, 12: 195).

2. Scott had a financial interest in promoting Laing's work. Laing's edition was printed by his business associate Ballantyne and published by Constable. Despite his lukewarm review of the work, Scott (1972) notes that Laing's volume is very attractively presented: "We have seldom seen a handsomer book in execution and external appearance" (p. 433).

3. Scott notes: "The specimens of his early poetry which remain are also deeply tinged with the peculiarities of the Celtic diction & character so that in fact he might be considered as a highland poet even if he had not left us some Earse translations or originals of Ossian unquestionably written by himself. These circumstances gave a great advantage to him in forming the style of Ossian which though exalted and modified according to Macpherson's own ideas of modern taste is in great part cut upon the model of the tales of the Sennachies & Bards" (*Letters*, 1: 323).

4. Scott adds that Burns seems to relish suffering the consequences of his actions, rather than learning how to avoid error in the future.

5. MS 911, National Library of Scotland. Hand-copy of a fragment of a letter from Anderson to Percy.

6. Despite his professed intentions, however, he does include some ballads from Aberdeenshire.

7. P. Fielding (1996) notes that "the *Minstrelsy of the Scottish Border* offered Scott a good opportunity for moving Scottish interests to the British centre, providing it could be handled carefully" (p. 50). See also Fielding's excellent discussion of the paradoxes of orality in the *Minstrelsy* (pp. 44–58).

8. R. Crawford (1992) suggests the "anthropological dimension in Scott's thought" (p. 112).

9. McMaster (1981) observes, "The Waverley novels have as their subject matter more the world of post-war Britain than the historical periods they are set in" (p. 127).

10. Scott's attitude to cultural change in Scotland has been hotly debated. Daiches (1951) suggests that "Scott's attitude to Scotland . . . was a mixture of regret for the old days when Scotland was a turbulent and distracted country, and of satisfaction at the peace, prosperity, and progress which he felt had been assured by the Union with England in 1707 and the successful establishment of the Hanoverian dynasty on the British throne" (pp. 84–85). Pittock (1991) suggests that "Although he was a Scotch patriot, he believed that Scotland's future lay in a Union which appeared to him to have healed what he believed to be otherwise incurable divisions in Scottish life. . . . Britain seemed to offer broader horizons than those hitherto encompassed by internecine strife" (p. 84). Pittock shows how Scott represents Jacobite beliefs to be "childish" in contrast to British patriotism (p. 85). See also Pittock's "Scott as Historiographer." Nairn (1981) takes a harsher view, reading Scott as indicative of the failure of Scottish nationalism. Nairn observes that Scott's "essential point is always that the past really is gone, beyond recall. . . . For all its splendour, his panorama of the Scottish past is valedictory in nature" (p. 115). Kidd (1993) sets that panorama in the context of an erosion of Scottish history, arguing that Scott's achievement as a historian of Scotland was "a mythopoeic encapsulation, in the *Waverley Novels* (1814–32) of the mid-eighteenth-century sociological and antiquarian deconstruction of Scotland's much-vaunted historical identity" (p. 256). According to Kidd, "by the time that Scott was explaining Scotland to the English, there was no grand narrative structure of national historiography by which to promote Scotland, other than that of her retardation. Scott's major contribution to Scottish national identity was one of national reconciliation—of Highlanders and Lowlanders, Covenanters and Jacobites—not of national asser-tion" (pp. 266–67). Other critics have looked fruitfully at the ambiguity of Scott's perspective. Recasting the work of translating culture as a more ambigu-ous practice than imposing metropolitan values on a periphery, Ferris (1997) observes that Scott complicates his representation of the Highlands by present-ing it in *Waverley* as "an ongoing *world*" and not just a picturesque space (p. 215). And Duncan (1992) has examined the way the romance genre accommo-dates the sentimentalism and violent contradiction of national identity: "Ro-

mance reproduces itself as the figure of mediation and synthesis by turning contradiction into ambiguity, which provides a vital margin of refuge between fatal historical fact and extravagant spiritual impossibility" (p. 15). Trumpener (1997) looks at Scott's contribution to the historical novel in relation to the national tale, noting the reciprocity between national and imperial interests (chapter 3).

11. See Benjamin (1968).

Conclusion: Runes of Empire

1. Burns's reference was in regard to his powers in song, not in writing verse.

2. Rajchman (1995), p. x.

Ahmad, Aijaz. *In Theory: Classes, Nations, Literatures.* London:Verso, 1992.

Anderson, Benedict. *Imagined Communities: Reflections on the Origin and Spread of Nationalism.* Rev. ed. London:Verso, 1991.

Anderson, James. *An Historical Essay, Shewing That the Crown and Kingdom of Scotland is Imperial and Independent.* Edinburgh: Heirs of Andrew Anderson, 1705.

Armitage, David. "The Scottish Vision of Empire: Intellectual Origins of the Darien Venture." In John Robertson, ed., *A Union for Empire: Political Thought and the British Union of 1707,* pp. 97–121. Cambridge: Cambridge University Press, 1995.

Armstrong, Nancy. *Desire and Domestic Fiction:A Political History of the Novel.* Oxford: Oxford University Press, 1987.

Arnold, Matthew. *The Complete Prose Works of Matthew Arnold.* 11 vols. R. H. Super, ed. Ann Arbor: University of Michigan Press, 1962.

Ashcroft, Bill, Gareth Griffiths, and Helen Tiffin. *The Empire Writes Back:Theory and Practice in Post-Colonial Literatures.* London: Routledge, 1989.

Atwood, William. *The Superiority and Direct Dominion of the Imperial Crown of England, over the Crown and Kingdom of Scotland.* London: J. Hartley, 1704.

———. *The Superiority and Direct Dominion of the Imperial Crown of England Over the Crown and Kingdom of Scotland . . . Reasserted.* London: John Nutt, 1705.

Backscheider, Paula. *Daniel Defoe:Ambition and Innovation.* Lexington: University Press of Kentucky, 1986.

———. *Daniel Defoe: His Life.* Baltimore: Johns Hopkins University Press, 1989.

Bakhtin, M. M. *The Dialogic Imagination: Four Essays.* Austin: University of Texas Press, 1981.

Baldick, Chris. *The Social Mission of English Criticism, 1848–1932.* Oxford: Clarendon Press, 1983.

Basker, James G. "Scotticisms and the Problem of Cultural Identity in Eighteenth-Century Britain." *Eighteenth-Century Life* 15 (Feb. and May 1991): 81–95.

Bate, Walter Jackson. *Samuel Johnson.* New York: Harcourt, Brace, Jovanovich, 1977.

Battestin, Martin. "Tom Jones and 'His Egyptian Majesty': Fielding's Parable of Government." *PMLA* 82, no. 1 (1967): 68–77.

———, ed. *The History of Tom Jones, A Foundling.* Oxford: Clarendon, 1974.

Beasley, Jerry C. "Smollett's Art: The Novel As 'Picture.'" *Tennessee Studies in Literature* 29 (1985): 143–83.

Beattie, James. *The Poetical Works of James Beattie.* London: Bell and Dalry, 1814.

———. *Scoticisms, Arranged in Alphabetical Order, Designed to Correct Improprieties of Speech and Writing.* Edinburgh: n.p., 1787.

Belhaven's Vision, or His Speech in the Union-Parliament. November 2, 1706. London: n.p., 1729.

Benjamin, Walter. "The Work of Art in the Age of Mechanical Reproduction." In *Illuminations,* pp. 217–52. New York: Schocken, 1969.

Bhabha, Homi K. *The Location of Culture.* New York: Routledge, 1994.

———, ed. *Nation and Narration.* New York: Routledge, 1990.

Black, Jeremy. *Culloden and the '45.* Stroud, England: Allen Sutton, 1990.

Boswell, James. *Boswell's Life of Johnson, Together with Boswell's Journal of a Tour to the Hebrides and Johnson's Diary of a Journey into North Wales.* 5 vols. G. B. Hill and L. F. Powell, eds. Oxford: Clarendon Press, 1934–64.

Bourdieu, Pierre. *The Field of Cultural Production: Essays on Art and Literature.* Randal Johnson, ed. New York: Columbia University Press, 1993.

Breuilly, John. *Nationalism and the State.* London: Manchester University Press, 1993.

Brown, Homer Obed. "Tom Jones: The 'Bastard' of History." *boundary* 2, no. 7 (1979): 201–33.

Burns, Robert. *Letters of Robert Burns.* 2 vols. J. DeLancey Ferguson, ed. [1931]; Rev. G. Ross Roy, ed. Oxford: Clarendon Press, 1985.

———. *The Life and Works of Robert Burns.* Alexander Peterkin, ed. Edinburgh: Macredie, Skelly and Muckersy, 1815.

———. *The Poems and Songs of Robert Burns.* 3 vols. James Kinsley, ed. Oxford: Clarendon Press, 1968.

———. *The Works of Robert Burns.* 4 vols. James Currie, ed. London: Cadell, 1800.

Butler, Marilyn. "Culture's Medium: The Role of the Review." In Stuart Curran, ed., *The Cambridge Companion to British Romanticism,* pp. 120–47. Cambridge: Cambridge University Press, 1993.

Buzard, James. "Translation and Tourism: Scott's *Waverley* and the Rendering of Culture." *Yale Journal of Criticism* 8, no. 2 (1995): 31–59.

Campbell, Jill. *Natural Masques: Gender and Identity in Fielding's Plays and Novels.* Stanford: Stanford University Press, 1995.

Campbell, R. H. "The Anglo-Scottish Union of 1707: The Economic Conse-
    quences." *Economic History Review* 16, no. 3 (1964): 468–77.

Cannon, John. *Samuel Johnson and the Politics of Hanoverian England*. Oxford:
    Clarendon Press, 1994.

Carlton, Peter J. "Tom Jones and the '45 Once Again." *Studies in the Novel* 20,
    no. 4 (1988): 361–73.

Carlyle, Thomas. "Burns." *Scottish and Other Miscellanies*, pp. 1–53. London:
    J. M. Dent, 1915.

———. *On Heroes, Hero-Worship, and the Heroic in History*. Michael K. Gold-
    berg, ed. Berkeley: University of California Press, 1993.

Černy, Lothar. "Reader Participation and Rationalism in Fielding's *Tom Jones*."
    Connotations 2, no. 2 (1992): 137–62.

Chandler, James. *Wordsworth's Second Nature: A Study of the Poetry and Politics*.
    Chicago: University of Chicago Press, 1984.

Chard, Leslie. "Bookseller to Publisher: Joseph Johnson and the English Book
    Trade, 1760–1810." *Library* (1977): 138–54.

Chatterjee, Partha. *The Nation and Its Fragments: Colonial and Postcolonial Histo-
    ries*. Princeton, N.J.: Princeton University Press, 1993.

———. *Nationalist Thought and the Colonial World: A Derivative Discourse*.
    London: Zed Books, 1986.

Clark, James. *Scotland's Speech to Her Sons*. Edinburgh [?]: n.p., 1706.

Cleary, Thomas. "Henry Fielding and the Great Jacobite Paper War of
    1747–49." *Eighteenth-Century Life* 5, no. 1 (1978): 1–11.

———. *Henry Fielding: Political Writer*. Waterloo, Ont.: Wilfred Laurier Univer-
    sity Press, 1984.

Coley, W. B., ed. *The True Patriot and Other Writings*. Oxford: Clarendon, 1987.

Colley, Linda. *Britons: Forging the Nation 1707–1837*. New Haven: Yale Univer-
    sity Press, 1992.

Court, Franklin E. *Institutionalizing English Literature: The Culture and Politics of
    Literary Study, 1750–1900*. Stanford: Stanford University Press, 1992.

Craig, Thomas. *Scotland's Sovereignty Asserted*. Trans. George Ridpath. London:
    n.p., 1695.

Crawford, Robert. "Bakhtin and Scotlands." *Scotlands* 1 (1994): 55–65.

———. *Devolving English Literature*. Oxford: Clarendon Press, 1992.

———, ed. *Robert Burns and Cultural Authority*. Iowa City: University of Iowa
    Press, 1997.

———, ed. *The Scottish Invention of English Literature*. Cambridge: Cambridge
    University Press, 1998.

Crawford, Thomas. *Burns: A Study of the Poems and Songs*. Edinburgh: Canon-
    gate, 1994.

Crawford, Thomas, David Hewitt, and Alexander Law, eds. *Longer Scottish
    Poems*. Vol. 2. (1650–1830). Edinburgh: Scottish Academic Press, 1987.

Cross, Wilbur L. *The History of Henry Fielding*. 2 vols. New Haven: Yale University Press, 1918.

Curley, Thomas M. *Samuel Johnson and the Age of Travel*. Athens: University of Georgia Press, 1976.

Currie, James, ed. *The Works of Robert Burns*. 4 vols. London: Cadell, 1800.

Daiches, David. *The Paradox of Scottish Culture: The Eighteenth-Century Experience*. London: Oxford University Press, 1964.

————. *Robert Burns*. London: Andre Deutsch, 1966.

————. "Scott's Achievement as a Novelist." *Nineteenth-Century Fiction* 6, no. 2 (1951): 80–96, and 6, no. 3 (1951): 153–73.

Davis, Leith. "James Currie's *Works of Robert Burns*: The Politics of Hypochondriasis." *Studies in Romanticism* 36 (summer 1997): 43–60.

Davis, Lennard. *Factual Fictions: The Origins of the English Novel*. New York: Columbia University Press, 1983.

Defoe, Daniel. *Defoe's Review, reproduced from the Original Editions*. 9 vols. in 22 facsimile books. Arthur Secord, ed. New York: Columbia University Press, 1938.

————. *An Essay, at Removing National Prejudices Against a Union With England*. Part 3. Edinburgh: n.p., 1706.

————. *A Fifth Essay, at Removing National Prejudices Against a Union With England: With a Reply to Some Authors, Who Have Printed Their Objections against An Union With England*. Edinburgh: n.p., 1707.

————. *A Fourth Essay, at Removing National Prejudices Against a Union With England; With Some Reply to Mr. Hodges and Some Other Authors, Who Have Printed Their Objections Against An Union with England*. Edinburgh: n.p., 1706.

————. *History of the Union Between England and Scotland*. Edinburgh: Andrew Anderson, 1709.

————. *Letters of Daniel Defoe*. Goerge Harris Healey, ed. Oxford: Clarendon, 1955.

————. *The Shakespeare Head Edition of the Novels and Selected Writings of Daniel Defoe*. Vol. 13. Oxford: Oxford University Press, 1927.

————. *A Tour Thro' the Whole Island of Great Britain*. London: G. Strahan et al., 1724–26.

————. *Two Great Questions Considered, 1. What is the obligation of Parliament to the addresses or petitions of the people, and what the duty of the addressers? II. Whether the obligation of the Covenant or the other national engagements, is concerned in the Treaty of Union? Being a Sixth Essay, At Removing National Prejudices Against the Union*. Edinburgh: n.p., 1707.

DeGategno, Paul. *James Macpherson*. Boston: Twayne, 1989.

Dickey, Laurence. "Power, Commerce, and Natural Law in Daniel Defoe's Political Writings." In John Robertson, ed., *A Union for Empire: Political*

Thought and the British Union of 1707, pp. 63–96. Cambridge: Cambridge University Press, 1995.

Dijkstra, Bram. *Defoe and Economics: the Fortunes of Roxana in the History of Interpretation*. Basingstoke, England: Macmillan, 1987.

Donaldson, William. *The Jacobite Song: Political Myth and National Identity*. Aberdeen: Aberdeen University Press, 1988.

Downie, J. A. *Robert Harley and the Press: Propaganda and Public Opinion in the Age of Swift and Defoe*. Cambridge: Cambridge University Press, 1979.

Duncan, Ian. *Modern Romance and the Transformations of the Novel: The Gothic, Scott, Dickens*. Cambridge: Cambridge University Press, 1992.

Dwyer, John. *Virtuous Discourse: Sensibility and Community in Late Eighteenth-Century Scotland*. Edinburgh: John Donald, 1987.

Eagleton, Terry. *The Ideology of the Aesthetic*. Oxford: Basil Blackwell, 1990.

———. *Literary Theory: An Introduction*. Minneapolis: University of Minnesota Press, 1983.

Eilenberg, Susan. "Mortal Pages: Wordsworth and the Reform of Copyright." *ELH* 56 (1989): 351–74.

An Elegy on the much Lamented Death of John Hamilton Lord Balhaven. Edinburgh: n.p., 1708.

Elegy on the never enough to be Lamented Death of Lord John Hamilton of Balhaven, &c. who departed this Life, (at London) 21. June 1708. Edinburgh: n.p., 1708.

Ewald, William Bragg. *The Newsmen of Queen Anne*. Oxford: Basil Blackwell, 1956.

A Faithful Narrative of the Base and Inhuman Arts That Were Lately Practised Upon the Brain of Habbakuk Hilding, Justice, Dealer and Chapman, Who Now Lies at His House in Convent-Garden, in a Deplorable State of Lunacy: A Dreadful Monument of False Friendship and Delusion. Attributed to T. Smollett. London: J. Sharp, 1752.

Feather, John. "The Book Trade in Politics: The Making of the Copyright Act of 1710." *Publishing History* 8 (1980): 19–44.

———. *A History of British Publishing*. London: Routledge, 1988.

Ferguson, William. "The Making of the Treaty of Union of 1707." *Scottish Historical Review* 43 (1964): 89–110.

———. *Scotland's Relations with England: A Survey to 1707*. Edinburgh: John Donald, 1977.

Ferris, Ina. *The Achievement of Literary Authority: Gender, History, and the Waverley Novels*. Ithaca, N.Y.: Cornell University Press, 1991.

———. "Translation from the Borders: Encounter and Recalcitrance in *Waverley* and *Clan-Albin*." *Eighteenth-Century Fiction* 9, no. 2 (1997): 203–22.

Fielding, Henry. *The History of Tom Jones, A Foundling*. 2 vols. Martin C. Battestin, ed. Oxford: Clarendon Press, 1974.

———. *The True Patriot and Related Writings.* W. B. Coley, ed. Oxford: Clarendon Press, 1987.

Fielding, Penny. *Writing and Orality: Nationality, Culture, and Nineteenth-Century Scottish Fiction.* Oxford: Clarendon Press, 1996.

Fry, Michael. *The Dundas Despotism.* Edinburgh: Edinburgh University Press, 1992.

———. *Patronage and Principle. A Political History of Modern Scotland.* Aberdeen: Aberdeen University Press, 1987.

Gaskill, Howard, ed. *Ossian Revisited.* Edinburgh: Edinburgh University Press, 1991.

Gellner, Ernest. *Nations and Nationalism.* Oxford: Basil Blackwell, 1983.

Goldberg, M. A. *Smollett and the Scottish School.* Albuquerque: University of New Mexico Press, 1959.

Grant, Damien. "*Roderick Random*: Language as Projectile." In Alan Bold, ed., *Smollett: Author of the First Distinction*, pp. 129–47. London: Vision, 1982.

Greenblatt, Stephen. "Towards a Poetics of Culture." In Aram Veeser, ed., *The New Historicism*, pp. 1–14. London: Routledge, 1989.

Greenfeld, Liah. *Nationalism: Five Roads to Modernity.* Cambridge, Mass.: Harvard University Press, 1992.

Hamilton, John (Lord Belhaven). *The Lord Belhaven's Speech in the Scotch Parliament, 2 November 1706.* Edinburgh: n.p., 1706.

———. *On the Affair of the Indian and African Company, and its Colony of Caledonia.* Edinburgh: n.p., 1701.

———. *A Second Defense of the Scotish Vision.* Edinburgh: n.p., 1706.

———. *Upon an Act for Security of the Kingdom, in case of the Queen's death.* Edinburgh: n.p., 1703.

Harvie, Christopher. *Scotland and Nationalism: Scottish Society and Politics, 1707–1994.* Rev. ed. London: Routledge, 1994.

Hatfield, Glenn. *Henry Fielding and the Language of Irony.* Chicago: University of Chicago Press, 1968.

Hayden, John, ed. *Scott: The Critical Heritage.* London: Routledge and Kegan Paul, 1970.

Healey, George Harris, ed. *Letters of Daniel Defoe.* Oxford: Clarendon Press, 1955.

Helgerson, Richard. *Forms of Nationhood: The Elizabethan Writing of England.* Chicago: University of Chicago Press, 1992.

Hobsbawm, Eric J. *Nations and Nationalism Since 1780: Programme, Myth, Reality.* Cambridge: Cambridge University Press, 1990.

Hodges, James. *Rights and Interests of the Two British Monarchies Inquir'd Into, and Clear'd.* London: n.p., 1703.

Hont, Istvan, and Michael Ignatieff, eds. *Wealth and Virtue: The Shaping of Politi-*

cal Economy in the Scottish Enlightenment. Cambridge: Cambridge University Press, 1983.

Hook, Michael, and Walter Ross. *The Forty-Five: The Last Jacobite Rebellion*. Edinburgh: HMSO, 1995.

Hudson, Nicholas. "Signs, Interpretations, and the Collapse of Meaning in *Tom Jones* and *Amelia*." *English Studies in Canada* 16, no. 1 (March 1990): 17–34.

Hunter, J. Paul. *Before Novels: The Cultural Contexts of Eighteenth-Century English Fiction*. New York: W. W. Norton, 1990.

———. "The Novel and the Contexts of Discourse." In Richard B. Swartz, ed., *Theory and Tradition in Eighteenth-Century Studies*, pp. 119–39. Carbondale: Southern Illinois University Press, 1990.

Jacobus, Mary. *Tradition and Experiment in Wordsworth's Lyrical Ballads*. Oxford: Clarendon Press, 1976.

Jameson, Fredric. "Third World Literature in the Era of Multinational Capitalism." *Social Text* 15 (1986): 65–88.

Johnson, David. *Music and Society in Lowland Scotland in the Eighteenth Century*. London: Oxford University Press, 1972.

Johnson, Samuel. *A Journey to the Western Isles of Scotland*. Mary Lascelles, ed. New Haven: Yale University Press, 1971.

———. *A Journey to the Western Isles of Scotland, 1775*. J. D. Fleeman, ed. Oxford: Oxford University Press, 1985.

———. *The Letters of Samuel Johnson with Mrs. Thrale's Genuine Letters to Him*. 2 vols. (1719–74). R. W. Chapman, ed. Oxford: Clarendon Press, 1952.

———. *The Works of Samuel Johnson, LL.D.* Vol. 5. London: Pickering, 1825.

Johnston, Arthur. *Enchanted Ground: The Study of Medieval Romance in the Eighteenth Century*. London: Athlone Press, 1964.

Jones, G. H. *The Main Stream of Jacobitism*. Cambridge: Harvard Unversity Press, 1954.

Kearney, Anthony. "Tom Jones and the '45." *ARIEL* 4 (1973): 68–78.

Kelly, Lionel. *Tobias Smollett: The Critical Heritage*. London: Routledge and Kegan Paul, 1987.

Kidd, Colin. *Subverting Scotland's Past: Scottish Whig Historians and the Creation of an Anglo-British Identity*. Cambridge: Cambridge University Press, 1993.

Klancher, Jon P. *The Making of English Reading Audiences, 1790–1832*. Madison: University of Wisconsin Press, 1987.

Kratzmann, Gregory. *Anglo-Scottish Literary Relations, 1430–1550*. Cambridge: Cambridge University Press, 1980.

Kristeva, Julia. *Nations Without Nationalism*. New York: Columbia University Press, 1993.

Langford, Paul. *A Polite and Commercial People: England, 1727–1783*. Oxford: Clarendon Press, 1989.

Leneman, Leah. "Ossian and the Enlightenment." *Scotia* 11 (1987): 13–29.

Lenman, Bruce. *Integration, Enlightenment, and Industrialization. Scotland, 1746–1832*. London: Edward Arnold, 1981.

———. *The Jacobite Risings in Britain, 1689–1746*. London: Eyre Methuen, 1980.

Lerner, Adam, and Marjorie Ringrose. *Reimagining the Nation*. Buckingham and Philadelphia: Open University Press, 1993.

Levack, Brian. *The Formation of the British State. England, Scotland, and the Union, 1603–1707*. Oxford: Clarendon Press, 1987.

Levinson, Marjorie. *Keats's Life of Allegory: The Origins of a Style*. Oxford: Basil Blackwell, 1988.

———. *Wordsworth's Great Period Poems: Four Essays*. Cambridge: Cambridge University Press, 1986.

Lindsay, Maurice. *The History of Scottish Literature*. London: Hale, 1977.

Liu, Alan. *Wordsworth: The Sense of History*. Stanford: Stanford University Press, 1989.

Lloyd, David. *Anomalous States: Irish Writing and the Post-Colonial Movement*. Dublin: Lilliput Press, 1993.

Locke, Miram Austin. *Henry Fielding, "The True Patriot," and the History of Our Own Times*. University of Alabama Press, 1964.

Lockhart, John, ed. *Memoirs of the Life of Sir Walter Scott*. 7 vols. Edinburgh: Cadell, 1837.

Lord, George de F., ed. *An Anthology of Poems on the Affairs of State, 1660–1714*. New Haven: Yale University Press, 1975.

Low, Donald, ed. *Burns: The Critical Heritage*. London: Routledge, 1995 [1974].

Lucas, John. *England and Englishness: Ideas of Nationhood in English Poetry, 1688–1900*. London: Hogarth, 1990.

Lynch, Deirdre. "'Beating the Track of the Alphabet': Samuel Johnson, Tourism, and the ABCs of Modern Authority." *ELH* 2 (summer 1990): 357–405.

Macaree, David. "The Flyting of Daniel Defoe and Lord Belhaven." *Studies in Scottish Literature* 13 (1978): 72–80.

Mackinnon, J. *The Union of England and Scotland: A Study of International History*. London: Longman's, Green, 1896.

Macpherson, James. *The History of Great Britain, from the Restoration to the Accession of the House of Hanover*. 2 vols. London: W. Strahan and T. Cadell, 1775.

———. *Introduction to the History of Great Britain and Ireland*. Dublin: n.p., 1771.

———. *Poems of Ossian*. 2 vols. Malcolm Laing, ed. Edinburgh: Constable, 1805.

———. *The Poems of Ossian and Related Works*. Howard Gaskill, ed. Edinburgh: Edinburgh University Press, 1996.

————. *The Rights of Great Britain Asserted against the Claims of America, being an Answer to the Declaration of the General Congress.* London: T. Cadell, 1776.

————. *A Short History of the Opposition During the Last Session of Parliament.* London: T. Cadell, 1779.

Macqueen, John. *Progress and Poetry: The Enlightenment and Scottish Literature.* Edinburgh: University of Edinburgh Press, 1982.

Manning, Susan. *The Puritan-Provincial Vision: Scottish and American Literature in the Nineteenth Century.* Cambridge: Cambridge University Press, 1990.

Mason, Roger. "Scotching the Brut: Politics, History, and National Myth in Sixteenth-Century Britain." In Roger Mason, ed., *Scotland and England, 1286–1815,* pp. 34–59. Edinburgh: John Donald, 1987.

————, ed. *Scots and Britons. Scottish Political Thought and the Union of 1603.* Cambridge: Cambridge University Press, 1994.

Mathieson, William Law. *Scotland and the Union. A History of Scotland from 1695 to 1747.* Glasgow: J. Maclehose, 1905.

McCracken-Flesher, Caroline. "Speaking the Colonized Subject in Walter Scott's *Malachi Malagrowther* Letters." *Studies in Scottish Literature* 29 (1996): 73–84.

McCrea, Brian. *Henry Fielding and the Politics of Mid-Eighteenth-Century England.* Athens: University of Georgia Press, 1981.

McCrone, David. *Understanding Scotland: The Sociology of a Stateless Nation.* London: Routledge, 1992.

McGuirk, Carol. "Burns and Nostalgia." In Kenneth Simpson, ed., *Burns Now,* pp. 31–69. Edinburgh: Canongate, 1994.

————. "Burns, Bakhtin, and the Opposition of Poetic and Novelistic Discourse: A Response to David Morris." *The Eighteenth Century: Theory and Interpretation* 32, no. 1 (1991): 58–72.

McIntyre, Ian. *Dirt and Deity: A Life of Robert Burns.* London: HarperCollins, 1995.

McKeon, Michael. *The Origins of the English Novel, 1600–1740.* Baltimore: Johns Hopkins University Press, 1987.

McLeod, W. R. and V. B. McLeod. *Anglo-Scottish Tracts, 1701–1714.* Morgantown: University of Kansas Libraries Series 44, 1979.

McMaster, Graham. *Scott and Society.* Cambridge: Cambridge University Press, 1981.

Meikle, Henry. *Scotland and the French Revolution.* London: Frank Cass, 1969.

Millgate, Jane. *Scott's Last Edition: A Study in Publishing History.* Edinburgh: Edinburgh University Press, 1987.

Mitchison, Rosalind. "The Government and the Highlands." In N. T. Phillipson and Rosalind Mitchison, eds., *Scotland in the Age of Improvement: Essays in Scottish History in the Eighteenth Century,* pp. 24–46. Edinburgh: Edinburgh University Press, 1970.

Morris, David. "Burns and Heteroglossia." *The Eighteenth Century: Theory and Interpretation* 28, no. 1 (1987): 3–27.

Murphy, Peter. *Poetry as an Occupation and an Art in Britain, 1760–1830.* Cambridge: Cambridge University Press, 1993.

Nairn, Tom. *The Break-Up of Britain: Crisis and Neo-nationalism.* Rev. ed. London: NLB, 1981.

Nash, Andrew. "The Cotter's Kailyard." In R. Crawford, ed., *Robert Burns and Cultural Authority*, pp. 180–97. Iowa City: University of Iowa Press, 1997.

Newman, Gerald. *The Rise of English Nationalism: A Cultural History, 1740–1830.* New York: St. Martin's Press, 1987.

Noble, Andrew. "Burns and Scottish Nationalism." In Kenneth Simpson, ed., *Burns Now*, pp. 167–92. Edinburgh: Canongate, 1994.

Noyes, Russell. "Wordsworth and Burns." *PMLA* 59 (1944): 813–32.

O'Brien, Timothy. "The Hungry Author and Narrative Performance in *Tom Jones.*" *Studies in English Literature* 25, no. 3 (summer 1985): 615–32.

Ortiz, Ricardo. "Fielding's 'Orientalist' Moment: Historical Fiction and Historical Knowledge in *Tom Jones.*" *Studies in English Literature* 33 (1993): 609–28.

Owen, John B. *The Eighteenth Century, 1714–1815.* New York: Norton, 1974.

Parry, Benita. "Problems in Current Theories of Colonial Discourse." *Oxford Literary Review* 9, nos. 1–2 (1987): 27–58.

Percy, Thomas. *Reliques of Ancient English Poetry.* 3 vols. New York: Dover, 1966.

Pittock, Murray. *Inventing and Resisting Britain: Cultural Identities in Britain and Ireland, 1685–1789.* Houndmills, England: Macmillan, 1997.

———. *The Invention of Scotland: The Stuart Myth and the Scottish Identity.* London: Routledge, 1991.

———. *Poetry and Jacobite Politics in Eighteenth-Century Britain and Ireland.* Cambridge: Cambridge University Press, 1994.

———. "Scott as Historiographer." In J. H. Alexander and David Hewitt, eds., *Scott in Carnival*, pp. 145–53. Aberdeen: Association for Scottish Literary Studies, 1993.

Plumb, J. H. "The Commercialization of Leisure in Eighteenth-Century England." In Neil McKendrick, John Brewer, and J. H. Plumb, eds., *The Birth of a Consumer Society: The Commercialization of Eighteenth Century England*, pp. 265–85. London: Europa Publications, 1982.

Potkay, Adam. "Virtue and Manners in Macpherson's *Poems of Ossian.*" *PMLA* 107 (1992): 120–30.

Prebble, John. *Culloden.* London: Secker and Warburg, 1961.

Pryde, G. *The Treaty of Union of Scotland and England, 1707.* London: Nelson, 1950.

Rajchman, John, ed. *The Identity in Question.* New York: Routledge, 1995.

Reddick, Allen. *The Making of Johnson's Dictionary, 1746–1773.* Cambridge: Cambridge University Press, 1990.

Rendall, Jane. *The Origins of the Scottish Enlightenment.* London: Macmillan, 1978.

Report of the Committee of the Highland Society of Scotland Appointed to Inquire into the Nature and Authenticity of the Poems of Ossian. Edinburgh: Constable, 1805.

Riley, P. W. J. *The Union of England and Scotland: A Study in Anglo-Scottish Politics of the Eighteenth Century.* Manchester: Manchester University Press, 1978.

Robertson, Fiona. *Legitimate Histories: Scott, Gothic, and the Authorities of Fiction.* Oxford: Clarendon, 1994.

Robertson, John, ed. *A Union for Empire: Political Thought and the British Union of 1707.* Cambridge: Cambridge University Press, 1995.

Robinson, Jeffrey. "The Structure of Wordsworth's *Memorials of a Tour in Scotland, 1803.*" *Papers on Language and Literature* 13 (winter 1977): 54–70.

Roe, Nicholas. "Authenticating Robert Burns." In R. Crawford, ed., *Robert Burns and Cultural Authority,* pp. 159–79. Iowa City: University of Iowa Press, 1997.

Rogers, Pat. *Johnson and Boswell: The Transit of Caledonia.* Oxford: Clarendon Press, 1995.

Ross, Ian, and Stephen Scobie. "Patriotic Publishing as a Response to the Union." In T. I. Rae, ed., *The Union of 1707 and Its Impact on Scotland,* pp. 94–119. Glasgow: Blackie, 1974.

Ross, Trevor. "Copyright and the Invention of Tradition." *Eighteenth-Century Studies* 26, no. 1 (fall 1992): 1–27.

Rudy, John. "Beyond Vocation and Ego: Self-displacement in Wordsworth's 1803 *Memorials.*" *SEL* 29 (1989): 637–53.

Said, Edward. *Orientalism.* New York: Vintage Books, 1994.

———. "Orientalism Reconsidered." *Cultural Critique* 1 (1985): 89–107.

Schellenberg, Betty. "Imagining the Nation in Defoe's *A Tour Thro' the Whole Island of Great Britain.*" *ELH* 62 (1995): 295–311.

Schonhorn, Manuel. "Fielding's Ecphrastic Moment: Tom Jones and His Egyptian Majesty." *Studies in Philology* 78 (1981): 305–23.

Scotland's Parliament. Scottish Office, 1997.

Scott, Walter. *The Journal of Sir Walter Scott.* W. E. K. Anderson, ed. Oxford: Clarendon Press, 1972.

———. *Letters of Sir Walter Scott.* 12 vols. Herbert Grierson, ed. London: Constable, 1932–37.

———. *Minstrelsy of the Scottish Border.* 4 vols. Edinburgh and London: William Blackwood and Sons, 1902.

———. *The Poetical Works of Sir Walter Scott, Bart.* 12 vols. John Gibson Lockhart, ed. Edinburgh: Cadell, 1833–34.

———. "Review of *Reliques of Robert Burns.*" Quarterly Review (1809): 19–36.

————. "Review of *Report of the Committee of the Highland Society* and Laing's *Poems of Ossian.*" Edinburgh Review (1805): 429–62.

Sher, Richard B. *Church and University in the Scottish Enlightenment: The Moderate Literati of Edinburgh.* Edinburgh: Edinburgh University Press, 1985.

————. "Those Scotch Imposters and Their Cabal: Ossian and the Scottish Enlightenment." *Man and Nature: Proceedings of the Canadian Society for Eighteenth-Century Studies.* London, Ont.: Faculty of Education, University of Western Ontario, 1982.

Simpson, David. *Romanticism, Nationalism, and the Revolt Against Theory.* Chicago: University of Chicago Press, 1993.

Simpson, Kenneth. *The Protean Scot: The Crisis of Identity in Eighteenth-Century Scottish Literature.* Aberdeen: Aberdeen University Press, 1988.

————, ed. *Burns Now.* Edinburgh: Canongate, 1994.

Sinclair, John. *Prospectus of the Intended Publication of Ossian's Poems in the Original Gaelic, with a Verbal Translation Into Latin.* London: Bulmer, 1804.

Smart, J. S. *James Macpherson: An Episode in Literature.* London: David Nutt, 1905.

Smith, Anthony. *National Identity.* Harmondsworth, England: Penguin, 1991.

Smith, G. Gregory. *Scottish Literature: Character and Influence.* London: Macmillan, 1919.

Smollett, Tobias. *Poems, Plays, and "The Briton."* O. M. Brack, ed. Athens: University of Georgia Press, 1993.

————. *Roderick Random.* Paul-Gabriel Boucé, ed. Oxford: Oxford University Press, 1979.

Smout, T. C. "The Anglo-Scottish Union of 1707. 1. The Economic Background." *Economic History Review* 16, no. 3 (Apr. 1964): 455–67.

————. "The Road to Union." In Geoffrey Holmes, ed., *Britain After the Glorious Revolution, 1689–1714,* pp. 176–196. London: Macmillan, 1969.

Speck, W. A. *The Butcher: The Duke of Cumberland and the Suppression of the '45.* Oxford: Basil Blackwell, 1981.

Spivak, Gayatri Chakravorty. *In Other Worlds: Essays in Cultural Politics.* New York: Methuen, 1987.

Srebrnik, Patricia. *Alexander Strahan, Victorian Publisher.* Ann Arbor: University of Michigan Press, 1986.

Stafford, Fiona. *The Sublime Savage: James Macpherson and the Poems of Ossian.* Edinburgh: Edinburgh University Press, 1988.

Stewart, Susan. *Crimes of Writing: Problems in the Containment of Representation.* Durham, N.C.: Duke University Press, 1994.

Strong, Roy. *Art and Power. Renaissance Festivals. 1450–1650.* Woodbridge, England: Boydell, 1984.

Sutherland, Graham. *The Life of Walter Scott.* Oxford: Blackwell, 1995.

Trumpener, Katie. *Bardic Nationalism: The Romantic Novel and the British Empire.* Princeton, N.J.: Princeton University Press, 1997.

Turnbull, Gordon. "James Boswell: Biography and the Union." In Andrew
    Hook, ed., *History of Scottish Literature*, vol. 2, *1660–1800*, pp. 157–74.
    Aberdeen: Aberdeen University Press, 1987.
Vance, John A. *Samuel Johnson and the Sense of History*. Athens: University of
    Georgia Press, 1984.
Viswanathan, Gauri. *Masks of Conquest: Literary Study and British Rule in India*.
    New York: Columbia University Press, 1989.
Watson, Roderick. *The Literature of Scotland*. Houndmills, England: Macmillan,
    1984.
Weinbrot, Howard. *Britannia's Issue: The Rise of British Literature from Dryden to
    Ossian*. Cambridge: Cambridge University Press, 1993.
Whatley, Chris. *"Bought and Sold for English Gold"?: Explaining the Union of
    1707*. Glasgow: Economic and Social History Society of Scotland, 1994.
Wilkes, John. *The North Briton*. London, 1763.
Williams, Raymond. *Culture and Society, 1780–1950*. Harmondsworth, England:
    Penguin, 1963 [1958].
————. *Marxism and Literature*. Oxford: Oxford University Press, 1977.
Withers, Charles. *Gaelic Scotland: The Transformation of a Culture Region*. London:
    Routledge, 1988.
Wordsworth, William. *The Letters of William and Dorothy Wordsworth: The Middle
    Years, 1806–1820*. 7 vols. Mary Moorman and A. G. Hill, eds. Oxford:
    Oxford University Press, 1969–70.
————. *Poems, in Two Volumes, and Other Poems, 1800–1807*. Jared Curtis, ed.
    Ithaca, N.Y.: Cornell University Press, 1983.
————. *The Poetical Works of William Wordsworth*. Ernest de Selincourt and
    Helen Darbishire, eds. Vols. 1, 3–5. Oxford: Clarendon Press, 1940–49. Vol. 2,
    2d ed., rev. Helen Darbishire. Oxford: Clarendon Press, 1952.
————. *The Prose Works of William Wordsworth*. 3 vols. W. J. B. Owen and Jane
    Worthington Smyser, eds. Oxford: Clarendon Press, 1974.
————. *William Wordsworth: The Poems*. 2 vols. John Hayden, ed. New Haven:
    Yale University Press, 1977.
Wright, William. *The Comical History of the Marriage-Union Betwixt Fergusia and
    Heptarchus*. Edinburgh: n.p., 1706.

INDEX

In this index an "f" after a number indicates a separate reference on the next page, and an "ff" indicates separate references on the next two pages. A continuous discussion over two or more pages is indicated by a span of page numbers, e.g., "57–59." *Passim* is used for a cluster of references in close but not consecutive sequence.

Library of Congress Cataloging-in-Publication Data

Davis, Leith
    Acts of Union : Scotland and the literary negotiation of the
British nation, 1707–1830 / Leith Davis.
        p.   cm.
    Includes bibliographical references and index.
    ISBN 0-8047-3269-8 (alk. paper)
    1. English literature—18th century—History and criticism.
2. National characteristics, British, in literature.   3. Nationalism
and literature—Great Britain—History—18th century.
4. Nationalism and literature—Great Britain—History—19th
century.   5. English literature—Scottish authors—History and
criticism.   6. English literature—19th century—History and
criticism.   7. Scotland—History—The Union, 1707—
Historiography.   8. Literature, Comparative—English and
Scottish.   9. Literature, Comparative—Scottish and English.
10. Scotland—In literature.   I. Title.
PR448.N38D38   1998
820.9'358—dc21   98-35263

⊗ This book is printed on acid-free, recycled paper.

Original printing 1998
Last figure below indicates year of this printing:
07   06   05   04   03   02   01   00   99   98